THE INVISIBLE SCAR

The Invisible Scar

by CAROLINE BIRD

LONGMAN

New York and London

THE INVISIBLE SCAR

Longman Inc., New York
Associated companies, branches, and
representatives throughout the world.

First published 1966 by David McKay Company, Inc.
Twelfth printing 1978 by Longman Inc.

Library of Congress Catalog Card Number: 65-24266
ISBN: 0-582-28016-8 (previously ISBN 0-679-30119-4)

Manufactured in the United States of America

For my daughter Carol

ACKNOWLEDGMENTS

THIS is not a dispassionate book. I believe there is a difference between human rights and property rights, and when the two conflict, I'm for the human rights. Since I am a journalist, not a scholar, I write by the canons of journalism: I state my bias, evaluate my sources, listen to both sides, get facts as straight as possible, and seek help from experts, many of whom are scholars, historians, economists, and sociologists whose insights are their stock in trade. They have been unfailingly generous. But the opinions and conclusions are my own.

My first debt is to William Arthur, who encouraged me to write "The Day the Money Stopped" for *Look* magazine on the thirtieth anniversary of the Bank Holiday of March 6, 1933. Alice Leslie Koempel, Professor of Sociology at Vassar College, has been a continuing source of information and technique and a friend through the loneliness of thinking hard for a long time about times gone by. Others who reacted helpfully to all or part of the manuscript are Raymond Corry, Vivian Cristol, Pendleton Dudley, Vivienne Marquis, William Barton Marsh, Mabel Newcomer, Karl Pretshold, H. S. Smith, Sara Welles, and Tom Yutzy.

Among those who made time in busy schedules to let me question them were Dr. Alvan L. Barach, A. A. Berle, Jr., James Bird, W.

Randolph Burgess, Carl N. Degler, William Dignam, Raymond S. Franklin, Lawrence M. Gelb, Lancaster Greene, Charles C. Griffin, Helen Lockwood, James E. McClellan, Edna Macmahon, Wilfred May, Margaret Mead, Raymond Moley, Richard B. Morris, Franz Pick, Adolphus Roggenburg, Raymond Rubicam, A. M. Sullivan, and Laurence Winship. Special thanks go to Libby Ruch, Vassar '64, who shared her Senior thesis on the impact of the Depression on the family, to Vassar sociology majors Sarajane Heidt, '64, and Jane Ratcliffe, '65, who helped me frame a survey for Depression college graduates, and to Peggy Pike Gesell, Vassar '35, and other members of my class who filled out the questionnaire at a reunion. John F. Maloney lent me biographical material on the Princeton class of 1935, as did Norman A. Hall and Frank W. Knowlton, Jr., for Harvard, Charles A. Seidle for Lehigh University. The alumni offices of University of Wisconsin, Wellesley, and City College of New York were helpful, too.

Anecdotes and other incidental information were kindly contributed by Dr. Nathan Adelman, Dr. George Blinick, Berton Braley, Helen Brattrud, Bert Briller, John H. Caldwell, Homer Calver, James A. Farley, John Fischer, Faye Henle, Chase Horton, Ed Kent, Sol Kimball, Hans Leon, James L. Lumb, Allen MacKenzie, Howard Marshall, William Ogilvie, Warren Phillips, Don Robinson, Richard Rodgers, Mary Schuster, William Swanberg, Kate Titus, Alden Todd, Al Toffler, Leonard Turk, Ray Vogel, Mort Weisinger, Stephen White, and Ben Zapolski. Among the people who answered my queries with time-consuming letters were J. A. Bancroft, Thomas A. Craig, James F. Donovan, Freeman F. Gosden, A. S. Puelicher, Carl Ruff, Edward Sard, Riley P. Stevenson, Rexford Tugwell, Henry Wallace, and Morton Yarmon.

Information specialists in libraries and research organizations helped locate specific material in the sea of printed matter on the Depression period. Among them are Frances Adrian, Paul D. Aird, Herbert Bienstock, Robert Deindorfer, Paul L. Evans, Jeannette Fitz-williams, Peggy Hubbard, Robert E. Lewis, Joseph Marshall, Geoffrey H. Moore, Joan Murphy, and Dorothy Alice Plum. I am especially indebted to the staff of the Franklin Delano Roosevelt Memorial

Library in Hyde Park, New York, for diving into their archives and coming up with the highest assay of usable material for the least sifting on my part. The Vassar College Library turned out to be so pleasant an open-stack library that we ended by buying a house as close to it as possible.

Authors depend on a frighteningly long list of people. Zetta Decker, Patricia Doherty, Helen McGinnis, and Esther Vail typed and reproduced research material. Blanche Harding and Mona Vaeth entertained my three-year-old son Johnny while I worked. To Johnny, I am indebted for delivering urgent bulletins from the door of my workroom instead of prancing in with them.

I am indebted to my husband, Tom Mahoney, for dozens of anecdotes and hundreds of facts; Tom was a United Press regional manager during the Depression, and he not only remembers everything that ever happened, but usually has a clip to prove it. I owe my general outlook to my father, the late Hobart S. Bird, who was brought up in the Progressive golden age of Wisconsin and campaigned for Robert M. La Follette in 1924. I think he would have liked this book.

I am appalled at how fast the firsthand sources on the Thirties are dwindling. Jules I. Bogen, Charles Bonner, Walter Dolgin, James M. Landis, Herbert Lehman, Eleanor Roosevelt, and Pascal Whelpton gave me information while I was writing the book. Now all of them are dead.

CAROLINE BIRD

CONTENTS

INTRODUCTION:
THE LONG SHADOW
OF THE DEPRESSION

WHEN I was growing up, I often heard people talking about "the good old days, before the war," meaning, of course, the supposedly golden era before the 1914 war. The phrase has no currency or meaning any longer. Nobody talks, glowingly or otherwise, about "the good old days" before World War II. And yet that war marked a sharper dividing line in the American mode of living, the economy, the culture, the thought, the politics, than did the first World War.

It is a curious fact that the Great Depression is in danger of disappearing altogether from the collective consciousness. Already it seems unreal, even to those who lived through it. Did those things really happen? We pinch ourselves. Wasn't it just a bad dream?

In spite of this tendency, the Great Depression was real, it was awful, and more to the point, it packed a bigger wallop than anything else that happened to America between the Civil War and the Atom Bomb. It had more far-reaching consequences, I happen to think, than either of the World Wars. Nobody escaped. Every individual in every walk of life was hit.

What is overlooked and frequently forgotten is this: when the stock market crashed in October 1929, America stopped growing and did not really get moving again until the attack on Pearl Harbor in December 1941 mobilized our resources. During those long intervening years of standstill everybody and everything marked time. There were years when we wore out our roads and factories and houses faster than we replaced them. We had so few babies and crippled so many promising careers that we are now desperately short of teachers and executives for the educational and industrial expansion to which our affluent society is now committed.

Americans were bewildered. From the beginning, this country had grown bigger and richer almost every year. Standstill challenged our Conventional Wisdom of progress, individual initiative, thrift, free enterprise, limited government—even our Conventional Wisdom of love and marriage. It was so puzzling that when the war rescued us from our dilemma we gratefully brushed the whole ideological mess under the rug and left it there.

Occasionally, today, some hard-bitten old hand on Wall Street warns that stocks can go down as well as up. Sometimes a veteran sales manager declares that no one under thirty really knows how to get out and sell, or an employer laments the passing of "an honest day's work for an honest day's pay." The young usually listen in pity and in boredom.

But while the Depression fades in memory, it continues to define economic problems for the business and government policymakers who succeeded under Depression conditions. One of the most powerful men in the United States is William McChesney Martin, Jr., Chairman of the Federal Reserve Board since Truman's Presidency, who started working as a stockbroker in 1929 and at 29 succeeded Richard Whitney as Governor of the New York Stock Exchange with a mandate to reform it. In May 1965, Martin broke the public silence to warn of "disturbing parallels" with the boom of the 1920s that ended in the Crash. He pointed out that now, as then, American dollars were powering a European boom that could be dented by the abrupt withdrawal of our credit (and this time American business was dependent on overseas markets for a larger proportion of its profits). Responsible leaders all over the country reassured investors with a recital of all the reasons why we cannot, in 1965, have the same kind of Crash that we had in 1929.

We have Federal deposit insurance and sounder banks. We have floors under consumption—Social Security, unemployment insurance, private pensions, more workers in salaried and non-profit jobs that hold up in hard times. We have a progressive tax system that takes away income from the rich, who might hoard it, and taxes business only when business is making a profit. Professional managers in big corporations have learned to manage inventory, to plan further ahead, and to measure the market and respond to it faster. We have economic tools and computers to report the whole economy faster and more accurately. The Government has finally learned to plan taxes and spending on the basis of the cash it pumps in or takes out of circulation.

The Depression could not, everyone agreed, happen again. Yet even as the experts were explaining why, individual traders were getting out of the stock market, and it began to drop. Economic forecasters lowered their sights for 1966 and almost all predicted a slowing of growth and more unemployment. The most sophisticated economists were uneasy. Our safeguards were, after all, safeguards against 1929-style Crash. Our statistical measures were based on a smaller and simpler economy, and we might understand as little about the present economy as the speculators of 1929 understood about theirs.

These forebodings did not get far. They were cut short by the war in Vietnam and the recognition that it would take more men and money than previously admitted. In September 1965, the escalation of the war appeared to be exactly big enough to take up the slack that was forecast for the first quarter of 1966.

There is, of course, nothing new about generational lag. The world has always been run by men in their late fifties as if it were—or at least ought to be—the world of their early twenties. But unlike other ruling generations, the leaders of 1965 are not talking up the world of their youth, but doing their best to forget it. The penalty for this amnesia is not the loss of those copybook lessons in economic virtue that the Depression supposedly taught us. It is not even the prospect that we may have to repeat those portions of our history which we have forgotten. The penalty is worse. The victim of a selective memory loses touch with himself.

The college rebels of the 1960s who have grown up in an affluent society see a gap between public policy and reality. They accuse the Depression-bred authorities of asking the wrong questions. They are marching for peace against older people who unconsciously perpetuate the cold war because defense programs make jobs. They find their elders cynical and hypocritical. The placard-carriers on the campuses confront the presidents of the multiversities and wonder "how guys like that ever made the scene so big." It is a fair question.

The stony standstill of the 1930s favored the careers of young men with tough hides or private incomes, just as a long dry summer favors weeds and hothouse plants. In the 1960s, it is those who best endured adversity, the survivors, who have advanced to the front offices of the nation, including the White House, where they preside—with crossed fingers—over the longest and steepest economic expansion of record. What are our leaders doing that would have been done differently by the gentler, and perhaps more imaginative, souls screened out of the running in the bad old days? The very question arises only because the Depression shook our faith in the automatic elevation and superiority of the fittest.

A full answer would be long. It would have to map all the far-flung ways in which economic standstill frustrates, limits, and demeans. The total human bill for the Great Depression has never been added up, but it would contain thousands of sizable items. For a few weeks I picked up nonfiction books at random from library shelves and flipped to the indexes. The words "Depression" or "Great Depression" appeared in accounts of everything from the insurance business to the ballet.

The Depression expanded the role of government, and of Federal government at the expense of the states. It stimulated business to social conscience and professionalized corporate management. It changed the balance of power in family life in favor of women while discouraging marriage and motherhood. It held back and isolated Negroes, Jews, and women by making it easy to discriminate against them in employment, and it converted the public school from stepping-stone to refuge for the unemployed. It turned intellectuals to the left, slowed the application of technology, kept most of the nation ill housed, and prevented the natural spread of population to suburbs. It influenced fashions in women's clothing, amusements, architecture, lovemaking, and child rearing.

It drew fellow-sufferers together for good (there was time for conversation and camaraderie) and for evil (couples stayed together because they couldn't afford divorce). It slowed our induction into the contemporary world and shoved us into it with reservations; every worry expressed about automation is a retread of Depression discussions of technological unemployment. It spread abroad, gaining us enemies, and it cut us off from Europe until the war engulfed us, first as a shock and then as a bonanza. Our guilt over preferring war to Depression is one of the reasons we hate to think about the bad old days before the war.

The self-perpetuating poor who dismay us now are the children of the people the New Deal left out, and the remedies President Johnson suggests are lifted whole cloth from President Roosevelt. The principal difference is in numbers: in those days, one out of every four employable people was unemployed, instead of one out of twenty; Roosevelt saw one third of America poor, instead of one fifth.

If you went by contemporary references to the Depression, you might get the idea that the Depression was a faceless menace. In truth, it was as explicit as a statistic, as tangible as a wound. Above all, it was a series of real events in actual time.

It began with a financial crash, reached nadir in paralysis, and ended with unexpected death from the skies. The beginning, the rock bottom, and the end were three days so vivid that most adults can remember what they were doing on those days:

• On Black Thursday, October 24, 1929, the bottom dropped out of the stock market, pulling everything else down after it.

• On March 6, 1933, the Bank Holiday that Roosevelt declared as his first Presidential act, economic activity of every kind stopped dead.

• On December 8, 1941, the day after Pearl Harbor, we declared a war that put every employable man and woman to devil's work.

• Those twelve years in between were filled with lower-case tragedies: mean stratagems, unspeakably petty economies, lost time, lost hope, lost opportunities, monotony, envy, and bitterness. Regarded from the other side of World War II, they added up to a major tragedy rousing pity and fear. These emotions were dissolved by the threat of instant, universal destruction of the human race.

Sophocles could have written the script.

THE INVISIBLE SCAR

1

$ $ $ $ $

CRASH

1929. That number always means a year, and that year means
the crash of prices on the New York Stock Exchange in the last
week of October. Like 1492, 1776, and 1914, the bare number
1929 has passed into the language as the term for a vivid event
and the big changes it brought.

The big change of 1929 was the end of the rich.

I was fourteen years old at the time, and I can remember
everyone in our car laughing when my father pointed to an
Italian Renaissance-style mansion on the Grand Concourse of
the Bronx. "See, Caroline? That's the poorhouse for millionaires!"

I told him I didn't believe there was such a thing. "Yes,
it's true," he said. "It's a charity for the rich so they won't have
to go to a public institution and live like other people if they
lose their money." This was the Andrew Freedman Home.

During the next few years so many people in comfortable
circumstances "lost everything" that Mr. Freedman's concern
for the impoverished rich seemed neither improper nor un-
timely. Every time we passed his mansion—and since we lived

1

in Westchester, that meant every time we drove in to New York —I half expected any number of people I knew to peep out of the stately windows.

In 1965, I finally got around to checking up on my father. He was absolutely correct. According to its charter, the Andrew Freedman Home was founded to maintain, in the style to which they had been accustomed, "people in good circumstances who through no fault of their own had lost their money." It was set up not in 1929, as I had imagined, but under a will dated 1907, the year of the biggest stock-market panic before 1929. Freedman was a poor boy who made a fortune in real estate. Experience in several walks of life had convinced him that reduced circumstances were harder on the rich than on the poor.

The rich did not actually become poor in 1929. The great American fortunes held together very nicely, and much of the money the new-rich lost was on paper. Only one or two of the rich became apple sellers. But after 1929 the rich no longer glittered as they walked. Never again were they to have it so good.

It took surprisingly little money to be rich in 1929—less than $6,000 a year if you define being rich as enjoying a family income greater than that of 95 percent of the population. Nor did the rich of 1929 have more things than the rich have now. In those days $6,000 bought only $10,000 worth of goods and services at 1963 prices, and there were no automatic washing machines, dishwashers, television sets, air conditioners, home movie cameras, home freezers, Fiberglas fishing rods, or hi-fi phonographs for anyone.

Instead of things, the rich had the priceless luxury of a commanding share of the wealth, the income, and even the regard of the American people. No one who has grown up since the Crash can know how it felt to be rich before 1929. In 1929, the last year of their glory, the rich got more of everything that could be bought for money than the rich of 1960 could. They gobbled up nearly a third of all the goods and services the

2

United States consumed. In 1960 their share was less than a fifth.

In 1929 the rich did not have to work for a living. Interest rates were high, and income taxes negligible. A nest egg of little more than $115,000 could assure you of a safe, coupon-clipping (and tax-free) income of $5,000 a year, the target of aspiring young men. You could live like a king on $5,000 a year in France, where the cost of living was even lower than in the United States and dollars commanded a premium in demoralized francs. In 1960, only one rich family out of every hundred lived entirely on unearned income. All the other 99 had someone out working for a living, and one out of four made the top-five-percent bracket only because the wife was working as well as the husband.

In 1929, more of the rich were very, very rich. A record 513 individuals admitted to an income of a million dollars or over, a larger number than in the 1960s, when there were more than half again as many people in the country. The contrast is significant even if it is more apparent than real. In 1929 a man could boast about his income without worrying about what the Internal Revenue might think.

In 1929 the rich were really rich. It is hard now to realize how much more a 20-dollar bill meant to some people than to others. Downtown in the Manhattan piece-rate sweatshops a girl might sew two weeks of long days for it. Uptown, at F. Scott Fitzgerald's Plaza, one of the very, very rich might hand a twenty to the headwaiter of the Oak Room, if he did not happen to have a smaller bill on him. It was real money, his very own, one hundred cents to the dollar, and no mean calculation of tax deductibility spoiled the fun of spending it.

Before October 1929, a million stock-market speculators were glad that the rich were rich, because they expected to be rich soon themselves. Millionaires were being made every day.

3

It was as if a fairy godmother had decreed a coach for every Cinderella.

The Crash turned them back to pumpkins as fast as the stroke of twelve in the fairy story.

It was like a conjuring trick. The morning of Tuesday, October 29, 1929, stocks on the New York Stock Exchange had a real value. By 5:30 that night, when the ticker finally caught up with the 3 o'clock closing transactions, that value was $14 billion less. Two weeks later, $26 billion in stock values—40 percent of the value of all stocks listed on the New York Stock Exchange—had evaporated into thin air. And that was just the beginning. By July 1, 1932, another $47 billion had vanished.

The break started on Thursday, October 24. Three billion dollars went down the drain that day, but the really big speculators were not badly hurt. A little after noon, Richard Whitney, the Groton-and-Harvard acting head of the New York Stock Exchange, cleared the gallery of curious spectators, including Winston Churchill, who was visiting from England. Deliberate, dignified, a "Morgan broker" of the old school, Richard Whitney made his way to Post 2 on the Stock Exchange floor. Acting for a pool subscribed by bankers Thomas W. Lamont of Morgan, Charles E. Mitchell of the National City Bank, William C. Potter of Guaranty Trust, Albert H. Wiggin of the Chase National Bank, and Seward Prosser of Bankers Trust, he dramatically offered $205 a share for 25,000 shares of U.S. Steel, 15 points above the boiling market. The market revived. The pool did not have to spend much of the $240 million they were supposed to have pledged to support prices, and what they did buy they quietly sold, during brief rises, at a small profit.

Most of the losers, that first Thursday, were small investors. In boardrooms all over the country they stood shoulder to shoulder for hours watching the ticker flash spot quotations, each one lower than the last. There was no talk, but once in a

4

while a low groan, "No!" They jammed the radio rooms of trans-Atlantic liners to hear the ruinous news by shortwave. In small towns they invaded newsrooms to watch the wire-service tickers. Long-distance phone service was overloaded.

The following Tuesday cleaned out the professional speculators. The drop in market values was so steep as to be vertical, from 20 to 25 times the earnings of the stocks, to 10 times earnings, and less. Steel dipped to 167, 38 points below Whitney's declared support price. Huge blocks of stock were offered "at market," and sometimes there was no market. When there were no takers for White Sewing Machine, a clever messenger boy bid $1 and found himself the owner of 10,000 shares.

The big bankers publicly admitted they could not support the market. Bowery bums, hearing that stocks were selling at a nickel, pooled change they had begged and advanced up Wall Street to invest in America. They were met by police. The Vanderbilts were out of yachts, it was said; taxi-driver reaction was that they richly deserved it.

Who got all the money that was lost? Suspicion turned first on the magical "big men in Wall Street," the rich who F. Scott Fitzgerald thought were a race apart from ordinary men. They could have profited by selling short, or by selling borrowed stock and paying it back later when it could be bought cheaper.

The notorious speculators ducked. Big Bear Jesse Livermore had dropped out of sight. He was supposed to be dueling with Big Bull Arthur Cutten, the Chicago grain speculator, who was sighted in Atlantic City. So many people in Cutten's original home town—Guelph, Ontario—followed his investment tips that Guelph's population of 20,000 lost $3 million on October 29, and Cutten found it expedient to announce that he had lost heavily, too. George F. Baker, chairman of the First National Bank, who had made $22 million in a single day, let it be known that he had dropped $15 million. It took a Congressional

5

investigation to discover that Albert H. Wiggin of the Chase had actually sold the stock of his own bank short, while telling reporters, "None of the corporations or institutions I am connected with is selling stocks at this time. We are buying."

The handiest villain was the broker. A great many simple people were convinced that the broker who had urged them to buy had somehow pocketed the money they had lost. In Chicago, Al Capone was supposed to have sent hundreds of thugs to the financial district to rub out the brokers held responsible for his losses. Many law-abiding citizens sympathized. During the last week of October, brokers called up hundreds of thousands of customers demanding money on pain of losing all that had been invested.

Margin was a magic multiplier that cut both ways. A speculator with $1,000 could win the rise on $10,000 worth of stock by buying on 90 percent margin. His broker would buy $10,000 worth of stock and find a lender who would take it as collateral for a loan of $9,000. A broker's loan was regarded as a safe investment, the nearest thing to ready cash. It was a "call loan," payable by either borrower or lender at a moment's notice. The stock that was used as collateral to secure it could be liquidated instantly on the stock market. Buyers gladly paid exorbitant interest rates because they expected the stocks they bought with the borrowed money to go up so high that the interest would become negligible. As long as the market kept rising, everyone was ahead. If it dropped, however, the borrower immediately had to put up more money to keep the "margin" of collateral required, or be sold out by the lender. That was what happened at the Crash.

The sellout was enormous. Since 1934, the Federal Reserve Board has regulated margins, but in 1929 a broker could make whatever margin arrangements he chose. Speculation drove stock prices higher and higher. Smart money poured in to the New York Stock Exchange from all over the world. Indian

6

princes sent their wealth to the fabulous New York "call-money market." By the middle of 1929, half of the $7 billion worth of brokers' loans then outstanding came from individuals and corporations rather than banks. Interest rates on brokers' loans rose as high as 20 percent. Corporate officers generally found they could make more money for their companies by lending to brokers than through manufacturing or selling. Sometimes they floated new stock issues in order to get the money to put out "on call." Some informed observers blamed the Tuesday drop on panicky company executives who were afraid the Board of Governors would close the New York Stock Exchange before they could sell the stock against which they had lent out company money. A few had quietly "borrowed" company funds to turn a quick, safe profit on the call-money market for themselves. In October 1929, $2.4 *billion* worth of brokers' loans outstanding on the New York Stock Exchange was liquidated.

Hardly a dollar was lost. This remarkable salvage job can be credited in part to the physical stamina of New York brokers. The official count of transactions on Tuesday, October 29, was 16,338,000, a record volume still, but some who were there think that many more shares were sold than were recorded. Some brokers sneaked in sales after the gong, or off the floor. The tape was half a day behind, the bookkeeping hopelessly snarled.

Brokers rested briefly in clubs, on billiard tables, in hotel rooms, and even in nearby Bowery flophouses. Girl clerks fainted. A 23-year-old broker's clerk collapsed and had to postpone his wedding. Goaded by the fear of losing collateral, brokers literally fought each other to buyers. They tore each other's collars and hair. They screamed. *The New York Times* described the sound emanating from the floor as an "eerie roar," but others thought it was like howling hyenas. Brokers lost shoes, glasses, false teeth, shirts. They clung to phones

7

tracking down customers who might have more collateral to put up. Some brokerage houses had a boy whose sole duty was to untangle phone cords on trading tables.

Brokers recovered the immediate loans in most cases, but they emerged without a livelihood. In 1929, they earned $227 million in commissions, by 1938 only $43 million. Dow-Jones tickers became a drug on the market. There was one of these secondhand machines for every two reporters covering the scattered events of the 1932 Olympic Games in Los Angeles.

Most of the hard-pressed customers tried desperately to save their holdings. They borrowed from relatives. They took money out of banks. They pawned jewelry. In November a policeman found a destitute parrot on Fifth Avenue crying, "More margin! More margin!" In Kansas City, a man who couldn't get up the margin shot himself through the chest, exclaiming, "Tell the boys I can't pay!" When the stock of the Union Cigar Company fell from $113.50 to $4, in one day, its president crawled out on a ledge of New York's Beverly Hotel. A waiter grabbed him by the leg, but he wriggled free and fell to his death.

Margin calls exposed wives speculating with the grocery money, bookkeepers embezzling the company's funds, and bankers playing the market with deposits. J. J. Riordan, head of the County Trust Company of New York, killed himself when he couldn't replace bank money he had "borrowed" from the till and lost on the market. The board of the bank kept the suicide secret while they passed the hat to make good the loss.

Suicide by jumping captured the popular imagination. A London newspaper sketched New York brokers falling like snowflakes into Wall Street. Comedian Eddie Cantor, himself a heavy loser, brought down the house when he had a hotel clerk ask a broker whether he wanted a room for sleeping or jumping. When a workman was spotted on the roof of a downtown building, a crowd gathered to watch him jump.

New York authorities announced that only 44 persons had

committed suicide in Manhattan between October 13 and November 19, compared to 53 for the same period in 1928, and none of them brokers, but people paid no attention to the statistics. They continued to see Wall Street strewn with fallen brokers. The actual suicides were mainly embezzlers and margin-short customers, and the evidence is that they used guns, ropes, water, and poison in the classic percentages. The image of the jumping broker may have taken hold because Wall Street means skyscrapers and a great many people would have enjoyed seeing their brokers fall as disastrously as their stocks.

The notion that somebody must have gained from all the loss dies hard. Charles Morton, of *The Atlantic Monthly* magazine, claims that a rich man in Boston sold all his stock in 1928 and put it all back into the stock market at the very bottom, in 1933, on the well-founded theory that money would not do him any good if the country were going to hell, but if it were not, then General Motors was dirt cheap at $14. Stories about people who quietly bought at the bottom persist into the 1960s. Every share that was sold, people tell you, was bought by someone. The trouble is that almost nobody held on until after the war, when prices really recovered. In deep Depression, some relief agencies had to open brokerage accounts to dispose of odd shares of stock that applicants for relief had clutched, sometimes through actual hunger, against the day the market would rise again. More sophisticated stockholders took their losses sooner. The quick winners on Tuesday were the telephone company (11,000 more calls than usual), the State of New York, which harvested $350,000 in transfer taxes on the day's record volume of stock sales, and the pawnbrokers.

The logical winners would have been the great American fortunes. There were moments, on Tuesday, when it looked as if a few well-deployed millions could have bought the whole country, but people were too panic-stricken to see the opportunity when John D. Rockefeller announced that he and his sons believed in America and were buying common stocks. Eddie Cantor cracked, "Sure. Who else has any money left?" John D. Rockefeller, Bernard Baruch, and other substantial holders had withdrawn from the market before the Crash because it looked too high to them, but there is no evidence that they took advantage of the lows. Those who tried usually lost their nerve and sold when the market kept going down.

The few who played the crashing market correctly were not members of the capitalist establishment in good standing. One frequently cited was Joseph Kennedy, father of President Kennedy, who later became a stern policeman of Wall Street as Chairman of the Securities and Exchange Commission. Floyd B. Odlum, a maverick, bought up investment-company portfolios at the bottom of the market to parlay $4 million into $100 million between 1929 and 1935. All but unknown at the time was future "richest-man-in-the-world" Jean Paul Getty, who had made his first million in 1926 and spent the 1930s picking up good oil companies that were going cheap. Norton Simon, famous corporate empire builder of the midcentury, got his financial start in 1931 when he bought a bankrupt cannery for $7,000 and used it to get control of booming Hunt Foods in 1942.

The people who had formerly boasted about how much they had made on the market spent the next few years boasting about how much they had lost. Previous panics had ruined gentlemen who tried to conceal their losses. In 1929 it seemed as if "everyone" was in the market. Actually, fewer than five percent of the population were involved, but they made a lot of noise. Many of the losers who had never owned stock before the boom were chauffeurs, taxi drivers, speakeasy bartenders, elevator operators, waiters, and barbers, who got into the market on tips from the people they served and so were in a position to spread the details of their losses. "Like all life's rich emotional

10

experiences, the full flavor of losing important money cannot be conveyed by literature," broker-humorist Fred Schwed wrote in a book on the stock market with the lovely title, *Where Are the Customers' Yachts?*

If so, it was not for lack of trying. Alexander Woollcott, Willard Huntington Wright ("S. S. Van Dine"), and many other exquisitely articulate citizens were heavy losers. Producer George White lost $4 million he had made on the famous George White *Scandals.* Composer Jerome Kern had sold his rare books and autographs for more than a million dollars in 1928 and lost nearly every cent of it in the Crash. "Marx, the jig is up," producer Max Gordon phoned his friend Groucho.

On Friday, the day after the first break, President Hoover officially announced that business was "fundamentally sound." H. L. Mencken likened the market to a carbuncle: "As well say that a pimple on a beautiful woman's behind is an essential part of her." Editorials pointed out that the factories, the farms, and the riches of America were intact. Winners who had recently rejoiced at unaccustomed riches now comforted themselves with the thought that they were only paper poor. "How could I lose $100,000?" a woman asked her broker when he called for margin. "I never *had* $100,000 in all my life."

It dawned on most people that the trouble was largely on the books. "People aren't going to quit riding in automobiles or eating or wearing clothes, are they?" a newspaper editorial reassured. But that very week *The New York Times* discovered that customers were canceling orders for automobiles. It was disclosed that the people who had been getting rich in 1929 were getting rich largely on paper too. Brokers' loans and new stock issues were "printing-press money." If the created money could have burned up at the Crash without affecting "real" money, it would have been possible to contain the speculation and the Crash in a big playpen or gambling casino on Wall Street, so that the stock-market disaster would not, in fact, hurt business. But the Wall Street speculators were creating real money when they piled loan on loan, and the debts eventually had to be paid in U.S. currency or repudiated.

In 1928 and 1929, investment bankers had literally forced money on manufacturers to expand capacity. The sober light of the Crash disclosed that industry was dangerously overbuilt. Industrial production had been leveling off since June 1929. Most lines were down in September and further off in October, before the Crash. In November, steel users told *The New York Times* that they would have been buying cautiously even if there had been no Crash. The stock-market drama simply publicized what astute observers had been whispering for months: everyone who could afford a house, a car, or a radio had one already.

Market losses made the rich count their pennies. Speakeasy prices fell with the market. Illicit champagne was down from $100 to $75 a bottle, and few were celebrating. Florists complained that standing orders were being canceled. New York stores reported a 50-percent cut in the sale of radio sets, which in those days cost more than $100. The London diamond syndicate, which stabilizes the price of diamonds by controlling the supply, stopped offering rough stones to cutters.

Good faith could no longer be assumed. The New York Stock Exchange publicly called for a daily report on short sales, to see who was making money on the market as it went down, and secretly set up a blacklist of margin-jumping customers whose telephone promises to pay would never be honored again. The National City Bank reneged on an agreement to merge with the Corn Exchange Bank when the new lower prices of bank stocks made it a less attractive deal, but hounded their own employees to keep up salary-deduction payments on bank stock bought at boom prices long after they had left the employ of the bank.

Steel, car loadings, automobile production, all went down further in November. Then, as Wall Streeters were marveling that all the brokerage houses were still solvent, the market took another sickening lurch. On November 13, gilt-edge securities hit lows for the year on a huge volume in large blocks. Banks were selling the stock they had taken as collateral to help substantial customers meet margin calls. Before the day was out, John D. Rockefeller publicly placed an order for a million shares of Standard Oil of New Jersey at $50 a share.

The Government tried to restore confidence. Secretary of the Treasury Andrew J. Mellon, Jr., recommended an income-tax cut that would have given a man supporting a family of two children on $4,000 a year an extra $6 to spend. With a Federal budget surplus of more than $700 million, Mellon went so far, a week later, as to recommend spending on public works $175 million more than the Federal Government had planned, provided this sum were spread over the next ten years. These, of course, were empty gestures.

Hoover told Congress that the economy was fundamentally sound and the stock-market drop due to "uncontrolled speculation," but he admitted that losses had reduced the "consumption of luxuries and semi-necessities" and thrown some people "temporarily" out of employment.

The President was more pessimistic in private. He called business leaders to the White House and scared them into publicly promising to spend $2 billion on expansion by telling them that "two to three million were unemployed by the sudden suspension of many activities." He begged Henry Ford to make some good news. Ford walked out into the pressroom of the White House and announced that he was going back to Detroit to raise wages from $6 to $7 a day, at a cost of $19.5 million a year. The stock market rallied briefly.

Henry Ford refused to recognize that the market for automobiles was saturated. Secondhand dealers had almost a million cars on their lots. Ford had dropped prices the week of the Crash, but the customers did not buy. In November 1929, fewer cars were built than in any November since 1919, except for the year 1927, when Ford closed down to change models. At Christmas, Senator James Couzens confided to the Michigan Manufacturers Association that the Government estimated unemployment had jumped from 700 thousand to 3.1 million in the two weeks following the Crash.

In December, everything was worse. Steel was operating at 40 percent. Bank deposits continued to shrink as brokers' loans were liquidated. Gold flowed out of the country back to the smart moneylenders all over the world who had been making loans to speculators. There was a record distribution of Christmas Club funds, and Christmas sales were almost as big as the year before, but merchants were not encouraged. On December 24, Chicago mail-order houses cut prices. Two weeks before Christmas, the American Piano Company (Chickering, Knabe, Mason & Hamlin) went bankrupt when it could not pay a $7,000 truckers' bill. The father of Tennessee Williams scolded the playwright's mother for buying a piano on the day of the Crash. She had felt encouraged to shop because of finding the showroom pleasantly quiet.

The decade ended appropriately with the bankruptcy of the Stutz Motor Car Company, manufacturers of the Bearcats that bore the raccoon-coated flappers of the booming Twenties. Many other proud little automobile makes went out of business or merged in the next few years. The factory that had manufactured the Edwardian Peerless became a brewery after repeal. In the next few years, Locomobile, Durant, Marmon, Franklin, Auburn, Cord, Duesenberg, Pierce-Arrow, and other fine automobile names vanished. The automobile industry was not to make as many passenger cars again until 1949.

In spite of the Crash, the New York Stock Exchange saw the Twenties out with the last of those wild annual outbursts that

14

had become customary during boom years. *The New York Times* called the party bigger and louder than ever before:

"The celebration at the Stock Exchange started at 1:30 with the arrival of the 369th Infantry band, thirty Negro musicians under Lieutenant J. W. Porter. A stand had been erected in the center of the trading floor and the music started with still an hour and a half of trading scheduled for 1929. Confetti started flying immediately, solo dances were given at almost every trading post and soon the brokers had forgotten trading for sport. Dances were interrupted to close trades which had to be made, but the main endeavor of those around each post was to originate some form of impromptu entertainment that would surpass that given at other posts.

"Noise-makers had been supplied to everyone on the floor and the galleries were crowded with visitors who had procured the few invitations available for the families and friends of the members of the Exchange. Even the staidest of the floor traders became frivolous under the influence of the band. Pinning tails on the traders became the popular sport of the afternoon. At one of the trading posts the newspaper record of the trading on October 24, the 16,000,000-share day, was burned as an indication of desiring never to be reminded of it again.

"E. H. Simmons, president of the Exchange, personally sounded the gong at 3 o'clock to announce the end of trading for 1929. As the gong was still reverberating, the members broke into a pandemonium of noise, everything in the Exchange that had noise-making possibilities being utilized. The din could be heard as far away as Broadway. This outbreak in celebration of the passing of the year lasted over five minutes, members yelling until they were hoarse." *

New Year forecasts were bright. The Department of Labor predicted that 1930 would be a "splendid employment year."

* Copyright 1930 by The New York Times Company. Reprinted by permission.

The New York Times rejoiced that brokers' loans were at last liquidated and counted the nation's blessings: low inventories, rising population, sound government, sound money, a balanced Federal budget. Speculators who had been smart enough to stay out of the market in 1929 thought the bottom was at hand and rushed in to buy. In March, Hoover predicted that the worst would be over in 60 days. Sixty days later he announced that the worst *was* over, and added, at the end of May, that business would be normal in the fall. Instead, banks that still held stocks as collateral for sour loans took advantage of the rise, sold their stocks, and overloaded the market. There was a sharp break in June, and the market continued to go down, ending the year below the lows of 1929.

All during 1930 the wake of the Crash moved like a tidal wave, wrecking parts of the economy that seemed far removed from the turbulent market on Wall Street. In 1929, wheat had been hurt by reports of bumper crops abroad. When stocks dropped, wheat, cotton, corn, and other commodities dropped in sympathy, weakening little country banks that carried farmers until their crops could be marketed. Then a drought caused the topsoil of Western states to dry up and blow away, destroying some crops completely. Country banks could not pay back the money they had borrowed from city banks.

The Crash cut off the flotations of bonds of German and South American governments that had supplied the domestic demand for "securities" and provided foreigners with dollars to buy our goods. In June, we raised the high Hawley-Smoot tariff against imports. Foreigners could not pay their debts to us. They could not sell to us. They stopped buying from us. They raised their own tariffs in retaliation. By mid-1930 the Depression was worldwide.

The Crash made us see, in a blinding flash of insight, that we had more buildings than we were going to need for the next generation. More new floor space had been built in 1928 than

16

would be constructed again until the war expansion of 1942. It would be 30 years before New York City required a new hotel or theater. The Crash struck down financing for new ventures overnight. On October 6, 1929, for instance, ebullient real-estate men in New York had announced plans for a 150-story skyscraper to top the Empire State Building. The plan was dropped hastily, and the Empire State Building itself stood half empty for years, after being finished in 1931. Some buildings were abandoned literally in midair. In Detroit, the Elks stopped work on an 11-story building, and it stood like a skeleton on East Jefferson Street for the next 34 years.

Bankruptcies peppered the 1930 news. In November, a Nashville brokerage house, Caldwell & Company, failed, carrying with it banks in half a dozen states. In December, the Bank of the United States failed in New York, damaging nearly half a million depositors, many of them small immigrant businessmen who thought they were banking their money with the United States Government. Investigation disclosed glaring irregularities in which the state bank examiners had connived, at least in part, to maintain "confidence."

On New Year's Day, 1931, *The New York Times* reasoned that things were so bad they simply had to get better: people had held off buying so long they must have a lot of money saved up to replace their "worn-out private belongings," and prices were so low they surely would be tempted to buy. The president of U.S. Steel said that the peak of the Depression had passed 30 days before. Owen D. Young, board chairman of General Electric, added that the "dead center of the Depression" had come and gone. Thomas Lamont, Secretary of Commerce, took a deep breath and proclaimed, "The banks of this country generally are in a strong position."

Then, in May, a bank in Vienna failed. Germany refused to let gold leave the country. "Hot money"—the liquid balances held by certain capitalists who specialized in foreign currencies

17

—was hastily moved to wherever its owners thought it would be safe. Britain extended herself trying to help shaky Germany; this scared the currency specialists into demanding gold for their paper pounds, putting further strain on the British. The United States in turn tried to help the British. Nevertheless, the British were forced off the gold standard in 1931, and the international money speculators began to worry about the gold backing of the dollar.

Many Americans with money took fright. They turned in their dollars for gold and shipped it out of the country without the slightest feeling of disloyalty, at the same time denouncing ordinary depositors, who questioned the soundness of their banks, as "unpatriotic." To make dollars attractive to hold, the Federal Reserve raised interest rates so that capitalists could get more return on their money. The move tightened credit so much that no one would borrow.

For thousands of American banks, the consequences of the European currency crisis provided the last straw. Loaded with frozen assets, these banks were carrying mortgages that could not be foreclosed at a figure even close to their face value. New York City real estate fell to about 60 percent of 1929 values, and since mortgages were usually for 60 percent of market value, equities generally were destroyed, so that mortgages became risky investments. Banks that had been holding mortgages as collateral for sour loans, in hopes that values would improve, were getting desperate. When Hoover called a secret meeting of big New York bankers and begged them to form a pool to support the weaker banks, they told him there was nothing they could do.

After Britain went off gold, American banks began to liquidate in panic. They called loans. They sold stocks and bonds they had been holding as collateral since the Crash. They sold off so many bonds that prices fell 20 percent. When they took their losses, their real condition showed up on the books,

18

triggered even more desperate moves. More than half of the $5 billion shrinkage of bank deposits between 1929 and 1931 took place in the last three months of 1931. More banks failed during that year than in all the years between 1900 and 1929.

Factories responded to sales figures more sensitively than they do now. Most manufacturers made no attempt to build inventory. When orders were filled, they simply laid off the hands to shift for themselves until more orders came in. During 1930, workingmen had longer and longer waits for work, but the hourly rates were maintained. In 1931, manufacturers cut wage rates to lower their labor costs. On October 1, 1931, bellwether U.S. Steel cut wage rates 10 percent. Soon afterward, Henry Ford retreated from the seven-dollar day he had announced in December 1929, to fight the Depression. Cities could not collect property taxes and had to cut the pay of their teachers and policemen. Salaries and piece rates were cut. At one point Southern cotton planters were paying as little as 20¢ to get 100 pounds of cotton picked—a rate that amounted to a wage of 60¢ a 14-hour day for the strongest and most skilled.

An orgy of saving and hoarding made money even scarcer. Some of the economies were frantic. Newspapers pulled out electric clocks to save the cost of the current. Paper mills made their employees use mill cuttings for toilet paper. Bethlehem Steel discharged 6,000 of the 7,500 workers they had brought to Lackawanna, New York, and then tried to evict them from company housing so that it could be torn down to save property taxes. The National Chain Store Association canceled its 1932 convention and printed in *Chain Store Age* the speeches and toasts that would have been given, thus saving money that normally would have made business for hotels, railroads, restaurants, and bootleggers.

Before the Crash, the more exuberant boosters had proclaimed a New Era. Poverty was to be vanquished by mass consumption. "We do not ride around in automobiles because we are prosperous," the saying went. "We are prosperous because we ride around in automobiles." With this lovely doctrine, living it up became a patriotic duty. The trouble was that the only people who could afford the new mass-produced marvels were the five percent who were rich, and by the end of 1929 the rich were shaken.

Some were completely broke. Thousands of families who had converted everything into cash in hopes of meeting margin calls had dismissed the servants and were huddling in partly heated white elephants of houses that were all they had left. In New York City, taxis went off the streets for lack of business, more than half the legitimate theaters were dark for the 1931 season, and in the suburbs thousands of cars were not relicensed. Detroit was so sensitive to this situation that licenses were extended just to keep cars on the road. The formerly rich reneged on their charities, and some of them even wrote plaintive notes begging the return of last year's contributions. They passed up their churches and resigned from their clubs. Vassar College had to spend more money to feed its students because the girls did not have money for off-campus snacks. Self-help dormitories were set up so that hard-up girls could save money on college expenses by doing their own housework. The economy persisted. Today all Vassar students scrape their own dishes.

Others simply did not feel like spending when their friends were broke. J. P. Morgan and others who did not have to count costs laid up their yachts. Debutantes gave up big parties, or joined together to give them. Society weddings that used to cost $25,000 were held to $5,000. *Fortune* calculated that Gobelin tapestries, fine jewels, rare books, antiques, and castles were going so cheap that families living on $100,000 could afford them for the first time. A string of polo ponies actually fell into the hands of a club of news photographers on *The Detroit Free Press*.

20

Restaurants and hotels were half empty. Conrad Hilton wooed permanent guests with rents below costs, cut off whole floors to save heat, took telephones out of rooms to save 15¢ a month, and urged clerks to dole out stationery sheet by sheet and ink drop by drop. New York's Plaza Hotel, hangout of the gilded rich, could not afford to clean the marble, tapestries, or bronze, or even the panels of the fabled Oak Room.

2

$ $ $ $ $

THE DISCOVERY OF POVERTY

YOU could feel the Depression deepen, but you could not look
out of the window and see it. Men who lost their jobs dropped
out of sight. They were quiet, and you had to know just when
and where to find them: at night, for instance, on the edge of
town huddling for warmth around a bonfire, or even the municipal incinerator; at dawn, picking over the garbage dump for
scraps of food or salvageable clothing.

In Oakland, California, they lived in sewer pipes the manufacturer could not sell. In Connellsville, Pennsylvania, unemployed steelworkers kept warm in the big ovens they had formerly coked. Outside Washington, D.C., one Bonus Marcher
slept in a barrel filled with grass, another in a piano box, a
third in a coffin set on trestles. Every big city had a "Hoover-
ville" camp of dispossessed men living like this.

It took a knowing eye—or the eye of poverty itself—to understand or even to observe some of the action. When oranges
fell off a truck, it wasn't always an accident; sometimes they
were the truck driver's contribution to slum kids. A woman
burning newspapers in a vacant lot might be trying to warm a

22

baby's bottle. The ragged men standing silent as cattle, in a flatrack truck parked on a lonely public road, might be getting the bum's rush out of town. In the Southwest, freight trains were black with human bodies headed for warm weather. Railroad dicks shooed them off at stations. Deming, New Mexico, hired a special constable to keep them out of town. When the Southern Pacific police ordered the men off the train, the special constable ordered them back on again.

Everyone knew of someone engaged in a desperate struggle, although most of the agony went on behind closed doors. The stories were whispered. There was something indecent about them. A well-to-do man living on the income from rental property could not collect his rents. His mortgages were foreclosed, and his houses sold for less than the debt. To make up the difference, he sold his own home. He moved himself and his wife into a nearby basement and did odd jobs for the people upstairs in exchange for a room for some of his six children. He mowed lawns, graded yards, and did whatever common labor he could find in order to pay for groceries, until his health broke down under the unaccustomed work. The doctor told him that he needed an operation and would have to rest for a year afterward.

A 72-year-old factory worker was told that he could no longer be employed because he was too old. He went home and turned on the gas. His 56-year-old widow, who had worked as a proofreader before developing heart trouble, sat alone staring at their few sticks of furniture for three days after her husband's death. Then she too turned on the gas. The neighbors smelled it in time and saved her life.

Neither the property owner nor the widow was an uncommon case. They merely were lucky enough to be among the Hundred Neediest Cases chosen by *The New York Times* for 1932. Unlike the hardship cases of the 1960s, who are often urgently in need of psychiatric help, these people were in trouble only because they were physically sick and had no money.

By the charitable standards of the rich at that time, they were regarded as the "deserving poor," as distinguished from the undeserving poor, who were thought to be unwilling to work or to save.

If the "deserving poor" had been few, charitable help might have sufficed. But there were too many, and more all the time. In December 1929, three million people were out of work. The next winter, four to five million. The winter of 1931–1932, eight million. The following year, no one knew exactly how many, but all authorities agreed that additional millions were unemployed. In 1965, unemployment is a "problem" when one in twenty is idle. In the fall of 1932, *Fortune* thought that 34 million men, women, and children—better than a fourth of the nation—were members of families that had no regular full-time breadwinner. Estimates differed, but none included farmers unable to make both ends meet, in spite of the blessing of seven-day, sunup-to-sundown employment, or factory hands who were making out on two or three days' work a week.

There were too many in want to hide. There were too many in want to blame. And even if the poor were shiftless, a Christian country would not let them starve. "Everyone is getting along somehow," people said to each other. "After all, no one has starved." But they worried even as they spoke.

A few were ashamed to eat. The Elks in Mt. Kisco, New York, and Princeton University eating clubs were among the organizations that sent leftovers from their tables to the unemployed. A reporter on *The Brooklyn Eagle* suggested a central warehouse where families could send their leftovers for distribution to the needy. John B. Nichlos, of the Oklahoma Gas Utilities Company, worked out a leftover system in detail and urged it on Hoover's Cabinet. It provided:

"Sanitary containers of five (5) gallons each should be secured in a large number so that four (4) will always be left in large kitchens

24

where the restaurants are serving a volume business. The containers should be labeled 'MEAT, BEANS, POTATOES, BREAD AND OTHER ITEMS.' Someone from the Salvation Army with a truck should pick up the loaded containers every morning and leave empty ones. The civic clubs, restaurants, the proprietors and the workers should be asked to cooperate in order to take care of all surplus food in as sanitary a way as possible. In other words, when a man finishes his meal he should not (after lighting his cigarette or cigar) leave the ashes on the food which he was unable to consume."

Many more fortunate people turned away from the unemployed, but some tried to help in the traditional neighborly way. A Brooklyn convent put sandwiches outside its door where the needy could get them without knocking. St. Louis society women distributed unsold food from restaurants. Someone put baskets in New York City railroad stations so that commuters could donate vegetables from their gardens. In New York, Bernarr Macfadden served six-cent lunches to the unemployed and claimed he was making money. In San Francisco, the hotel and restaurant workers' union arranged for unemployed chefs and waiters to serve elegant if simple meals to the unemployed.

But there was more talk than help. A great many people spent a great deal of energy urging each other to give, to share, to hire. President Hoover led a national publicity campaign to urge people to give locally and to make jobs. At the suggestion of public-relations counsel Edward L. Bernays, the first President's Emergency Committee was named "for Employment" (PECE) to accentuate the positive. In 1931 it was reorganized more realistically as the President's Organization for Unemployment Relief (POUR). Both undertook to inspire confidence by the issuing of optimistic statements; POUR chairman Walter Gifford told a Senate committee offhandedly that he did not know how many were unemployed and did not think it was the committee's job to find out.

Local groups responded by pressing campaigns of their own to "Give-A-Job" or "Share-A-Meal" until people grew deaf to them. Carl Byoir, founder of one of the country's biggest public-relations firms, declared a "War against Depression" that proposed to wipe it out in six months by getting one million employers to make one new job each.

Results of such appeals were disappointing. Corporation executives answered the pleas of PECE and POUR by saying that they had no right to spend stockholders' money hiring men they did not need. Even in New York City, where the able and well-supported Community Service Society pioneered work relief, there were enough hungry men without money to keep 82 badly managed breadlines going, and men were selling apples on every street corner. Newspapers discovered and photographed an apple seller who was formerly a near-millionaire.

The well of private charity ran dry. A Westchester woman is said to have fired all her servants in order to have money to contribute to the unemployed. "Voluntary conscription" of wages helped steelworkers weather the first round of layoffs in little Conshohocken, Pennsylvania, but the plan broke down as there were more mouths to feed and fewer pay envelopes to conscript. Local charities everywhere were overwhelmed by 1931, and the worst was yet to come.

Kentucky coal miners suffered perhaps the most. In Harlan County there were whole towns whose people had not a cent of income. They lived on dandelions and blackberries. The women washed clothes in soapweed suds. Dysentery bloated the stomachs of starving babies. Children were reported so famished they were chewing up their own hands. Miners tried to plant vegetables, but they were often so hungry that they ate them before they were ripe. On her first trip to the mountains,

26

Eleanor Roosevelt saw a little boy trying to hide his pet rabbit. "He thinks we are not going to eat it," his sister told her, "but we are." In West Virginia, miners mobbed company stores demanding food. Mountain people, with no means to leave their homes, sometimes had to burn their last chairs and tables to keep warm. Local charity could not help in a place where everyone was destitute.

No national charity existed to relieve mass poverty. The American Red Cross was big and efficient, but it had been set up to mobilize outside help for "a temporary condition brought about by some uncontrollable act or acts." Chairman John Barton Payne contended that unemployment was not an "Act of God." If not controllable by the unemployed themselves, and he believed it was, it was the result of some Act of Man and so out of bounds for the Red Cross. Payne did not even want to distribute $25 million of Federal money for drought relief because drought was a natural disaster and so belonged to the Red Cross. Government help would ruin his fund drive. "Why should the Government be dealing in this sort of thing when the people have plenty of money?" But the police could not keep hungry people out of the Red Cross warehouse in Hazard, Kentucky.

A Quaker himself, Hoover went to the American Friends Service Committee. The Philadelphia Meeting developed a "concern" for the miners. Swarthmore and Haverford students ventured into the hollows, winning the confidence of suspicious miners. They systematically weighed the children, so they could feed those in greatest need first. Hoover gave them $2,500 out of his own pocket, but most of the contributions seem to have come from the Rockefellers.

"No one has starved," Hoover boasted. To prove it, he announced a decline in the death rate. It was heartening, but puzzling, too. Even the social workers could not see how the unemployed kept body and soul together, and the more they

27

studied, the more the wonder grew. Savings, if any, went first. Then insurance was cashed. Then people borrowed from family and friends. They stopped paying rent. When evicted, they moved in with relatives. They ran up bills. It was surprising how much credit could be wangled. In 1932, about 400 families on relief in Philadelphia had managed to contract an average debt of $160, a tribute to the hearts if not the business heads of landlords and merchants. But in the end they had to eat "tight."

Every serious dieter knows how little food it takes to keep alive. One woman borrowed 50¢, bought stale bread at 3½¢ a loaf, and kept her family alive on it for 11 days. Every serious dieter knows how hunger induces total concentration on food. When eating tight, the poor thought of nothing but food, just food. They hunted food like alley cats, and in some of the same places. They haunted docks where spoiled vegetables might be thrown out and brought them home to cook up in a stew from which every member of the family would eat as little as possible, and only when very hungry. Neighbors would ask a child in for a meal or give him scraps—stale bread, bones with a bit of good meat still on them, raw potato peelings. Children would hang around grocery stores, begging a little food, running errands, or watching carts in exchange for a piece of fruit. Sometimes a member of the family would go to another part of town and beg. Anyone on the block who got hold of something big might call the neighbors in to share it. Then everyone would gorge like savages at a killing, to make up for the lean days. Enough people discovered that a five-cent candy bar can make a lunch to boom sales during the generally slow year of 1931. You get used to hunger. After the first few days it doesn't even hurt; you just get weak. When work opened up, at one point, in the Pittsburgh steel mills, men who were called back were not strong enough to do it.

Those who were still prosperous hated to think of such things and frequently succeeded in avoiding them. But professional people could not always escape. A doctor would order medicine for a charity case and then realize that there was no money to pay for it. A school doctor in Philadelphia gave a listless child a tonic to stimulate her appetite and later found that her family did not have enough to eat at home.

A reporter on *The Detroit Free Press* helped the police bring a missing boy back to a bare home on Christmas Day, 1934. He and his friends on the paper got a drugstore to open up so they could bring the boy some toys. *The Detroit Free Press* has supplied Christmas gifts for needy children every year since.

A teacher in a mountain school told a little girl who looked sick but said she was hungry to go home and eat something. "I can't," the youngster said. "It's my sister's turn to eat." In Chicago, teachers were ordered to ask what a child had had to eat before punishing him. Many of them were getting nothing but potatoes, a diet that kept their weight up, but left them listless, crotchety, and sleepy.

The police saw more than anyone else. They had to cope with the homeless men sleeping in doorways or breaking into empty buildings. They had to find help for people who fell sick in the streets or tried to commit suicide. And it was to a cop that city people went when they were at the end of their rope and did not know what else to do. In New York City, the police kept a list of the charities to which they could direct the helpless. In 1930 they took a census of needy families, and city employees started contributing one percent of their salaries to a fund for the police to use to buy food for people they found actually starving. It was the first public confession of official responsibility for plain poverty, and it came not from the top, but from the lowest-paid civil servants, who worked down where the poor people were.

Teachers worried about the children who came to school to get warm. They organized help for youngsters who needed food

29

and clothing before they could learn. Sometimes Boards of Education diverted school funds to feed them. Often the teachers did it on their own. In 1932, New York City schoolteachers contributed $260,000 out of their salaries in one month. Chicago teachers fed 11,000 pupils out of their own pockets in 1931, although they had not themselves been paid for months. "For God's sake, help us feed these children during the summer," Chicago's superintendent of schools begged the governor in June.

Mayors discovered the poor. Mayor Harry A. Mackey of Philadelphia used to disguise himself as a hobo to check up on the city shelters for unemployed men. Detroit's Frank Murphy invited the unemployed into his office and insisted on allowing them to demonstrate. In the fall of 1931 there were 600,000 single men with no work in Chicago. The city was bankrupt. Only state funds could keep the breadlines going. "Call out the troops before you close the relief stations," Mayor Anton Cermak told the Illinois state legislature.

Official recognition of need, and even Hoover's appeals to private local charity, raised questions of principle in the minds of those in a position to think of poverty and unemployment in the abstract. "You make a bad mistake in talking about the unemployed," a businessman told the mayor of Youngstown when he tried to raise a bond issue to finance city relief. *"Don't* emphasize hard times, and everything will be all right." Businessmen feared that the talk was bad for business. They did not like to think of hard times. Without firsthand experience, it was easy to stick to the traditional view that it was a man's own fault if he was poor, that a man ought to take care of his own family and lay aside something for a rainy day. The suspicion persisted that most of the poor were not really "deserving" of charity, that they were better off now than they had ever been.

Men of old-fashioned principles really believed that the less said about the unemployed, the faster they would get jobs. They really believed that public relief was bad for the poor because it discouraged them from looking for work or from taking it at wages that would tempt business to start up again. According to their theory, permanent mass unemployment was impossible, because there was work at some wage for every able-bodied man, if he would only find and do it. Charity was necessary, of course, for those who were really disabled through no fault of their own, but there could never be very many of these, and they should be screened carefully and given help of a kind and in a way that would keep them from asking for it as long as possible. Those who held this view were not necessarily hardhearted or self-interested. Josephine Lowell, a woman who devoted her life to the poor, issued the bluntest warning: "The presence in the community of certain persons living on public relief has the tendency to tempt others to sink to their degraded level." That was in 1884, when cities were smaller, and fewer people depended on the ups and downs of factory work.

The view persists. In 1961, the mayor of Newburgh, New York, cut off relief to make the unemployed find jobs. In 1965, it was thought that raising the minimum wage would hurt the poor by pricing them out of jobs.

Thirty years earlier, respectable folk worried about the idea of public relief, even though accepting the need for it. On opinion polls they agreed with the general proposition that public relief should be temporary, hard to get, and less than the lowest wage offered by any employer. In the North as well as in the South, relief stations were closed at harvesttime to force the unemployed to work at getting in the crops, for whatever wages farmers offered.

It was a scandal when a relief client drove an old jalopy up to the commissary to lug his groceries home. In some places, a client had to surrender his license plates in order to get relief, even if the old car meant a chance to earn small sums to pay for necessities not covered by relief. Phones went, too, even when they were a relief client's only lifeline to odd jobs. It was considered an outrage if a woman on relief had a smart-looking winter coat, or a ring, or a burial-insurance policy, or a piano. She was made to sell them for groceries before relief would help her. The search for hidden assets was thorough. One thrifty family in New York was denied relief "because it does not seem possible for this family to have managed without some other kind of assistance."

When a woman on relief had triplets, newspapers pointed out that for every 100 children born to self-supporting parents, relief parents produced 160. It was hard even for the social workers to see that big families were more apt to need relief. Almost everybody thought relief caused the poor to become irresponsible and to have children they could not support—if, in fact, they did not have babies deliberately in order to qualify. In 1965, there still are people who believe that Aid to Dependent Children is raising the birthrate among the poor. During the Depression, if some way could have been found to prevent married couples on relief from indulging in sexual intercourse, there would have been those who would have demanded it.

People who took public relief were denied civil rights. Some state constitutions disqualified relief clients from voting, and as late as 1938 an opinion poll showed that one out of every three Republicans thought this was right. In some places, village taxpayers' organizations tried to keep the children of tax delinquents out of the local schools. People suspected of taking public relief were even turned away from churches.

During the first and worst years of the Depression, the only public relief was improvised by cities. Appropriations were deliberately low. If funds ran out every few months, so much the better. The poor would have to make another effort to find work. Every program was "temporary." In most cases, this was

32

sheer necessity. Cities could not afford otherwise. Their tax bases were too narrow. Some of them had lost tax money when banks folded. Detroit could not collect property taxes because landlords could not collect the rent from their unemployed tenants. Bankrupt Chicago was living on tax anticipation warrants doled out by bankers. Some well-heeled citizens refused to pay their taxes at all. Cities cut their own employees, stopped buying library books, and shot zoo animals to divert money to relief.

State governments were not prepared to help. No state even had a Department of Welfare until Governor Franklin D. Roosevelt organized one for New York State in 1929. Cities begged for temporary loans. Bankers were generally reluctant, because cities did not have tax resources from which to pay back the money. The bankers made conditions. Everything was done on an emergency basis. In January 1932, the New York City Department of Welfare did not have postage stamps on hand to distribute a million dollars raised and lent to the city by a committee of bankers.

Cities had to ration relief. In 1932, family allowances in New York City fell to $2.39 a week, and only half of the families who could qualify were getting it. Things were worse elsewhere. In little Hamtramck, Michigan, welfare officials had to cut off all families with fewer than three children. In Detroit, allowances fell to 15¢ a day per person before running out entirely. Across the country, only about a fourth of the unemployed were able to get help, and fewer than that in many cities. Almost everywhere, aid was confined to food and fuel. Relief workers connived with clients to put off landlords. Medical care, clothing, shoes, chairs, beds, safety pins—everything else had to be scrounged or bought by doing without food. Those on relief were little better off than those who couldn't get it. Private help dwindled to six percent of the money spent on the unemployed.

33

Still, Hoover kept insisting, no one starved. In May 1932, Hoover's Secretary of the Interior, Dr. Ray Lyman Wilbur, reassured the National Conference of Social Workers meeting in Philadelphia. "We must set up the neglect of prosperity against the care of adversity," he philosophized. "With prosperity many parents unload the responsibilities for their children onto others. With adversity the home takes its normal place. The interest of thousands of keen and well-trained people throughout the whole country in seeing that our children are properly fed and cared for has given many of them better and more suitable food than in past good times."

Social workers were indignant. "Have you ever seen the uncontrolled trembling of parents who have starved themselves for weeks so that their children might not go hungry?" social worker Lillian Wald demanded. Others told how fathers and even older brothers and sisters hung around the street corners while the younger children were being fed, for fear they would be tempted to eat more than their share. The social workers knew the facts. They also knew newspaper reporters. In 1932, the public began to listen.

"Mrs. Green left her five small children alone one morning while she went to have her grocery order filled," one social worker reported. "While she was away the constable arrived and padlocked her house with the children inside. When she came back she heard the six-weeks-old baby crying. She did not dare touch the padlock for fear of being arrested, but she found a window open and climbed in and nursed the baby and then climbed out and appealed to the police to let her children out."

Eviction was so common that children in a Philadelphia day-care center made a game of it. They would pile all the doll furniture up first in one corner and then in another. "We ain't got no money for the rent, so we's moved into a new house," a tot explained to the teacher. "Then we got the constable on us,

34

so we's movin' again." Philadelphia relief paid an evicted family's rent for one month in the new house. Then they were on their own. Public opinion favored the tenant. An eviction could bring on a neighborhood riot.

Landlords often let the rent go. Some of them needed relief as much as their tenants, and had a harder time qualifying for it. In Philadelphia a little girl whose father was on relief could not get milk at school, under a program for needy children, because her father "owned property." Investigators found some unemployed tenants sharing food orders with their landlords. In the country, where poor farmers had been accustomed to paying their taxes in work on the roads, tenants who could not pay their rent sometimes did the landlord's road work for him.

It was not true that "no one starved." People starved to death, and not only in Harlan County, Kentucky. The New York City Welfare Council counted 29 deaths from starvation in 1933. More than fifty other people were treated for starvation in hospitals. An additional 110, most of them children, died of malnutrition.

A father who had been turned away by a New York City welfare agency was afraid to apply for help after public relief had been set up. Social workers found one of his children dead; another, too weak to move, lay in bed with the mother; the rest huddled, shivering and hungry, around the desperate father.

A New York dentist and his wife died rather than accept charity. They left a note, and then took gas together. "The entire blame for this tragedy rests with the City of New York or whoever it is that allows free dental work in the hospital," the note read. "We want to get out of the way before we are forced to accept relief money. The City of New York is not to touch our bodies. We have a horror of charity burial. We have put the last of our money in the hands of a friend who will turn it over to my brother."

Health surveys were made to pound home the fact that poor

35

people are sicker than the well-to-do. Doctors, nurses, teachers, and social workers warned that privation was ruining the nation's health. In 1933, the Children's Bureau reported that one in five American children was not getting enough of the right things to eat. Lower vitality, greater susceptibility to infections, slower recovery, stunting, more organic disease, a reversal of gains against tuberculosis—all were freely predicted. Medical care for the poor was sketchy. Doctors were hard hit financially, and they did not always live up to the Oath of Hippocrates. Frequently, the poor were afraid to call a doctor because they did not have money. New York City surgeons sometimes demanded cash in advance or delayed operations until the family could get money together.

Middle-class people put off the doctor and the dentist. "Illness frightens us," John Dos Passos writes of his Depression days at Pacific Grove, California. "You have to have money to be sick—or did then. Any dentistry also was out of the question, with the result that my teeth went badly to pieces. Without dough you couldn't have a tooth filled." Hospitals could never fill the private rooms that helped to pay for their charity cases, with the result that they had fewer patients than they do now, but sicker ones. They learned to be tough in admitting people who could not pay.

The harder the middle class looked, the more critical poverty seemed. It did not seem possible that people could stand lack of regular food, unstable homes, medical neglect. The Depression would leave its mark in the future. "If we put the children in these families under a period of malnutrition such as they are going through today, what sort of people are we going to have twenty years from now?" Karl de Schweinitz of the Philadelphia Community Council asked a Senate committee in 1932. "What will we say at that time about them?"

Senator Robert M. La Follette pursued the point in the same hearing. "What do you think would happen to your standard of living and the health conditions of your dependents if you were forced to exist on $5.50 a week?" he asked Walter Gifford, president of American Telephone and Telegraph Company and chairman of POUR. Walter Gifford conceded they would be bad. Senator La Follette cited some of the evidence of overcrowding. "Do you think this is an adequate meeting of the problem of relief?" La Follette pressed.

"In prosperous times I regret to say, unfortunately, you find conditions like that," Gifford stammered. "Whether we can, as much as we might like to, under these conditions, and in these times, remedy conditions which we could not remedy in more prosperous times, I doubt."

He was right. The Depression did not depress the conditions of the poor. It merely publicized them. The poor had been poor all along. It was just that nobody had looked at them. The children of Depression grew up to be bigger and healthier than their parents, who had enjoyed the advantages of a prosperous childhood. World War II recruits were more fit in every way than doughboys drafted in World War I. The death rate did not rise in the Depression. It kept going down. The health record of the Depression parallels that of rapidly industrializing societies everywhere: infectious diseases dropped, but mental illness, suicide, and the degenerative diseases of an aging population rose.

One explanation may be that people do not need as much food as they think. Since the Depression we have learned that the thin rats bury the fat rats. In 1965, some of the richest Americans are restricting themselves to a calorie intake United Nations Food and Agriculture specialists define as starvation. Food standards are relative. In 1929, we imagined America's amber fields of grain feeding everyone the hearty meals then regarded as necessary. Three years later, in 1932, when we weren't so sure everyone was eating, the Brookings Institution used a new Department of Agriculture definition of the cost of

37

an "adequate diet" to show that in prosperous 1929 one out of every eight families was fighting hunger. Nutrition researchers are less arbitrary than they used to be. Man seems to be an omnivore with unsuspected resources for converting wildly unbalanced foods.

But the most likely explanation for our surviving poverty is grimmer. The poor survived because they knew how to be poor. The Milbank Foundation found more sickness among the poor than among the well off, but they also found that the newly poor were sicker more often than those who always had been poor. In the 1960s, social work provides steady jobs for people who often are close to poverty themselves. In the 1930s, charity was work for middle- and upper-class volunteers, who were charmed and awed by the techniques for survival that they discovered.

A family eating tight would stay in bed a lot. That way they would save fuel, as well as the extra food calories needed in cold weather. The experienced poor, particularly the Negroes, knew about eating the parts of the animal normally rejected. And the poor generally did not spend as much money on food as their middle-class advisers thought they should be spending.

The poor worked at keeping warm. A family with no money for the gas company would economize by cooking once a week. When it was cut off, they would cook in the furnace. They gathered scrap wood to keep the furnace going. They saved by heating only the kitchen. When fuel was low, the experienced poor would sneak into a movie house. Even if they had to spend ten cents to get in, they could sometimes keep out of the cold for two double features. When the electricity was turned off, some men found ways to steal current by tapping a neighbor's wire.

Shoes were a problem. The poor took them off when they got home, to save them. Do-it-yourself shoe-repair kits were popular with the middle class, but if you could not afford the dime-store item you could resole a pair of shoes with rubber cut from

38

an old tire, or wear rubbers over a worn-out sole. Clothes were swapped among the family. One mother and daughter managed to get together an outfit both could wear. They took turns going to church.

The poor whose lives were laid bare by the Depression lived in the same world of poverty that Michael Harrington has recently described in *The Other America,* and Oscar Lewis in his studies of the working classes in Mexico. They lived for the present without much thought for their own past or future. They ate quite literally from hand to mouth. Even when they had a little money, they did not lay in stocks of food. They paid high interest rates on what they bought or borrowed, and seldom got their money's worth. Their world was small, limited to the people they saw every day, and they did not venture out of it. A trip to the relief office was a daring undertaking. They had few friends. They did not read. Without outside contacts, they could not organize or revolt or escape.

A year after his defeat by Roosevelt, Hoover—who had repeated so many times that no one was starving—went on a fishing trip with cartoonist "Ding" Darling in the Rocky Mountains. One morning a local man came into their camp, found Hoover awake, and led him to a shack where one child lay dead and seven others were in the last stages of starvation. Hoover took the children to a hospital, made a few phone calls, and raised a fund of $3,030 for them.

Before the Crash, it was easy for the middle classes to forget about the poor, because soon everyone was going to be rich. Some of the poor themselves were carried along on the tide of illusion. When they thought about their poverty, they thought they were exceptions, or victims of bad luck, or that it was true they did not deserve any better. Unemployment was high in the good years. Farmers, seamen, textile workers, coal miners had hard going all through the prosperous Twenties, but many believed that soon all this would change.

Before the Crash, nobody suspected how many Americans were poor. Senator Paul Douglas, then a social worker, figured that it took almost $2,500 a year to support a family of four on what he called "the American standard of living." In 1929, more than two-thirds of the people were living on that amount or less. After the Crash, manufacturers and farmers talked about overproduction, but they did not have the capacity to produce an "American standard of living" for everybody. Those who were black, or didn't speak English, were not even expected to live "like white folks."

The Depression gave the middle classes a double vision of the poor. They did not give up the notions that the poor should have saved or that they did not want to work, or that their poverty was their own fault. These were concepts hard to change. While firmly holding to these ideas, however, they saw contradictory facts before their eyes. When the Depression forced them to scrutinize the condition of the working people, they could see that wages were too low and employment too intermittent for most wageworkers to save enough money to see them through emergencies, or old age, even if banks had not failed. A favorite cartoon of the times pictured a squirrel asking an old man sitting on a park bench why he had not saved for a rainy day.

"I did," said the old man.

3

$ $ $ $ $

SUPERFLUOUS PEOPLE

A FEW years ago a well-paid staff specialist retired early from a corporation famous for its lush fringe benefits so that he and his wife could paint, travel, and enjoy their country house. Almost at once, his wife began worrying about money. Within six months, she recognized the irrationality of her distress and consulted a psychiatrist. With his help she discovered that as a little girl she had learned that whenever her adored father stayed at home to play with her during the day, it meant that he was out of work, and disaster quickly followed. The psychiatrist suggested that the husband offer his services to a nonprofit organization. As soon as he began leaving the house at the same time every morning, the wife rapidly recovered.

This could have happened only in America. Americans not only say they would continue working if sudden riches struck them, they really do it. One of the reasons is that most American men and women over 50 spent their youth running away from a fate that, but for the grace of God, could have happened to almost anyone.

The image was specific and graphic: a bent, graying man

turning away from a factory gate that bore the sign "No Help Wanted Today."

Cartoonists used the figure so often that all the misery of unemployment came to be symbolized in the sagging shoulder line of a man shuffling aimlessly away from the reader, carrying the bad news back to his wife and children.

As conservatives repeated all through the Depression, the poor we have always had with us. But all along there had been more of them than we realized. After the Crash we discovered how many, and how poor they were, because for the first time the poor were also idle and they became conspicuous. They were poor, not because they did the lowest-paid and hardest work, but because they were of no use. In non-Catholic America they did not even provide the rich with an opportunity to practice the Christian virtue of charity. They were superfluous people.

What happens to people when they are not needed? What happens to a society loaded with superfluous people? Any serious study of the impact of mass unemployment must begin with the Depression. Men who remember the Depression personally look back to it for their answers, and as long as Lyndon B. Johnson is President such men will be making policy.

It is hard to realize now that so many were idle for so long. In the 1960s, the President's Council of Economic Advisors officially sounds the alarm when unemployment rises to five percent of the labor force. In 1931, 16 percent of the people who wanted to work could not find jobs, and the rate kept straight on up to 25 percent in 1933. In 1937, there was "prosperity" because real income per capita had climbed back almost to 1929 levels and unemployment had broken a few decimal places below 15 percent. In 1938, however, unemployment was up again to 19 percent. In 1941, when we thought we were rearming at full blast, we rejoiced because unemployment was down to 10 percent. Ten percent is more than twice the proportion of the labor force we are willing to have idle under President Johnson.

The Depression unemployed were not the hard-core poor alone. They were a good fat sample of people of all kinds. During the 1930s, one in every four or five persons of working age was unable to find work for long enough periods to learn how it feels to be unwanted.

It was as if the law of supply and demand was being applied to human beings. The unemployed treated themselves as a glut on the market and tried to get rid of themselves. There was something "dead" about them. There were so many superfluous people around during the Depression that it did not seem quite decent for the others to act fully alive. Careful studies showed that the unemployed moved more slowly than the employed poor, were sicker more often, more unhappy, more suicidal, more distrustful, and less self-confident. The decade in which American society was visibly loaded with superfluous people was a time of life-denying morals and manners. During the 1930s we played down sexual passion, regarded pregnancy as a disaster, treated children as burdens, and thought of food as an exercise in nutrition.

The economic waste was easy enough to see, and it was, of course, astronomical in terms of the value of goods and services the unemployed could have produced. Less calculable but more tragic was the waste of human skills. People took any kind of job they could get, regardless of training or aptitude. When the Government needed skilled war workers, a test survey in Kokomo, Indiana, disclosed that, as a result of Depression emergency, almost half the workers in town were in the wrong jobs: a sheet-metal worker was a shipping clerk; a diemaker was running a sewage plant; a drill-press operator was a janitor, a molder was a policeman, and a barrel reamer was digging ditches.

Skilled workers laid off by factories clerked in stores, slung

43

food across lunch counters, washed dishes, tended gas stations, wrapped packages, delivered groceries, swept out beauty parlors. So few people were able to pay for medical care that airlines were able to hire registered nurses to serve as stewardesses. At $4 a day, jury duty was a break. Construction was so hard hit that you could have an architect for an office boy if you wanted one. Many employers did not. The personnel problems of hiring people who "thought they were too good for the job" were indignantly discussed. Meanwhile, skills rusted with disuse. Unemployed stenographers hired on work relief were known to break down and cry, out of sheer nervousness, the first time they tried to take dictation on their new jobs.

Almost unnoticed at the time were the questionable management practices encouraged by an "easy labor market." Enough skills were waiting outside the gate for Detroit automobile makers to put most of the operations on piece rates, thus shifting to the workers the burden of time lost due to machine breakdowns or lack of planning. Once Hudson called back a small-parts assembler and then kept her waiting three days for a half-hour's work, so that she spent 60 cents in carfare to earn 28 cents. Laborsaving devices were not economic when muscle was cheap. Machines that handled materials, such as fork-lift trucks and loaders, were not widely installed before the labor shortage of World War II. Skilled workers and professionals could be wasted on unprofitable little stores and gas stations, attempts to farm bad land, and marginal, door-to-door peddling.

At a time when established farmers were being foreclosed and wheat growers talked of lighting out to the sub-Arctic brush country with a hog and a cow and a gun to kill moose, urban workers were drifting back to the country looking for something to eat. Between 1930 and 1935, a million acres went into cultivation in farms of ten acres and less. While a few may have been high-powered cash truck farms, most yielded only enough

44

vegetables and chickens to feed a single family. Many were on land so poor that it never had been seriously farmed.

Some of the unemployed were pathetically enterprising. One relief client concealed from social workers the little income he made on the side from selling cast-off corsets salvaged from garbage dumps. People on relief actually starved themselves to save up enough money to start a little business. Five million people bought a book entitled *Think and Grow Rich,* which Dr. Napoleon Hill said he wrote while advising Franklin D. Roosevelt in the White House.

We have no way of knowing how many people borrowed on life insurance or shot their last few hundred dollars to go into business and fail, but there must have been millions. In 1960, only one man in seven earned a living in his own business, but at the end of the war a survey in Oakland, California, indicated that probably one man out of three had been in business for himself at some time. Turnover was high among the two million or more "firms" employing one to three people. They failed quietly and looked for jobs.

Ways were found to exploit these eager entrepreneurs. Certain oil companies encouraged the unemployed to open gas stations that boosted sales slightly for the refinery, but returned less than relief subsistence to the "owner." Millions of painfully saved dollars were wasted on gas stations that never had a chance. Beauty "schools" flourished on the unpaid labor of students. Manufacturers set women up in little front-parlor shops and got rich selling them beauty equipment for $250 down and $25 a month. Giving a wash, set, and manicure for a dollar, these amateurs could return a handsome rate of interest to the supplier who was bankrolling them. Like nurses, professional beauticians began to lobby for state licensing to limit entry into their field.

People invested their savings in "parlor" grocery stores. Between 1929 and 1939, while retail sales dropped $6 billion,

45

nearly 400,000 *more* people were trying to make a living from little stores. Suppliers flourished meeting the demand for cash registers, but some of the little grocery-store proprietors barely sold enough to be able to replenish the stock they ate off the shelves. At a time when people were cutting their own hair, washing their own clothes, and resoling their own shoes to save money, thousands hopefully started one-chair barber shops, diaper laundries, shoeshine stands, cleaning and pressing shops, antiques shops, tearooms, and catering services. At a time when money was scarce, thousands plodded from door to door peddling books, magazines, vacuum cleaners, pressure cookers, and other nonessential consumer articles—no more efficiently than household goods were purveyed in Homer's day.

Companies increased sales at little expense by inducing the unemployed to sell on a commission basis. The harder the times, the better the talent that sales managers were able to enlist. Alfred C. Fuller reports that sales of his Fuller Brush Company "suddenly upended, like a tired freighter, and headed toward the bottom" during the prosperous closing years of the boom, but jumped from $15,000 to $50,000 in the doldrum month of August 1932 alone, and grew at the rate of a million dollars a year all through the Depression.

Salesmen thought up sales arguments that were often little short of appeals to pity. The pressure to sell insurance was intense. Salesmen for the "industrial insurance," sold door-to-door to working-class people, sometimes invented sales to meet the quotas set by their companies, and paid out of their own pockets to maintain these "tombstone" or "lamppost" policies. When pressed to reduce claims, they sometimes deliberately allowed policies of very sick people to lapse just before death. At a slightly higher level, insurance companies took on recent college graduates just to sell the few policies their relatives would take to help the young men get started. The more resourceful salesmen sometimes beat the competition by becom-

46

ing "insurance counselors," charging a fee for showing big holders how to save money by rearranging their policies. The companies called them "twisters."

Door-to-door salesmen of all kinds swarmed from town to town competing with local merchants for any loose change the lady of the house might have on hand. Cities tried to stop them by instituting licensing and fingerprinting. Green River, Wyoming, originated a widely adopted ordinance forbidding anyone to solicit a home without invitation. Fuller Brush fought back by offering the housewife a gift if she invited the salesman inside. Empty hotels, straining to meet boom-time mortgage payments, posted signs saying, "Patronize firms that keep salesmen on the road!"

Most of all, the unemployed eagerly exploited themselves. They took on piecework at ruinous rates. In Connecticut, a family of six worked at stringing safety pins on wires late into the night for less than $5 a week. Unemployed textile workers set up looms in their homes, reviving the evils of the early industrial revolution in England. At a time when oil and gas were forcing coal-mine operators to mechanize mines for greater efficiency or abandon them, unemployed coal miners were bootlegging coal by the most primitive and dangerous hand methods and selling it cut-rate in cities.

Bootleg coal became a big industry. In some years it accounted for 10 percent of the anthracite consumed in New York City. More than 6,500 miners made a living of sorts out of it, some hiring others for as little as 50 cents a day. Bootlegging hastened the bankruptcy of the Philadelphia & Reading Coal Company, which estimated that four million tons of coal a year were diverted from legal channels by the individual enterprisers of the mountains. The bootleggers organized an Independent Anthracite Miners Association for mutual defense and to keep each other from such dangerous practices as digging under highways. The preamble of this extraordinary organization was frank:

> "We must dig the coal out of these mountains as a means of supplementing our measly income that we receive in the form of relief, in order to keep the wolf from our doorsteps. Knowing that the coal which is in these mountains was put there by our Creator and that this mineral wealth was stolen away from us by the greedy rich class, the coal operators and the bankers . . ."

What the unemployed really wanted was a job, in spite of the clichés to the contrary, and some went to heroic lengths to find work. Job-hunting stories became Depression folklore. A persistent one was about the man in the Northwest who set a fire in order to get a job putting it out. Another was about the employment-agency head whose business was so bad that he took the first job he was asked to fill. Still another reports that a man whose "Situation Wanted" ad was put in the "Help Wanted" column by mistake drew 45 "applicants." A girl is supposed to have landed a job as a secretary by offering to cope with the flood of replies received by a man who had advertised for one.

In Detroit, men stood outside automobile plants all night long to be at the head of the line when the office opened. They built bonfires to keep warm. They wrapped their feet in gunnysacks to keep them from freezing while they waited.

Untold foot-pounds of energy were spent just in looking for work. In 1931, commercial employment agencies reported 5,000 applicants for every 100 job openings. The unsuccessful 4,900 simply wasted their shoe leather. This was no joke. The unemployed worried about their shoes. Jack Conroy, a miner's son, described what a hole in a shoe could mean to a man walking the streets for a job:

> "Maybe it starts with a little hole in the sole; and then the slush of the pavements oozes in, gumming sox and balling between your

48

toes. Concrete whets Woolworth sox like a file, and if you turn the heel on top and tear a pasteboard innersole, it won't help much. There are the tacks too. You get to avoiding high places and curb-stones because that jabs the point right into the heel. Soon the tack has calloused a furrowed hole, and you don't notice it unless you strike something unusually high or solid, or forget and walk flat-footed. You pass a thousand shoe-shops where a tack might be bent down, but you can't pull off a shoe and ask to have *that* done—for nothing."

The picture of the retreating father, with his sagging back, goaded the unemployed to seek work as relentlessly as the starving picked over garbage dumps for food, but it really spoke to everybody. The cartoonist's national emblem of un-employment conveyed a profound uneasiness, a malaise that getting a job could not cure. The image haunted millions who lived in fear that momentarily they might lose their jobs. It told millions of others not even to try to find work: until World War II, we never realized how many employable people had never worked for pay because they had taken it for granted that the nation's economy did not want them.

"Get lost," the silent figure seemed to say, and it gave dif-ferent reasons to different people. "You are too black or too Jewish or too old or the wrong sex to work here."

"Move on," it said to the newcomers. "Why don't you go back where you came from?" So many country boys got the message that there were years when more people went back to the farms than came to the cities.

"Stay home," it said to women. "Don't take a job from a man. And you'd better not have a baby, either."

And to men it said, "Keep away from women. Don't get hooked. If you can do it, keep away from your wife. You don't need children."

"Be careful," it said to everybody. "Save your money. Don't

49

spend. Don't get your hopes up. Keep clean and sober. Don't ask for anything. Don't take any chances."

"Light out," it seemed to say to some fathers. "You're just a mouth around the house. They'll be better off without you. Drop dead."

Many deserted their families, and a few killed themselves. There is such a thing as psychosomatic suicide. My great-grandmother's hundredth birthday killed her. "Nobody lives to be a hundred years old," she kept saying, "that's too old," and a few weeks later she quietly died.

Unemployed heads of families were the certified superfluous. They, too, felt that there was something unseemly about being alive at all. They crept around the house trying to act as if they were not there. They made as few demands as possible, sexually and otherwise. They did not think they had a right to beget children. And they thought a great deal about suicide.

Men who killed themselves rather than go on relief, or so that their families could collect their insurance, were classified by sociologist Emil Durkheim as "altruistic" suicides. One of the most dramatic was Albert R. Erskine, president of the Studebaker Company, who kept announcing that the Depression was over, and paid out five times the net profit of his company in dividends in the attempt to prove that he was right. When Studebaker went bankrupt in 1933, Erskine invited his wife's family to their house so she would not be alone when he was found, wrapped a bath towel around his middle, and shot himself to death in the bathroom. Erskine's estate collected his $900,000 life insurance and paid his debts.

Suicide was a staple of proletarian fiction. The unemployed hero of *The Happiest Man on Earth,* by Albert Maltz, insists on taking a well-paid but lethal job driving a dynamite truck, hoping to last long enough to provide for his wife after his death. "I'm going to feel proud of myself for the first time in seven years," he exults. In real life, these suicides were often

50

masked as accidents, or noted only on police records. In Mamet's *The Pension,* an elderly worker is put on a "killer machine" by an employer who hopes the man will die before he can claim his pension. The worker kills himself.

Harvard epidemiologists Brian MacMahon and Thomas Pugh find that suicides go up with unemployment. Suicides rose gently all through the Twenties and passed October 1929 without a visible hump, but they rose faster in 1930, 1931, and 1932. They peaked in 1933, the year of deepest unemployment, and then fell jaggedly down. They dropped sharply in the war years, when everyone who could work was in the armed forces or on a defense job, sloped more gently when the soldiers were coming home, but still kept going down until in the mid-Sixties the suicide rate of the United States is about half what it was in the gilded Twenties. The suicide rate has been more sensitive to unemployment than to any other economic indicator.

The birthrate reflects unemployment, too. The decline was dramatic in the Depression. In some years we did not produce enough girl babies to be sure of reproducing ourselves. We came out of the Depression with nearly three million fewer babies than would have been born at 1929 rates, and if the birth rate had continued as low as it was in 1933, nearly 30 million people alive in 1965 would never have been born at all.

Most couples lowered their sights to two children, less than the 2.6 average per couple required for replacement. In the 1930s, statisticians forecast a 1960 population of 134 million, or at most 147 million—some 40 million short of the 179 million counted at the census of 1960. Stuart Chase is worth quoting at some length on the outlook, not so much because the opposite happened in every particular, but because he expressed the Depression foreboding so vividly:

"Manufacturers of infants' clothing—and presently youths' and misses' clothing—of toys, bicycles, perambulators, bottles, baby

51

carriages, kindergarten equipment, must prepare for a slackening demand. As children become scarcer, they may be valued more highly, and spoiled more thoroughly. Fees to pediatric specialists may hit the stratosphere. But there will be less call for obstetricians, wet nurses and lying-in hospitals."

(The only prophecy of this batch that came true was the decline in the call for wet nurses: breast feeding is in fashion, but today's mothers want to nurse their own.)

Most couples said they aspired to no more than two children because they did not think they could support more, but this could not have been the whole story. Most sociologists blamed the decline on the spread of birth control because they assumed that women did not want babies and had them only when they could not help it. Conservatives like Louis Dublin, of Metropolitan Life, opposed birth control because it tempted "people most fit to become parents to shirk their duty to the state."

Feminists and liberals worried more about getting means of birth control to the poor than about keeping them from the rich. They pointed out that half of the births were in families on relief, or with less than $1,000 a year, and that families on relief accounted for more than their share of children. When Catholic Monsignor Ryan objected that the country really needed more consumers, liberal journalist Dorothy Dunbar Bromley retorted that it really needed fewer unemployed.

The earnest public discussion did more than help overcome scruples against using birth control. It taught people how to ask for it. Gas stations began to sell contraceptives, and soon they were offered in the Sears, Roebuck catalog. Although rich white women had a head start in adopting birth control, the poor caught up rapidly. Opinion polls reported overwhelming public sentiment for making birth control widely available.

Moralists blamed women for "selfishness" in preferring consumer goods to babies, but selfishness was not the reason for

52

limiting families. The cliché of the times states the real reason straightforwardly: "I don't want to bring children into a world that has no use for them."

The world had less use for some, of course, than for others. This is always true, but the tragedy of a world full of superfluous people was that it could afford the irrational preferences we now outlaw as "discrimination in employment." Not only could it afford them, it actually needed them, in order to choose among the hordes who were equally qualified. Consider, for instance, what happened when a "Secretary Wanted" ad drew scores of crackerjack applicants. An employer could interview the first ten, but when he discovered that all were competent, he still had to find some reason for preferring one over the others.

Some of the reasons for discrimination were bizarre. A hospital rejected an applicant for nursing school on the ground that her crooked teeth might disturb patients. Women who hoped to teach did not dare to smoke, drink, or dress too fashionably, at least in public. One Rose Freistater was refused a permanent job teaching in New York City, for instance, because she weighed 182 pounds—too fat, the examiners said, to move quickly in a fire drill. Rose was a spunky girl. She protested to the newspapers, and the examiners gave her six months to get down to 150 pounds. When Major General John F. O'Ryan became police chief of New York City in 1934, he looked over 75 patrolmen qualified to serve as his chauffeur and decided to make his decision on the basis of height. "Some of the men who drive the cars now are too tall," he explained to reporters. "They have to bend down when they get into the cars. That does not look so good. A man should be able to get in without lowering his head."

It was more impersonal, of course, to rule out whole classes of applicants on the basis of age, sex, color, or marital status. These exclusions were so generally accepted that most people

53

did not stop to think that they were purely arbitrary, or at least archaic, criteria for organizing industrial work, and it was not until the war brought full employment that people saw how unreasonable they really were. When people were superfluous, everyone, including the victims, tended to take the mythical disqualifications for real. In the effort to get jobs, men dyed their hair, women took off their wedding rings, Jews changed their names and their noses, and Negroes enriched the lotion manufacturers who promised to straighten their hair.

Before the full employment of World War II, there were no black faces in department stores. There were no black faces in offices. There were not even very many in that outpost of equal opportunity, the Post Office. There were "nigger jobs" and "white men's jobs," but during the Depression the distinction broke down. White men wanted the "nigger jobs," and in any case the "nigger jobs" were so vulnerable that the Negro job market was what we would now call an "early economic indicator" of downturn. The Negro newspaper in Chicago, *The Defender*, noticed the slowdown before the Crash, and for the first time in its history warned Southern Negroes to stay in the South.

The Negroes took more than their share of the Depression damage. They got it from all sides. Unions hated them because many of the Negroes in Chicago and East St. Louis had come originally as strikebreakers, but when under Communist influence unions began to admit them and force them to charge union rates, they could not get jobs at all. Low relief standards were tolerated in part at least because welfare clients were predominantly Negroes who had "never known anything better." In Chicago, for instance, four out of ten relief clients in 1939 were Negro.

White relief clients felt that equal treatment was an injustice. "It makes me boil," an unemployed white relief client told a reporter. "Where do I come in to be compared with the col-

54

ored people? They have always lived like animals." In Baltimore, in 1935, *The Sun* reported it as a scandal that the Federal Government was running a work relief camp where "colored women live in screened-in cabins, possess a beautifully furnished main room for recreation and study, and have tennis courts, swings, and a croquet ground for sports." Worse yet, the women were given chicken and ice cream for Sunday dinner.

The Negroes were the most superfluous of the superfluous people and they adjusted, as did the white unemployed, by lying low. Like the rest of the unemployed, they clung desperately to anything that passed for a "place" in the world, no matter how humble. Negro children learn early that their place is literally low. On the play table psychological test, a little Negro boy was given various toy objects and told to make up a story about them; he carefully arranged them *under* the table. Child psychiatrist Erik Erikson thought he did so because he felt that he belonged under the table himself. Once a Negro woman quietly removed a hat she had bought at a rummage sale when she discovered that Eleanor Roosevelt was wearing one like it. The Negro professional people who should have led protests against discrimination were so scared by the Depression that even as late as 1954 they still were unable to stand up and demand compliance with the Supreme Court decision integrating the public schools. The Negro protests of the 1960s were led by Negroes who had grown up during the war when people were needed so badly that war plants and the armed forces could not afford discrimination.

Jews fared better than Negroes, but we forget how openly they were barred thirty years ago. Big law firms excluded them, or relegated them to the back room. Medical schools had a Jewish quota, which meant that a Jewish boy had to be brighter than a Christian boy to get in, reason enough for the recognized superiority of medicine as practiced in Jewish hospitals compared to that in Catholic hospitals. When *The New York Times* refused ads specifying "Christian," Jews were warned away by such phrases as "out-of-towner preferred," or "near churches." Hitler's persecution of the Jews seems to have struck a responsive chord in people looking for a scapegoat for their business troubles, particularly small retailers who complained that the Jews were unfair competition because they stayed open on Sundays.

During the Depression, a surprising number of otherwise decent people commented (in lowered voice betraying their moral uneasiness) that maybe Hitler "had something"—Jews were getting pretty aggressive in this country, too. Anti-Semitic jokes flowed freely, and many newspapers identified Jews in their columns as Jews, whether this was pertinent to the rest of the story or not, much as Southern newspapers carefully identified Negroes. Few saw the unconscious bias in the protest that "some of my best friends are Jews." Many other clichés that the mid-Sixties ear detects as bias were not identified as such when Hitler was in power. It was not until we had full employment that Jewish organizations were able to press effectively for an end to "gentlemen's agreements" and to real-estate covenants excluding Jews from clubs and summer resorts. The war and postwar demand for talent helped break down discrimination against Jewish professional and staff specialists everywhere but in the most stately executive suites.

Married women workers suffered from discrimination as much as Negroes and Jews. A surprising number of people thought the Depression could be cured if married women were sent back home and their jobs were given to men. In 1931, a majority of cities had laws against hiring married women as civil servants, and for a while even the Federal Government would not let both a husband and a wife draw Federal paychecks. The laws were repealed later on in the decade, when it turned out that sending the women home did not open up jobs for men, but deprived some households of their only means of support.

Most school systems forced a teacher to give up her job when she married. The rule had no foundation in merit or mercy. People thought men teachers would be better than women for schoolboys more than 13 years old, but there was no move to employ men. A teacher no sooner got to know her job than she was forced to choose between her job and marrying the man she loved. When he did not have a job, which was frequently the case, she was tempted to marry in secret or live with him out of wedlock. The National Association of Women Lawyers reported that teachers were marrying, then heading for Reno to get a quickie divorce during the summer months, before they could be fired. Most of them, said the Association, intended to remarry their husbands when the men found work.

It is hard to escape the conclusion that the rule against married teachers was intended to benefit the *husband* of the teacher rather than the children or the teaching staff itself. It seems to have been one of those backhanded reasons of the heart rather than of the head, but it was based on emotional realities everyone understood. The plain truth was that unemployment hurt men much harder than women.

The hourly-paid factory and construction work most men did was more subject to layoff than the lower-paid but steadier clerical and service work performed by women. The result was that more households than would admit it were in fact supported by women. Most families simply could not—or it was thought that they could not—survive this radical reversal of roles. Then, too, wives of unemployed men fared much better than their husbands. Even when there was not a cent in the house they had an occupation. They were still in command of "their" homes. Men were displaced persons, moping around the house, interfering with the routine. Relief investigators reported more quarreling among families of the unemployed.

"Have you anybody you can send around to tell my wife you have no job to give me?" a husband asked a social worker.

"Certainly I lost my love for him," a wife told another social worker matter-of-factly. "How can you love a husband who causes you so much suffering?"

Unemployment is less damaging in Latin America, where men do not have to support a family to prove their masculinity. In the United States the threat to male pride was sensed as a threat to civilization itself. Because women were so much less vulnerable, it was easy to blame them for undermining the confidence of their men. The contemporary folklore of the sexes pictured women as aggressive. A popular notion of the time was that women were getting control of all the money and property in the country. Another notion was that women were ruining men by egging them on to make money and then withholding from them sexually, like the "Bitch Goddess" movie heroines, or castrating them emotionally, like Philip Wylie's "Mom." Sex, like color or religion, is not relevant to most industrial employment, but Americans are not willing, as the Russians are, to leave sex a private affair. It has economic work to do.

Generations after Ibsen's *Doll's House*, Americans continue to talk incessantly and obsessively about the role of women. Books and articles and conversation make the problem sound intrinsically insoluble. Meanwhile, American women continue to suffer more discrimination in employment than women in Europe, or even in Asian and African countries that we like to think keep women "in their places." American women scold themselves and each other both for working "outside the home" and for staying in it.

Why do we make such a problem out of the role of women? The answer may be that when our economy stalled the orderly transition to paid work, we made women the scapegoats along with members of minorities. Negroes, Jews, married women— even the old and the teen-age young who were unable to find

58

work because of their age—could not escape the feeling that they were intrinsically inferior, not good enough to work.

A recent attempt to measure the will-o'-the-wisp of happiness has shown employment to be a key discriminator between those who say they are happy and those who say they are unhappy. One third of the unemployed studied by Dr. Norman M. Bradburn of the University of Chicago admitted they were "not too happy" compared with 12 percent of the employed and only nine percent of the self-employed. Fear of unemployment casts a pall, too. The poor and old in communities with high unemployment were more apt to say they were unhappy than those where unemployment was less threatening.

When Bradburn further broke down the replies of his sample he discovered something that sounds startling until you think a moment. Negative feelings of worry and trouble did not make people unhappy as much as the lack of positive feelings of elation or pleasure. According to him, the bluebird of happiness is the balance between fun and misery. You can have lots of both and be happy; you can have little of both and be happy, provided the fun stays ahead of the misery.

The Depression hurt people and maimed them permanently because it literally depressed mind and spirit. Hoover chose the word "Depression" in 1929 because it sounded less frightening than "panic" or "crisis," the words that had formerly been used for economic downturns. If he had consulted Dr. Bradburn, he would have stuck to the words suggesting excitement, for if it is lively enough, trouble can be fun, too. To its unemployed victims, the Depression was a dull misery in the bones, rather than an interesting illness calling for dramatic remedy.

When Bradburn broke down the "positive feelings" the unhappy lacked, he uncovered the most plausible link between unemployment and unhappiness—a link that could easily be the point of departure for a midcentury assault on the evil of idleness. Of all the positive factors he counted, a cluster meas-

59

uring "social interaction" proved to be the best indicator of happiness. Social interaction was scored on the basis of seven factors, all of them reducible to a number: organizations belonged to, phone calls per day, distance traveled from home in past week, meetings attended, friends visited, auto rides taken, restaurant meals eaten.

All seven of these activities declined during the Depression. Clubs and churches lost membership. During the first half of the decade the spending of recreational groups dropped to half, a third of the Grange and rural women's clubs disappeared, and millions of telephones were taken out. Even the mails were lighter. Travel dwindled. Meetings and church services were poorly attended. Restaurants lost business.

When a man lost his job, he shunned his former friends and refused invitations. One reason was that it took money to see people, and often there was not money enough to offer a visitor so much as a cup of coffee. Children had to have at least a penny to put on the collection plate at Sunday School, and they needed shoes for school. A great many children stayed at home because they lacked clothes to go out. It took carfare—at least a dime, a nickel going and a nickel coming back—to get almost anywhere. Housewives rarely got a chance to leave the house. Hard times isolated women in the city as traumatically as the farms had tethered an earlier generation of mothers who taught their daughters to look for jobs in town.

People intuitively know that human contact heals and isolation deranges. Volunteers shut up in darkened space capsules for days on end wind up seeing things. There is now medical evidence that boredom can cripple and even kill. Doctors do not recommend bed rest as they used to. Patients suffering from chronic diseases are urged to get out and see their friends. Isolation made the unemployed suspicious, or at least more fearful of being snubbed than it is possible for anyone who has never lacked for carfare to imagine.

60

"As soon as you are out of the dough, your friends don't want to know you any more," they said gloomily, whether it was true or not. When Robert and Helen Lynd returned to their "Middletown" during the Depression, they detected a streak of meanness and suspicion that was out of character with the Middletown they had studied before the Crash. Men who had lost money said their old friends cut them on the street for fear of being "touched" for a loan. Everywhere the unemployed were excluded. Children whose parents were on relief hung back from the others at school. High-school girls needed clothes for dates, and without them they avoided beaux. Older people tried to keep out of sight when they lost their teeth and could not afford bridgework.

Like prisoners in solitary confinement, the superfluous people got up every morning as late as they could and fought time as if it were an enemy. Some of them went to the public library and read, or simply sat for hours on end. Communist demonstrators, or anyone else offering a free show, could always be sure of an audience. People came for the animal presence of other people. The message did not matter. And it was not the unemployed alone who had time on their hands. Factories spread work so that in factory towns most of the "employed" were working only two or three days a week, often taking home little more than the totally unemployed could get on relief. Many offices gave up the traditional half day's work on Saturday so that salaried people had an extra day, a day uncommitted by the traditional churchgoing and visiting of Sunday.

There was more time for everybody, and less to do in it. It had to be "killed" at home, either alone or with people who were fellow prisoners at home. According to a National Recreation Association survey of 1934, people were killing time in sedentary, solitary, and spectatorial activities, when what they really wanted was to go somewhere, do something, or make something. People told the investigators they had given up out-

61

side group activities because they had "no money for carfare" and "no proper clothes" or were "too discouraged or worried because of loss of job to concentrate on anything." The most commonly mentioned leisure-time activities were reading newspapers and magazines, listening to the radio, and going to the movies, in that order; what people would have enjoyed most was, first, tennis, followed by swimming, boating, and other activities that have boomed in the affluent Sixties. Stamp collectors quadrupled during the Depression. Double-feature movies were a dark hole into which a superfluous person could crawl when he was supposed to be looking for a job. There were fads for knitting, games, and jigsaw puzzles.

The spectatorial recreations that alarm social critics no longer dominate leisure as they did in the Depression, television notwithstanding. The radio was a Depression success, and it addicted millions. People who yearned to be out and doing consumed activity vicariously, like the retired farmers who watched the world go by from their front porches. Amateur photography, the spectatorial sport *par excellence,* gained almost as dramatically as the radio.

Spectacle loomed bigger to people living a limited life, and it seemed to be more prized, like the fiestas that break the monotony of peasant routine. The movie palladium with its ornate lobby where the lonely crowd could see and be seen is no longer in taste for those who do go to movies. The Seattle World's Fair of 1963 and the New York World's Fair of 1964–65 aroused less enthusiasm than the Chicago World's Fair of 1933 and the New York World's Fair of 1939. The burlesque show, the splashy big-name band, the musical movie with a cast of thousands, the extravaganza double length for good measure (*Gone With the Wind* was a four-hour sensation)—all these routine-breakers attracted people who in the 1960s often prefer to make their own occasions. Television and the competition of active amusements such as boating have cut the gate receipts of

62

sports events, and the movie theaters of the Thirties have been made over into supermarkets, banks, and even churches. Many of the spectacles have gone the way of the drugstore cowboys who used to hang around watching the girls go by and hoping for something to happen.

Idleness did not precipitate a gross crime wave, although comparisons are inexact because police were so shorthanded that they could not afford to notice any crime that did not demand immediate attention. The best observers think that crimes of violence did not increase, but petty offenses against property did. If the "bezzle" (to use J. K. Galbraith's word for the amount of money misappropriated by employees) rose with stricter checkups when times were hard, the "pilfer" in grocery stores was harder to control when people put their wits to scrounging food.

Crimes that seemed like games against the rich multiplied. The idle constructed false claims against insurance companies. In some New York City neighborhoods, small-business people resorted to arson to bail themselves out of failing stores so frequently that no one really believed any fire to be accidental. One fantastic plot against an insurance company is notable because it delayed noncancelable health insurance for thirty years.

In December, 1933, a lawyer and a salesman for the Maccabees, an old-line insurance company experimenting with health insurance, cooked up an extraordinary scheme for milking the company by simulating heart-attack symptoms by the use of digitalis. Extended to insured persons whose names were abstracted from the company files, the scheme eventually involved hundreds of people and millions of dollars. When the racket was uncovered, insurance companies were so disillusioned with health insurance that many of them bought back the few policies they had issued and discontinued the coverage.

Box-top contests were ideal pastimes—cheap, solitary, and time-consuming, with the hope of something for nothing to cherish, however remotely. Two million people entered the Old Gold contest offering $100,000 to the winner of a series of rebus riddles. Tip-sheets to the answers were sold, and Post Office inspectors coped with a flood of real and fake contests in the mails. Some became professional prize winners. Actress Thelma Ritter's husband, Joe Moran, won so many radio slogan contests that Young & Rubicam, the advertising agency that ran many of them, hired him as a copywriter.

The great chain-letter craze of 1935 swept millions into passing along a dime to the top name on a list of six mailed to him, adding his own to the bottom, and writing a letter to the other five asking them to do likewise. Nearly every adult in Colorado was involved. The scheme burned itself out when no new prospects remained, but it left three million dead letters in the post office and required special mintings of dimes. Even people who disapproved could not bring themselves to break the chain.

When pari-mutuel betting on horse racing was legalized in the dark year 1933, enough money mysteriously appeared to triple the receipts. But the really big boom was in the low end of gambling—the bingo games, the bank nights of movie houses desperately seeking to attract trade, and above all the "one-armed bandits" installed in beer parlors to sedate the restless.

The slot machine was simply an automatic vending machine designed to give back the nickels, dimes, or quarters put into it at a rate that favored the machine over many turns. Its fatal attraction was that it might or might not belch forth a jackpot of change at each crank. The appeal was hypnotic. You put in your quarter and pulled the lever. The symbols whirled. They might be plums, apples, cherries. If all three windows showed the same fruit, a jingle of change notified you that you were in luck. It didn't matter that the machine was rigged to keep from 20 to 70 percent of all coins put into it. It didn't matter that half the take went into organized crime, which had moved in on the slots after Prohibition was repealed. What mattered was the anesthetic of the whir, punctuated by the momentary thrill of getting something for nothing. By the time Pearl Harbor produced some real excitement, the slots were gobbling up more than ten times as much change as they had taken at the time of the 1929 Crash.

Dance marathons took the country by storm in 1933. June Havoc recalls them as a "tiny pocket of the human struggle during the Great Depression." They were held in armories and usually started with 60 couples dancing or moving in dance positions 45 minutes of every hour, 24 hours a day, eating Army-style food from a board on sawhorses while the audience came and went, sometimes bringing picnic-style meals, throwing money, and sometimes offering food to the contestants or buying little postcard pictures of them. After 1,000 hours, partners took turns sleeping while leaning on each other and lapsed into a shadowy, subconscious state called "squirrelly," which June Havoc says provided amusement for the other marathoners, if not the audience. "Horses" were professional marathoners with thick, carefully tended calluses who went from contest to contest for the prize money. "Endurance shows" were so popular that the show-biz magazine *Billboard* devoted a special column to them. Six-day bicycle races staged a comeback, putting audience and contestants alike into a trance induced by the monotonous, whirring motion of the wheels around the track.

The endurance shows acted out the mood of the time just as goldfish swallowing and flagpole sitting had done before the Depression, and hula hooping and packing as many people as possible into a telephone booth were to do later. Flagpole sitters, more in tune with an earlier America that valued individual heroism, elevated themselves above their fellows and sat alone. Hula hooping seemed to express the mood of aimless but pleasurable motion characteristic of postwar prosperity. The telephone-booth packers seemed to be acting out the adaptation to

65

a densely populated society. The marathons of the Thirties were more transparent than these. For people trying to endure, to make money last, to hold out for a break, they were a ritual murdering of the enemy—time.

The mood of the marathon was very similar to the aimless, endless movement of superfluous people around and around the country in rickety cars or on freight trains. Like the marathoners, the wanderers were impelled by a vague hope that something might break for them, although they were not surprised when it did not. In 1933, between one and two million people were on the road, "Address Unknown." A reporter asked a girl in a crowded jalopy headed south from Seattle where her party was going. "Going?" she echoed. "Just going."

There were all kinds. Some were Okies blown off their farmlands in the Dust Bowl by a dry spell that coincided with the Depression to create the conditions John Steinbeck immortalized in his novel *The Grapes of Wrath*. There were occupational wanderers, the stoop-crop pickers, the gandy dancers and construction stiffs and lumberjacks and many other seasonal semi-skilled workers of a simpler technology. Many of them were hoboes who, in good times or bad, took to the wandering life from choice, or as modern psychiatry would put it, from inner compulsions to escape from authority in general and the home authority of women in particular.

Their numbers increased with unemployment. Boys could not face parents who expected them to get out and work. One frank woman wrote a magazine article to complain that she had to share her home, her friends, and the family car with a grown daughter and son who wouldn't "face life on their own." A high-school graduate thanked a newspaper columnist for writing a column that convinced his father it was not his fault that he could not find work. "Dad keeps throwing up to me all he has done for me, and it is a lot," the boy wrote. "But I am not going to be dependent upon him a minute longer than I can get away with it even if I have to take to the road." Moving on was so squarely in the Horatio Alger tradition (one Alger illustration has the hero waving goodby to his mother, who is weeping into a washtub) that Henry Ford thought the boys on the road were getting a good education out of their experiences. The U.S. Public Health Service and the Labor Department did not agree. Studies of the migrants showed that the boys were often half-starved and suffered cruelly from exposure, illness, and accident.

Sadder even than the boys were the grown men, the unemployed fathers who, one night, simply could not bear going home and headed for a freight train instead. Sometimes they acted on a rumor that there was work in another city, only to find that there was none. Once footloose, it did not matter much where they went. Hope of warm weather, word of a friend, memory of relatives perhaps never actually known, was excuse for a jaunt across the continent. It is hard for people who have jobs and careers, who sleep in beds, and have neighbors, to appreciate how planless a man cut loose can be.

President Herbert Hoover simply could not understand the Bonus Army. He could not grasp that 20,000 war veterans could pick each other up and roll—like a red tide, some thought —into Washington. All he could see was a great plot. But it was not that way.

The Bonus March started in Portland, Oregon, early in 1932 with 300 veterans led by ex-Sergeant Walter W. Waters. Their aim was to march across the country and ask Congress to pass the Patman Bill for immediate payment of a bonus that World War I soldiers were scheduled to get in 1945. Because they were all veterans, they fell into military discipline. They caught freight trains and camped. As word of their mission spread, thousands of unemployed veterans drifted along to join them. It was better than staying at home, and the idea of being in an "Army" again was appealing. The numbers grew. On June 8,

67

1932, 8,000 veterans paraded down Pennsylvania Avenue. Neither Waters nor the Communists, who were accused of starting the March, nor the Washington police had expected so many, but there was no violence, no disorder. Crime actually declined in the District of Columbia while they were there. So many of the veterans were violently anti-Communist—their *B.E.F. News* praised Hitler and Mussolini—that the Communists who tried to infiltrate their ranks appealed to Washington Police Commissioner Pelham D. Glassford for protection.

Once they arrived in Washington they did not seem to know what to do. When news of the defeat of the Patman Bill was announced to them, Hearst columnist Elsie Robinson whispered to Waters that he should tell the men to sing "America." They did. Hoover flatly refused to talk to them. Instead, he ordered regular Army troops to disperse the men. General Douglas MacArthur burned their shacks and routed them out with gas. Stunned, they broke and fled.

Local authorities passed along the routed Bonus Marchers like so many hot potatoes. Virginia and Maryland stationed troopers along their boundaries to turn the men back. Maryland provided trucks to take them to Johnstown, Pennsylvania, where the mayor offered asylum, but the Pennsylvania trucks were misdirected to take them out of the state. A Washington Negro who happened to be in the veterans' camp when MacArthur attacked could not escape, and was trucked all the way to Indianapolis. The nimble made their way back to friendly Johnstown. The president of the Baltimore & Ohio Railroad finally offered to haul them home free on B. & O. trains. Cities of destination plotted to get rid of them. Kansas City scraped together $1,500 to keep the train from stopping. Discovering that they were objects of pity, many of those "passed along" turned to begging for a living.

Hoover thought that the Bonus Army was a mixture of hoodlums, ex-convicts, Communists, and a few veterans, and he stuck to this view even after careful investigation by the Veterans Bureau and the Pennsylvania State Department of Welfare failed to substantiate it. Most people who read about the Bonus March in the newspapers thought the Marchers intended to start a revolution.

The truth was more frightening. The unemployed veterans of the war to save democracy were superfluous people—thousands and thousands of them marching, camping, and huddling together for sheer human warmth.

4

$ $ $ $ $

THE FAILURE OF WISDOM

1930 . . . 1931 . . . 1932 . . .   The average man not only was giving up his dream of getting rich, it was dawning on him that a majority of Americans were hopelessly poor. It began to look as if human beings, as producers, could become obsolete. The recognition of reality came slow and hard. This was not the way things were supposed to turn out. What had gone wrong? What could be done? People gathered around the radio.

Don't worry, said the wise men.

One of the first things Hoover had done as President was to ask the leading social scientists to examine the state of the economy. They found it great. They wrote 950 pages describing American prosperity. "Acceleration rather than structural change is the key to an understanding of our recent economic trends," they began. After crediting "prudence on the part of management . . . skill on the part of bankers," they concluded that "our situation is fortunate, our momentum is remarkable." *Recent Economic Trends* was written in the spring of 1929, but it did not come out until after the Crash.

Hoover stuck to the line. When the unemployed sold apples,

he was capable of saying that "many people left their jobs for the more profitable one of selling apples." He appealed to Weber and Fields and to Will Rogers for jokes that would cheer people up, and begged Rudy Vallee to sing a happy song, and told Christopher Morley that maybe a great poem would help. He worried about words. Instead of talking about Crisis (in Europe, *La Crise*), or Panic, with its suggestion of mob stampede into the woodlands of the unreliable god Pan, he adopted the chart-word "Depression," which suggested, at worst, a mood of sobriety.

This optimism was deliberate policy. The wisest and most learned believed that the country would become rich if businessmen could be made to believe that every day in every way they were getting closer and closer to prosperity. Influential Americans were willing not only to look stupid and calloused to save their country, but even to lie for it. At the December 1929 meeting of the American Economic Association in Washington, reputable economists sacrificed their scholarly honor to the cause by deliberately reporting outdated forecasts indicating recovery by June 1930. They felt that the current reports they had just received were so gloomy that it would be against public interest to publicize them.

"There are just two great dangers to the continuance of prosperity," a remarkable article entitled "Why We Are Prosperous" in the *Reader's Digest* of January 1930 declared. "The first is the false idea that business is still governed by a cycle of boom and depression, and the second is that the leaders of business will think that the country is broke because some of their friends are." The author, Samuel Crowther, was Henry Ford's biographer and public-relations man. Henry Ford practiced what he preached. In the first few months after the Crash he cut prices, raised wages, and built a new plant he did not need in Edgewater, New Jersey. Later he bought back over-age jalopies he thought were barring new car sales and ran 300,000

71

of them through a demolition line that systematically stripped them of all usable parts. Windows were used over again, leather went for workmen's aprons, bronze was melted down for connecting rods.

But most of the boosters tried merely to talk prosperity back. "Buy Now" programs sprouted. The International Association of Lions Clubs declared a Business Confidence Week. The merchants of El Paso kept windows of vacant stores filled with merchandise for morale's sake. A committee of Muncie, Indiana, businessmen journeyed to Detroit to petition General Motors not to board up the Muncie factory that could be seen from through trains. The press bristled with free advice. Corporations should pay out more money in dividends. Each family should buy goods worth $100 on the installment plan. Manufacturers should spend more on advertising. Retailers and newspapers urged people to buy. "Buy something from somebody: we all prosper together," a utility association advertised, "We'll go to the movies—that's one way to spend," said a Hearst ad.

Boosters fired to the possibilities of new products, new industries that would create new jobs, as the automobile industry had just done. Charles F. "Boss" Kettering, the engineering wizard of General Motors who had invented the electric self-starter, called on his fellow inventors to think big. "When we continue to produce the same things, the same model indefinitely," he diagnosed, "the people don't want to buy it." Oliver Mitchell Sprague, economic adviser to the Bank of England, had a suggestion big enough for General Motors: the "Fordization" of houses everyone could afford.

Housing was an attractive solution, because new homes would make family life better and put men to work in many industries, but there were sober Americans who contended that the United States could drink its way to prosperity. The United States Brewers Association and the Association Against the Prohibition Amendment figured that legalizing beer alone would employ more than a million men not already gainfully employed in bootlegging. Stuart Chase once suggested that the Depression might be cured if a group of benevolent millionaires hired an army of workers to bail out Long Island Sound.

The cheerful wise men were businessmen who hoped to revive or save the boom spirit. Manufacturers and especially retailers and newspapers dependent on retail advertising had learned from Henry Ford that it is worth cutting prices and profits to keep products moving and potential customers employed. But business—dealers in products—did not dominate the economy then, as they do now. Richer and more prestigious were the bankers and investors who lived on the interest from their money. Interest payments loomed much bigger in the national income then. The boom had increased debt. The Depression made money dearer and debt harder to pay back. As long as debts were honored, the creditors could not help getting richer still. Their play was to stand pat.

Whatever is wrong, there is nothing you can do about it, these wise men said. "No government can legislate away the morning after, any more than it can legislate away the effect of a tornado," Hoover wrote later. When asked what the stock market would do, J. P. Morgan had once answered, majestically, "It will fluctuate." Economists, then a small and academic group, generally disdained business cycles as accidents that had nothing to do with economic theory. When the stock market did not recover as he predicted, Professor Irving Fisher labeled the whole slump irrational and, therefore, not his professional concern. All the metaphors likened stock prices to a tide of nature. Like the weather, the Crash was inscrutable, a topic of conversation that could be used to express the speaker's feelings about life in general.

It was possible to demonstrate that whenever the temperature of the United States had risen above normal for the season, business conditions had fallen below normal. Good and bad

73

harvests had made trade cycles in preindustrial times, and the English economist W. S. Jevons (1835–1882) had gathered impressive circumstantial evidence incriminating sunspots. No one, of course, took this seriously. In 1932, a Birmingham judge ruled that the Depression was not an Act of God within the meaning of a clause letting the tenant out of a lease in the event of divine intervention. But if the Depression was an Act of Man, it was an act for which no particular man could be legally responsible. All manner of people and things were blamed.

In 1930, Sir Henry Deterding, director of Royal Dutch Shell, later called the "richest man in the world," solemnly ascribed the Depression to the Soviet regime in Russia, which was keeping more than half the world too poor to buy oil. He advocated stopping credit to the Bolsheviks and letting them "stew in their own juices" until they stopped their propaganda.

Rene Leon, onetime foreign-exchange expert for the Guaranty Trust, thought the Chinese were at the bottom of it. Falling silver prices depreciated their silver-based currency so low that no one on gold could compete with them. The remedy was to join them in monetizing silver. The British blamed us for demanding payment of war debts in gold, and we blamed the British for not buying our products.

The French, the Germans, Hoover, Roosevelt, Mrs. Roosevelt, and John Maynard Keynes were some of the many agents accused of bringing on the Depression. When John L. Lewis was added to the list, he returned the compliment. "A horde of small-time leaders in industry and finance," he declared, "looted the purse of the population." When President Hoover blamed the "malign inheritance of the Great War," peppery little Senator Carter Glass, the Democrats' financial authority, retorted that the Depression of the Thirties had no more to do with that war than with the "war of the Phoenicians or the conquest of Gaul by Caesar." Unlike the inflation of the boom years, the

74

inflation of the first World War had been fully liquidated in the short, sharp shakeout of 1921 and 1922.

Like the weather, the real issue was not so much why it was bad, but when it would end. The *New York Times* financial editor, Alfred Dana Noyes, did his best every New Year's to see grounds for optimism. A walking morgue of financial history, he delved further and further in the past to bolster confidence in the future. As the Depression of 1929 lengthened, so did the Panic of 1907:

• In January 1930, *Times* readers learned that "severe trade reaction after the October panic of 1907 lasted until the following August."

• In January 1931, they read that the cause commonly assigned to the "recovery of 1909" was "discovery that production had been cut far below consumption."

• In 1933, *The Times* confided that "the real turn in the depression following 1907 came in 1912, nearly four years after the panic."

• In 1935, the sixth year of depression, Noyes had to work a little harder. "Probably 1911 was the low point of reaction after the panic of 1907, and the rapid recovery of 1912 fairly duplicated 1933 and the first half of 1934," he speculated in print. "But the outbreak of Balkan War in 1912, foreshadowing a general European conflict, interrupted the progress of the cycle. Real American recovery came only in 1915."

• In 1938, in the space reserved for the annual New Year's forecast, Noyes discovered both a 20-year cycle and a "midcycle reaction." For the 1907 Panic, this mid-cycle reaction came in 1913 rather than in 1911, as previously reported. The lesson of history, he added, was that the mid-cycle reaction was severe, but always came "when recovery was vigorously under way."

Just before Roosevelt took office in 1933, Senator Pat Harrison of Mississippi asked 250 of the nation's business leaders to tell Congress what they thought should be done about the Depression. Most of them acted as if the question were impertinent, and many replied facetiously. John W. Davis, Democratic candidate for President in 1924 and favorite lawyer for big-business men, ascribed the Depression to "human folly," a malady he cheerfully wrote off as incurable. When pressed, Jackson Reynolds, president of New York's First National Bank, suggested that "ninety-nine out of a hundred persons haven't good sense." U.S. Steel president Myron Taylor had no remedy, but he speculated that maybe the trouble was a surplus of raw materials.

Most Americans were puritan enough to take the economic catastrophe as a punishment. Spartans blamed indoor plumbing. Moralists blamed the installment plan, which encouraged workingmen to "live beyond their means." Soft living undermined character, and when character went, so did the economy. "Business depressions are caused by dissipation, dishonesty, disobedience to God's will—a general collapse of moral character," devout Roger Babson wrote to a YMCA convention. He begged the godly to start a spiritual revival for the sake of business. By 1932 he was more specific: "If you can't think yourself into a job, work yourself into one," he advised the jobless. "Insist on working even without pay."

The morality at stake was the morality of paying what you owed in dollars—even if the dollars were worth much more than when you borrowed them. As the Depression worsened, creditors feared repudiation of debts by Government action or inflationary measures to lighten the load of debtors. They stood to gain if Government did nothing and private debtors pulled in their belts and paid.

"We cannot have any permanent prosperity when there is a load of debt around our necks," Eugene R. Black, Governor of the Atlanta Federal Reserve Bank, said in his prepared speech to warn a thousand bankers attending the convention of the

Investment Association in October 1930. "I believe we have got in America to assert our character." The sound assertion of character, it developed, was to economize and pay off the bank. The bankers in the audience were setting a good example. They had cut the agenda of the convention from six days to four to save expenses. DEPRESSION IS LAID TO AMERICAN LUXURY, *The New York Times* reported.

"Liquidate labor, liquidate stocks, liquidate the farmers, liquidate real estate," demanded Secretary of the Treasury Andrew Mellon, the leading spokesman for the Conventional Wisdom. "Enterprising people will pick up the wrecks from less competent people." After testifying to a personal income of $60,000 a year, Richard Whitney, then president of the New York Stock Exchange, advised a Senate committee to cut the salaries of veterans, Government employees, and Senators, in order to balance the budget. A balanced budget, he maintained, would end the Depression by restoring "confidence" among investors.

The cheery wise men hoped to spread confidence among consumers and get them to buy. The gloomy wise men threatened to withhold investment if they were not assured of getting the full value of the deflation that was making dollars worth more all the time. People with substantial capital acted—or at least talked—as if they were a sort of foreign nation situated inside the United States but not subject to it. Stripped of moralistic verbiage, their message was clear: prosperity was in their gift, so everybody had better treat them gently until the warm blood of confidence rose in their veins and they felt like lending money to get business going again.

Their alarms made them sound like a skittish lot. Confidence, they warned, was impaired whenever anyone suggested that the Federal Government might handle relief or look into the mysterious channels through which capital flowed. If the unemployed were going to need help, then let it be done, they insisted, by local governments "close" to the "people" or more responsive to property owners and bond underwriters than the Federal authorities. The relationship between the willingness of a capitalist to invest and an unbalanced Federal budget was never made clear, nor exactly what the unconfident would do with their money if the Government did something that scared them.

Other voices questioned the foundation of the system. The Communists grew steadily in influence. But until 1933 the wise men dictated what was actually done—or left undone. Some believed in cutting wages and prices until demand "picked up." Others—and perhaps a majority—wished they could have made jobs or built new plants to help prosperity, as Hoover begged them to do. Although "cutting down" was the orthodox remedy for hard times, opinion polls seldom mustered a majority of businessmen for cutting wages. Few had the heart to argue that wages should drop until it was worth employing everyone, but fewer still felt responsible for the standards of living of their employees.

John E. Edgerton, president of the National Association of Manufacturers, was simply voicing the conventional economic wisdom when he scorned the concern of a Senator who pointed out that men could not live on one or two days' wages a week. "Why, I've never thought of paying men on a basis of what they need," he said. "I pay men for efficiency. Personally, I attend to all those other things, social welfare stuff, in my church work." The crowd laughed.

By 1931 it did not matter much whether a businessman wished he could have expanded to save the country or whether he believed he was saving it by letting supply and demand "shake down" to a sound basis. He had to cut, and he did. Even Henry Ford could no longer throw his vast resources into bolstering the market. The new plant had to be closed, and the wage rises were first undermined and then withdrawn. Meanwhile, Hoover

78

kept urging business—and drafting businessmen to urge each other—to hire and expand. When businessmen complained that even Gulf Oil Company was laying off men, Secretary of the Treasury Mellon inquired of his Gulf management and reported to the President that the men in question had been laid off under an agreement Hoover himself had suggested to limit production. Voluntary cooperation was not fine even in theory. It did not tell a businessman which Government plea to heed, let alone how patriotic he ought to be at the expense of his stockholders. The most he usually could do was to divide the work among the regular employees so that several men would have a day or two a week.

Everybody seemed to approve this work-sharing. Baltimore & Ohio shopmen agreed to give up half a day's work a week to keep more men on the payroll. As the Depression deepened, thousands who were counted as employed and so ineligible for help were as badly off as those who had become public charges. At Republic Steel, the part-time work plan was paying $20 a month in 1931. Walter C. Teagle, of Standard Oil, persuaded 3,500 companies to go to the 40-hour week to spread employment, but only four of these companies had to hire extra men to do it. "Sharing unemployment" was a way to get the unemployed to take care of themselves. It could not increase total purchasing power or lower labor costs.

Hoover tried a great many of the measures Roosevelt was to develop.

His Federal Farm Board urged farmers to plant less, but with no law to stop them, farmers figured that prices would rise, and planted more.

He tried to use the fiscal power of the Government to stimulate business. Before the 1931 currency crisis, the Federal Government pared the rediscount rate to two percent and the income tax by one percent, and spent a few hundred million dollars on Federal public works. The moves were window dressing.

79

Low interest rates could not lure investors if they saw no hope of gain. The income tax was so small that a cut could not liberate much spending power. And billions, not millions, in public works were needed to restore the purchasing power lost by unemployment.

In 1932, his Reconstruction Finance Corporation began lending what was to be a total of $1.5 billion to save banks and businesses, but little of it "filtered down" to the unemployed. Much of the money simply stayed in the till or paid off debts.

His Federal Home Loan banks aimed to save homes from foreclosure by refinancing, but it did not get going in time to prevent mass evictions.

He was ingenious in finding ways the Government could ease distress. He made bankruptcy simpler. He ended the leasing of public oil lands to private prospectors. He urged oil producers to set production quotas to dry up the "hot oil" illegally shipped out of Texas to fuel gasoline-price wars that had brought gasoline down as low as 4¢ a gallon. He ordered the deportation of aliens illegally in the United States and made immigration harder, to keep jobs in the hands of American citizens.

He fed the drought-stricken cattle to help farmers as businessmen, but he did not think that the Federal Government should relieve individual human beings, so he worked out a clever plan under which his Federal Farm Board bought surplus wheat and cotton and the Red Cross processed and distributed it to the unemployed. Nobody appreciated his inventiveness. The Red Cross was reluctant to take on unemployment. The coal miners broke into the Red Cross warehouses. The man who had fed the Belgians after World War I and was concededly the most experienced organizer of relief for mass disasters stood accused of feeding cattle instead of people.

Hoover was determined and principled. He preserved the moral fiber of the unemployed by refusing to feed them on Federal money. He tried to balance the national budget. He cut

Federal salaries. He tried to save money on prisons. He steadfastly fought and defeated attempts to appropriate Federal penitentiaries and put prisoners in cheap work camps. He steadfastly fought and defeated attempts to appropriate Federal money for relief. He high-mindedly sacrificed the domestic economy to the international gold standard; in 1927 the Federal Reserve encouraged speculation by making money cheap, to help Britain attract enough dollars to stay on gold; in 1931 the Federal Reserve raised interest rates to keep gold in the country, even though the move made it so hard for banks to get money from the Federal Reserve on the basis of their loans to businessmen that many of them were forced to close. When declining business cut the mails to the point where Post Office deficits mounted, Hoover fired 6,000 employees, consolidated 810 rural free delivery routes out of existence, and raised first-class postage from two to three cents.

None of it helped. On the contrary, there were times when it looked as if Hoover were actually making things worse. Because his cheerful forecasts were intended to stave off or counter bad news, they sometimes seemed to cause the very disasters they were intended to combat. In the summer of 1930, Hoover's Federal Farm Board chief announced that he "saw no further decline in commodities." Almost immediately wheat plunged to 45¢ a bushel, a new low for the century.

The stock market so often broke after Hoover's public reassurances that the Republican National Committee once got out a full-page advertisement accusing John J. Raskob, the rich Chairman of the Democratic National Committee, of driving the market down by selling short to discredit the Administration.

Professional optimism had worn thin by New Year's Day 1932. A ground for optimism cited by *The New York Times* was "operating economies" (layoffs) promising lower costs. A bright spot of 1931 had been the record sale of one million refrigerators. The trade did not think that quite that many could be sold again, one of the few forecasts of the year to err on the side of pessimism. The forecasts showed evidence of shell shock. The *Architectural Record* worried, in print, that the declining birthrate might slow building in future years.

Disaster was much closer at hand. During 1932, residential construction was only 15 percent of what it had been in 1929, and all the important industries supplying building were paralyzed. The sheriffs put 273,000 families out of their homes, and mortgages were being foreclosed so fast that there was no chance of realizing on them. The Metropolitan Life Insurance Company had to take so many farms back on sour mortgages that it had to organize a farm department to take care of them. One fourth of the whole state of Mississippi was auctioned in a single day. Farmers gathered at the auctions to bid in their neighbors' farms for a few cents so that they would not be "set on the road." But thousands did not try to stay. Rather than face the bank and the dust that was drying up Oklahoma, thousands of farmers simply walked or drove away. "There's a mighty lot of real estate lying around the United States which does not know who owns it," Andrew Mellon remarked.

Some of the best housing in the country stood empty. Luxury apartments in New York City could not be rented. Every tree-lined nice neighborhood had a few dark houses with a "For Rent" sign, the former home of someone who had gone bankrupt or let his home go to pay business debts or simply left because neither he nor anyone else had the income to live in it. Many of the big old mansions were ill-suited to nonresidential use. They stood there, a burden to the banks that held them, while the families who had built them or made them home crowded into smaller quarters, or doubled up with a neighbor who needed extra income to hold onto his house.

When cities and counties could not collect taxes on empty

82

houses and deserted farms, they could not pay schoolteachers. Nearly a third of a million schoolchildren were out of school at some point during the 1932–33 term because money for schools ran out. Chicago issued tax anticipation warrants to teachers, but bankers would not discount them. In 1932 more than 800 Chicago teachers who had exhausted their savings and insurance had to borrow from loan sharks who charged them 42 percent interest.

The meanest housing was jammed. The evicted and the unemployed moved in with relatives. The newcomers slept in dining rooms, on living-room couches, and sometimes three or four to a bed. "Only the other day a family of ten moved in with a family of five in a three-room apartment," a social worker from Philadelphia told a Senate committee. "The demand for boxes on which people can sit or stretch themselves is hardly to be believed." In some communities, 15 percent of the housing units were sheltering extra families.

The whole country "dipped into capital." In the 1920s, American railroads had bought an average of 1,300 locomotives a year. In 1932, no American railroad ordered a single one. Institutions as well as individuals stopped investing. A third of all the investments life insurance companies made in 1932 were loans to policyholders.

At first, the deflation had merely wrung the water out of the boom. There was plenty of it to go. New stocks were issued and prices rose during 1929 until the total market value of all the stock outstanding reached a theoretical sum total of $100 billion. Everyone knew this was too high. The wise men talked of "getting back to reality." They likened the Crash to a purge that would restore economic health. People with money would be brought to their senses. Instead of speculating, they would put their money to useful work.

But it did not prove so easy. Once the liquidation started, it rolled on and on. After the patient shed his flabby fat, he began to waste away. No one could tell at just what point the line was crossed, but by 1932 it was obvious that values of stocks were too low. From 1929 peak to 1932 trough, the market value of all stocks outstanding fell $74 billion. Counted this way in dollars, on paper, stockholders "lost" three times as many dollars as the United States spent fighting World War I, or $616 for every man, woman, and child in the country.

In 1932, the deflation had wiped out all the economic progress the country had made in two generations; we were producing no more tons and bushels of actual commodities per capita than in 1899. Industrial production was at half its 1929 level. Steelmaking fell off until one week mills made only 12 percent of capacity. Farm prices fell so low that many farmers let their crops rot or burned them for firewood, because it did not pay to harvest them. The historic tides of migration reversed: in 1932, more people left America than entered it; 1933 was the only year farms gained population from towns.

How could it happen to us? There is general agreement now that the Crash was inevitable, given the boom. Everybody now blames speculation, which raged unchecked by regulation of security issues or trading, and the loose regulation of banks, which made it possible for them to overextend credit. Speculation was worse in the United States than abroad, if only because we had always been boomers from our very foundation, and we had always resisted regulation—particularly regulation by a national government that alone could control a national speculative fever.

Everybody now agrees, too, that the boom put a fever flush of health on a very sick economy. Our exports were financed by the paper securities we issued to play games with ourselves. Our mass production was spotty, and we did not have a mass market to consume it. Dreams and theories had outrun performance. The longer we put off looking at the facts, the ruder the shock, and it was a long time after the Crash before responsible leaders would publicly concede that the economy was fundamentally unsound.

In retrospect it is easy to see how we could have avoided the most serious damage, or at least shortened the effects, of the Crash. Almost everyone will admit that the United States of America had a run of bad luck that was all the harder to bear because as a nation we were not used to bad luck. We had poor distribution of wealth, overcapitalized corporations, an under-regulated banking system, bad foreign balance, a one-sided foreign trade, and very poor economic intelligence. We were steering by obsolete economic theory, so we did everything wrong and sometimes embarked on remedies that canceled each other out. There is agreement that many evils piled up to spell disaster, but the emphases vary with political faith, and the principal views taken then survive today:

Orthodox Communists blamed the "internal contradictions" of capitalism, and the Chinese Communists are still waiting for the other shoe to fall.

Orthodox sound-money men blamed the Federal Reserve System for allowing banks to encourage the boom by expanding credit, and in the 1960s there are still some economists who think it is dangerous for the Government to have any discretion in issuing money. In 1963, Murray N. Rothbard, a Ph.D. in economics, wrote a book to prove that the Crash developed into a Depression because Hoover prevented the "healthy readjustment" of wages and prices downward that would have cleared the decks. In 1965, Dr. Franz Pick criticizes every move of the Federal Reserve Board that looks like inflation. He has papered the wall of the office of *Pick's World Currency Report,* at the foot of Manhattan, with *assignats,* the worthless paper money the French Revolutionists issued. Less extreme conservatives deplore "Government spending," "Government interference," "big unions," and the unwillingness of workers nowadays to do a day's work for a day's pay. These are creditor positions. Those who hold them have an interest in maintaining or increasing the value of money. They like the status quo.

Most explanations fell somewhere between these extremes. The more popular view today is that people did not buy during the Depression because most of them did not have enough money. The symptom was labeled "underconsumption," and early proponents of this viewpoint invited ideas for getting more goods and services flowing into the economy. The Brookings Institution and liberals in general urged manufacturers to lower prices in the effort to increase sales. In the 1960s, Kennedy and Johnson were acting on this reasoning when they urged the steel industry not to raise prices. Attacks on monopoly, and more recently on prices "administered" by big companies, are in the underconsumptionist tradition. But in 1933 even the common people were scarcity-minded.

Four years after the election of Roosevelt, the American Institute of Public Opinion asked a cross section of people what they thought should be done to remedy unemployment. Everyone literate enough to be queried must have been familiar, by then, with the notion that men could be put to work if the economy would only grow. Yet all the popular suggestions assumed that the volume of production and hence the volume of employment were unchangeable. All were proposals for sharing scarcity. Not one contemplated increasing the size of the pie so that each piece would be bigger:

1) Shorten hours
2) Less government in business
3) Force people on relief into employment by slashing the WPA and other forms of relief
4) Retire the worker at the age of 60
5) Prohibit married women from holding jobs in business and industry
6) It's up to business

7) Levy a tax on new laborsaving machinery to support the workers who are being displaced
8) Establish the unemployed on small self-sustaining farmsteads
9) Stop further foreign immigration and send unemployed aliens back to their own nations
10) Eliminate child labor and give the child worker's job to an adult

Executives divided almost evenly on whether machines could make jobs, but factory workers voted against them two to one. In 1937, Rep. Hatton W. Sumners of Texas introduced a bill to stop patents for the duration of the Depression. "Now, is it good, old-fashioned common-sense trading," he inquired, "to go out in the market and buy some more idle people by offering whoever will invent a machine that will give you some more idle people an inducement of 17 years of a monopoly on the right to use such a machine?" The same year, J. Roy Ellison, of Portland, Oregon, proposed outlawing machines by reducing all taxes to one: a "Protax" on machines, based on the jobs they displaced. Businessmen were urged to hold back laborsaving devices until prosperity made it easier to find new jobs for men displaced. In Los Angeles, a Utopian Society proposed making jobs by keeping everyone in school until the age of 25 and retiring everyone at 45.

Work-sharing still appeals. In the 1960s, unions have pressed for the five-hour day; President Johnson has suggested double-time pay for overtime to force employers to take on more men; Secretary of Labor W. Willard Wirtz has urged raising the legal school-leaving age to 18 to keep youngsters off the job market, and the Protax suggestion survives in proposals to finance the retirement of workers displaced by automation by a tax on the new laborsaving machines.

People who sat around listening to the radio talked economics as well as politics. There was plenty of time, and the issue was pressing. What was the matter? What should we do? In 1933,

Harvard's F. W. Taussig, dean of American economists, warned that economists knew as little about the causes of the Depression as physicians about the causes of cancer—just enough to denounce all known remedies as quackery.

The most popular remedy was inflation. Californians suggested that the Government grubstake the unemployed to pan gold dust out of abandoned gold mines and so increase the supply of money while earning their keep. Traditional easy-money schemes were revived. Silver-state Senators demanded that "Free Silver" be coined at a rate that would expand the base of the currency. Farm economists proposed devaluing the dollar by cutting the gold content or raising the price of gold at the mint. The veterans demanded immediate payment of their bonus. Yale economist Irving Fisher prescribed inflation or "reflation" of the currency back to its boom-time value and local issues of nonhoardable "stamp scrip" that had to be spent before the date stamped on the back. Marriner Eccles, a Utah banker, broke with his profession to propose Government spending to get business moving again. Stuart Chase, an accountant turned writer, who flirted with just about every solution proposed by anyone, including Russian Communism, once prescribed a "stiff dose of inflation."

Inflation was a farm solution for the lack of money. Businessmen who wanted to spread purchasing power favored public works that would make jobs. In 1932, publisher Paul Block urged Hoover to issue $4 billion worth of bonds to finance public works, and William Randolph Hearst, no radical, was willing to go as far as $5 billion. As publishers, they were the natural spokesmen for merchants, their biggest advertisers. Fourteen years before the Marshall Plan, Belgian Professor Paul Otlet suggested that the United States turn over its credits in Europe to building a gigantic neutral World City, on the Scheldt River, which would employ the world's 30 million idle.

Intellectuals proposed ways to put idle money to work creating jobs. Henry S. Dennison and Lincoln Filene of Boston shocked fellow businessmen by recommending a stiffly graduated income tax, repeal of the tax exemption on Government bonds, and a punitive tax on undistributed corporate earnings. John Maynard Keynes of Cambridge was more outspoken. Capitalists being what they were, "the duty of ordering the current volume of investment cannot safely be left in private hands." Alvin Hansen, a once-orthodox American economist, concluded that the frontier was gone, the population declining, new inventions less stimulating, and the demand for capital so low that the Government would have to plan permanent public works to keep everyone employed.

There were all sorts of schemes for managing the economy. Some hoped to regulate business into active competition, thus lowering prices and raising output. Both Gerard Swope, of General Electric, and Sidney Hillman, of the Amalgamated Clothing Workers, favored industrywide planning of production and prices, although they naturally differed on the role of management and labor in the plan making. William T. Foster, an unusually articulate professor of economics ("the nation wasted its substance in riotous saving"), and David Cushman Coyle, a structural engineer, wanted the government to build public works.

1932 was a year for utopias. In Florida, Fabian Socialist Prestonie Martin, faculty wife at Rollins College, devised a National Livelihood Plan under which everyone 18 to 26 years old would serve a term of work, as boys now do military service. These "Commons" would raise and process food, and make clothes and all other necessities of life for the Government, which would hand them out to everyone free of charge. Food and other regularly needed products would be delivered to every door by a huge parcel post system. After serving their terms of work, the Commons would then become "Capitals," free either to loaf and live on the goods produced by the Commons or to produce luxuries for money that could be spent on the luxuries produced by other Capitals. Mrs. Martin was frankly visionary. "The young husband tires of loafing," she wrote. "Lovemaking begins to pall, so he takes a job in the Capitals and proudly brings home money . . . She immediately goes shopping" Impractical as the scheme now seems, Mrs. Roosevelt was so fascinated by it in March 1933 that she publicly recommended Mrs. Martin's book, *Prohibiting Poverty*, and the White House ordered six copies.

Howard Scott's "Technocracy" burst on public attention in August, 1932, when Columbia University proposed making an energy survey of America. Technocracy was seriously discussed by almost every literate adult. The system provided that engineers would rule, goods would be priced in terms of the joules and ergs of energy required to produce them, machines would run full blast, and everyone would enjoy a fair share of a national product ten times as high as we had in 1929 by working an average of 16 hours a week. It enlisted Stuart Chase, Upton Sinclair, and Leon Henderson, among other respectable figures, and generated hundreds of jokes. Al Smith cracked that we had not done so well under government by that great engineer Hoover. Within six months Technocracy was as dead as an Empress Eugénie hat. Howard Scott was declared bankrupt the week Roosevelt became President.

The schemes were discussed endlessly, obsessively, with an excitement economics no longer generates. It was not that people expected Technocracy to be adopted, or even that they thought it would work. It was rather that the schemes made it easier to grasp what was wrong with the present setup. The interest was genuinely intellectual. The exciting thing was that the new concern for general ideas about the basis of society was not confined to intellectuals alone. College students debated economic systems late into the night, but workmen debated over their lunchboxes, too. General ideas were aired in smoking

90

cars and on front porches, where gossip, anecdote, and jokes had been the rule. People who were not at home with abstractions wrestled wtih them, were drawn to them like the tongue to a sore tooth. During 1932 the consensus grew: somebody—"they"—the Government had better do something. Nobody was sure what ought to be done, but it had to be dramatic and decisive. Someone ought to take hold of things.

Hoover resisted this conviction. He did not think the Government should do anything it could get anyone else to do. A Quaker, he stuck to what he thought was right against all opposition and put his faith in persuading people to act altruistically of their own free will. He became a symbol of the paralysis and finally the target of the discontent. Shantytowns were called Hoovervilles. The unemployed carried Hoover bags, slept on Hoover blankets, rode in Hoover wagons. A farm-strike placard declared, "In Hoover we trusted, now we are busted." If anyone smiled it was smart to ask, "Is Hoover dead?" Scurrilous stories circulated about him. One even accused him of bringing about the execution of Nurse Edith Cavell, the famous British spy of World War I.

It was not hard to paint Hoover black, but the irony of his unpopularity was that it was publicized not by liberals who deplored his inaction, but by a small group of extremely rich men who regarded him as a dangerous liberal. When Hoover was elected President, John J. Raskob, Pierre du Pont, Bernard Baruch, and other Democrats with substantial capital gave Charles Michelson at least a million dollars to mount the first professional four-year publicity campaign against an elected Administration. Michelson's backers did not foresee that they were paving the way for more aggressive Government than Hoover ever contemplated. Although Michelson operated under the Democratic National Committee, he was not allowed to refer to Governor Franklin Roosevelt when he was a leading contender for the Democratic nomination for President.

By the summer of 1932, it was clear that the next President would be a Democrat. Most people were ready for anyone who was not Hoover. Roosevelt was not then widely known, and he did not impress most people as a strong leader. He was intuitively conservative, and this they liked because the people were fundamentally conservative too. Like Hoover, he promised economy in Government and a balanced budget. Unlike Hoover, he was not associated with the discredited bankers, manufacturers, or traders. No intellectual, he shared the popular fascination with economic speculation, plucking out and presenting ideas and phrases that sounded good, even if they did not make consistent sense.

"These unhappy times call for the building of plans . . . that put their faith once more in the forgotten man at the bottom of the economic pyramid," he told a radio audience in April 1932, when he was campaigning for the nomination. The phrase won him millions of votes. Humbly born Al Smith and others objected to talk about class distinctions, but very few listeners knew that he took the phrase from William Graham Sumner, a social Darwinist whose "Forgotten Man" was the taxpayer who had to pay for the laziness and incompetence of others.

"I pledge you, I pledge myself, to a new deal for the American people," Roosevelt promised the Democratic National Convention when he flew to Chicago in June 1932 to make his dramatic acceptance speech. The phrase was casually appropriated by speech-writer Sam Rosenman from a 1932 article and book by Stuart Chase.

Hoover believed Roosevelt would ruin the country. He campaigned doggedly. Respectful of the Presidency, crowds usually listened to him sadly and silently, but Detroit was carrying a quarter of a million of people on relief, and when Hoover spoke there, some booed and spat.

As the election approached, Republican publisher Mark Sullivan reported that "nobody doubts the Depression is ended."

Time slipped its between-elections mask of impartiality so far as to allow, in the November 2 issue, that "After many a false alarm business seems in the act of struggling back to its feet." Readers jeered.

The Depression elected Roosevelt President.

5

$ $ $ $ $

CRISIS

PROPPED up in bed the morning after the election, Roosevelt scribbled a conventional acknowledgment across the back of Hoover's telegram of congratulation, saying that he held himself "in readiness to cooperate with you in our . . ." But the word "cooperate" bothered him and he changed it to read "ready to further in every way the common purpose to help our country."

The change was not a quibble. Who was to cooperate with whom? Hoover had been repudiated by a bigger margin than had any previous President, but under the Constitution he would be President until March 1933, and millions of Americans did not think they could hold out that long. Now that he had been elected, it was not at all clear just what it was that Roosevelt intended to do about the Depression.

A few days after the election, Hoover asked Roosevelt to come and see him about the refusal of the Allies to resume paying their war debts. Roosevelt went, but he made no promises. During the next four months, Hoover kept trying to get Roosevelt to issue statements endorsing Hoover's policy in the interest of "confidence." Roosevelt kept refusing on the ground that he would speak and act when the legal power was his. At issue was the responsibility for the Depression. Recovery, Hoover insisted, had begun in June. Banks continued to fail only because people were afraid of what Roosevelt would do. Unless he endorsed Hoover, Roosevelt would be responsible for catastrophe. Roosevelt believed that most people blamed Hoover, and he did not want to lose his free hand by endorsing a discredited policy.

Politics raged in a vacuum. Lame-duck Congressmen and Senators spent their last months in office laying the blame for the Depression on various persons. Earlier, Hoover had encouraged a Senate investigation of bear raids on the stock market in hope of establishing the notion that the market had nothing to do with business. After the election, the committee hired Ferdinand Pecora to probe Wall Street. The sworn testimony of the leaders of finance themselves shocked newspaper readers. Charles E. Mitchell, president of the National City Bank, borrowed money from his own bank to cover his stock-market losses. J. P. Morgan cut favorites in on sure-thing investments. Most of these fabulously rich men avoided paying income taxes. Most infuriating, they acted on the stand as if the public had no right to question them. When Wall Streeters complained that the disclosures were undermining "confidence," Roosevelt retorted that "they should have thought of that when they did the things that are being exposed now."

Democrats accused Hoover's Reconstruction Finance Corporation of favoring Republican applicants for Government loans over Democratic applicants.

In December, Representative John Garner, Speaker of the House, sponsored a resolution requiring the RFC to name the banks it had supported earlier in the year. Republicans and bankers argued that the publicity would shake confidence in all the banks that had been helped, when depositors discovered that the banks had been in trouble, and would deter others from asking for loans. Garner rejected the argument. "If the truth scares people, let it come."

Confidence became a burning issue. It is, of course, essential to banking and paper money. If a bank kept all its money in cash so that it could pay every depositor in full at any moment, it would not be able to lend the money out to work. It would be a vault, not a banking business. If every paper dollar were redeemable 100 percent in gold at the mint, the volume of currency would depend on gold mining rather than on the needs of business. Ordinarily, only a few depositors want cash, and only a few holders of cash want gold at any one time. The more certain everyone is that he can get it, the less likely anyone is to demand it. Banking and paper money are possible only because most people have confidence that the promise to pay in cash or gold will be fulfilled.

There are two schools of thought about how confidence is maintained, and the crisis brought them into sharp contrast. One school advises saying as little as possible to arouse questioning, especially when there is cause for concern. Its premise is that the world turns because sleeping dogs lie, and it relies on inertia to carry a system along. The other school insists that people should be told the truth, even when it is bad; only if they understand can they be trusted to act rationally.

The issue arises in wartime and whenever business or Government has to break bad news to the public. It shows up in private life. Conservatives generally prefer secrecy. Liberals tend to believe in full disclosure. There is reason on both sides. When there is no serious reason to worry, secrecy can be a balance wheel against needless alarms, but when it is clear that trouble is at hand, candid acknowledgment wins belief and support. The art of politics is in large part the art of knowing when to tell the facts and when to withhold them.

By December 1932, it was obvious that the banks were in trouble. People wondered and gossiped. Newspapers often hesi-

96

tated to print alarming news about banks, although in some towns they gleefully reported the downfall of banks that had made enemies by refusing credit. Bankers and people living on the income of capital discouraged disclosure. Wall Street bankers regarded the publication of the number of bank failures every week as a threat to business. Bank examiners believed they were supporting confidence by going easy on weak banks.

Financial strain uncovered enough embezzlements to cast doubt on the most upright bankers. Columnist Marquis Childs described the fictional bank president, R. William McSwirtle, as "gray, respectable, shiny, with cold, fish-colored eyes concealed behind pince-nez, and a pompous smile." McSwirtle lectured civic groups on "Banks and the Churches." He was so pious that the very sight of him reassured depositors. Yet when the pinch came, he was caught looting $300,000 from the personal accounts of leading citizens who had left their money with him for safekeeping.

The bankers of Texas had once offered a reward for anyone bringing in a dead bank robber, but people said that the bankers themselves heisted more from the inside than robbers ever had lifted from the outside. In Columbus, New Mexico, for instance, a bank president heard that the Mexican government had finally paid a local widow $10,000 indemnity for the murder of her husband when Pancho Villa raided Columbus in 1916. The banker personally persuaded the widow to deposit the big check in his bank the day before it closed forever.

Jokes on bankers thrived. When a stooge said "safe as a bank," the producer and musical comedy star George M. Cohan would bring down the house by inquiring with lively interest, "Which bank?" A banker is supposed to have begged his friend not to tell his mother what he was really doing. "She thinks I'm playing the piano in a sporting house." Senator Carter Glass, the father of the Federal Reserve System, was harsh in his denunciation of the "little corner grocerymen calling them-

selves bankers—and all they know is how to shave a note."
According to the diary of an acquaintance, this distinguished
Senator from Virginia was heard to say, "One banker in my
state attempted to marry a white woman and they lynched him."

Roosevelt had been elected because he sounded as if he would
do something. By election time, even the arch-conservatives who
feared that Hoover would expand the Government too much
were conceding that something must be done for "the common
sort." To most Americans, the only thing that the Government
really could do was to print more money. Roosevelt had stated
flatly that he would protect the dollar. He had promised to cut
Government expenses 25 percent and to balance the budget.
After the election it looked less and less likely that he would be
able to keep these promises. Pressure for inflating the currency
mounted in Congress. There were 50 different inflation bills in
process. People living on capital watched Roosevelt for clues,
but he blandly refused to give any. Production fell, halting the
"recovery" Hoover had hailed when production rose from the
low of the previous June. Businessmen were waiting to see.

In December, country banks began to blink out faster and
faster. Every such failure weakened the city banks that stood
behind the country banks and generated gossip and suspicion
that triggered runs on neighboring banks. Everywhere bankers
dug in as if for a siege, liquidating assets at a sacrifice so that
they could pay out cash. They dared not lend their money out,
forcing postponement of legitimate, normal expansion as well
as inventory and crop financing. As cash became scarcer, individuals began to hoard it. As scandals and bad news broke,
people began to wonder if their money would be good. Many
families had always given gold pieces to children and servants
at Christmas as a festive touch. The Christmas of 1932, little
velvet-lined boxes with 10-dollar gold pieces appeared under
the trees of families who had never given gold before. There
was something reassuring about gold.

Well-informed people were gloomy at New Year's. The *Bulletin* of the Cleveland Trust Co. frankly warned their limited audience that worse was yet to come, while the reasons found by the cheerful for optimism were almost as alarming as the warnings. "The vague and formless notion of impending general ruin has disappeared," *The New York Times* declared, citing a consensus of businessmen who favored the Republican view that the bottom of the Depression had been the low of June 1932. The worst was over, *The Times* said, including the "uncertainties of a Presidential year"; some nations were still on gold; more gold had been mined than ever before; and Americans who had shipped their money out of the country in the form of gold when the British devalued the pound in 1931 were bringing it back. But this recital of troubles "past" could not fail to remind informed readers of that headlong flight of gold and of the atmosphere of "impending general ruin" that still existed around them.

During January, banks in key cities began to go. There were failures in Memphis, Cleveland, San Francisco. The crisis was now feeding on itself. When little banks tried to save themselves, they called in deposits with big banks and created a crisis for them, too. When a bank closed, business enterprises could not meet payrolls. City and county money was lost, so that civil servants could not be paid. Money for relief was gone. In many places, Community Chest money was lost. People were stranded away from home. In Europe, expatriates who had weathered the currency crisis of 1931 could not draw on funds in closed banks at home. They milled around the American Express office in Paris demanding that somebody, maybe the American consul, advance passage money to get them home.

At home, whole towns were left without enough cash to make change in the stores. Where banks could not supply cash, employers paid off in IOUs of small denomination, which were good at least at local stores. Newspapers and cities sometimes

99

had to issue scrip. When Toledo bootleggers agreed to accept it, the papers carried the story as an important news item. In part, at least, to put a humorous face on the nuisance, Blaine, Washington, issued wooden nickels. Tenino, Washington, went Blaine one better by eventually selling enough of its wooden coins as souvenirs to buy the building of a bank that had failed. Just before Roosevelt was inaugurated, a million Americans in 300 small communities were getting along on some locally improvised substitute for cash money. The scarcity of change helped to make "Brother, Can You Spare a Dime" one of the most popular songs of the year.

It was at about this time that a truck rolled up to our house with a dozen enormous, dreadful oil paintings of storms at sea. When Father came home, he explained he had taken them from a client for a legal fee. Mother was furious. Father insisted they were beautiful. Mother conceded that the frames might be worth something because they were covered with gold leaf. In the end, of course, they could not be sold, so we hung them.

"Swaps" began to appear in newspapers. "Man's overcoat, in good condition, for slide trombone, piccolo, or French horn." At Ohio State University, students used cigarettes for currency; in some places they were scarce because local merchants did not have cash to pay the stamp taxes. Bills often were paid in kind. Colleges took eggs or even sacks of coal in exchange for tuition. Farmers paid the doctor or dentist in food. Members of the patient's family sometimes worked out the bill around the doctor's house.

Schemes for doing without money at all were eagerly discussed. This was the time, city intellectuals told each other, to go back to self-contained independent living on the land. People who were growing their own food, making their own clothes, gathering their own fuel, wrote books and magazine articles urging flight from the artificial life of the corrupt cities.

Barter exchanges for swapping goods and services sometimes

100

issued their own scrip. The barter systems brought unemployed skills and surplus commodities back into local circulation. One of the most elaborate was in Seattle, Washington. The unemployed cut unsalable timber for fuel, dug unsalable potatoes, apples, and pears, ran idle fishing boats, and distributed unsold fish in exchange for the services of doctors, barbers, carpenters, cobblers, and seamstresses. At Christmas, an unemployed Santa Claus distributed toys made by the unemployed workers to the children of unemployed fathers. When winter came and there were no more surplus foodstuffs, the barterers turned to politics. In February, thousands of them stormed the county-city building.

February came, and there was still no word from Roosevelt. Bankers and businessmen fed on crumbs of information and reacted to any move that could be considered a sign. Roosevelt's Vice President-elect, John Garner, joined with the Republicans in proposing a sales tax to "balance the budget." When Roosevelt disowned the proposal, the financial community concluded he was going to inflate the currency, instead. A new wave of fear rippled out when Senator Carter Glass turned down Roosevelt's offer of the post of Secretary of the Treasury. Glass refused in part because of his health, but the story went around that he could not get Roosevelt to commit himself, in advance, to "sound money."

Whenever Roosevelt lunched with a currency reformer, bankers shuddered. In February it began to look as if the paper money of the United States might become worth less than its face value in gold. Against that day, people demanded their money in gold when they took it out of a suspected bank. They put it in little black bags that split and sometimes scattered gold bars in the street. They squirreled it away in baking-powder tins, under floorboards, between walls. A spinster in Boston carefully glued five-dollar gold pieces into walnut shells. Some of the medium rich converted small fortunes into gold that they packed in cans, then drove out into the country and buried it in the dead of night, a shotgun handy against robbers.

The very rich were more dignified. They withdrew large fortunes from banks and shipped bullion out of the country. Every ship that sailed for Europe from New York in February carried a treasure in gold. Financial adviser Roger Babson recommended diamonds not only as a hedge against "printing-press inflation" but as a portable form of wealth that could be secreted on a person's clothing "in case anything happened." In Palm Beach, a rich man advised his friends to "step without the territorial boundaries of the United States of America with as much cash as you can carry just as soon as it is feasible for you to get away."

The rich were lying low. An advertising man in New York told his wife that it was "bad public relations" to be seen in a car driven by a chauffeur who sat in an open cab in the style of gangster movies. He felt that the arrangement was not only inhumane in cold weather, but likely to attract unfavorable attention from the unemployed. The Ritz Hotel reported that patrons who usually took suites in town for the winter said they were staying in the country. Some of them were laying in stocks of canned goods and mounting machine guns under the eaves of their country places so as to be ready for "anything." Dayton businessmen had a secret committee working out plans to keep the city going in case the railroad and telephone lines were cut. In Muncie, Indiana, well-to-do families were talking about where candles could be found if the power lines were pulled down.

People held on to their cash. They thought up supposedly safe places for it. They put it away so thoroughly that many of them could not find it again; caches of old, large-size bills still turn up when buildings are demolished. They put bills between the pages of books and pasted the pages together. They slipped them behind the back lining paper of pictures, in the handlebars

102

of a bicycle. One hoarder taped bills under the feathers of a pet parrot. In January 1932, a schoolteacher asked a 12-year-old boy why he was scratching himself and discovered $1000 in big bills taped to his chest. He explained that his parents were afraid of banks.

Banks paid out so much cash that the amount of money in circulation increased every week. Ordinarily, most money changes hands by check. Only one dollar out of every ten is spent in cash. As Roosevelt's inaugural approached, the overworked mint was providing one out of every seven dollars in cash, but it was not enough. People queued up at banks, took their cash, and stashed it away.

Small cities with established leaders were able to rally public-spirited support for a threatened bank. Leading citizens sometimes pledged their fortunes so that banks could withstand runs. Volunteer committees would telephone all night to get emergency loans. Women would contribute their jewelry. A man would throw an empty suitcase into his car and drive all night to bring back currency from a big city bank, so that the tellers could keep paying out cash.

Banks frequently needed only a day or two to get the necessary cash, but dared not ask for time for fear of stimulating a bigger run than they already faced. All during 1932, savings banks occasionally restricted withdrawals for short periods. In October, the State of Nevada declared a moratorium, but only nine of the state's twenty banks closed. (The happy concept of a bank "holiday" was born in Louisiana. Governor Oscar Allen gave a hard-pressed New Orleans bank a day's breather by proclaiming February 5, 1933, a holiday "in commemoration of the severance of diplomatic relations between the United States and Germany.")

By February, the big banks were threatened. The hardest-hit city was Detroit. The unemployed auto workers could not pay their rent; landlords could not pay taxes; banks could not

103

realize on mortgages; the city could not pay on its municipal bonds, and so could not borrow money to keep relief going. Water had been cut off for nonpayment of water taxes in so many households that some public schools were giving children showers when they arrived each morning. Meanwhile, the banks of Detroit were the pawns of two rich men who used their private fortunes to war against each other, without regard to consequences for the public.

Henry Ford's money was the mainstay of the Guardian group of banks in Detroit. Opposed were banks dominated by Senator James Couzens, rich by virtue of his early partnership with Ford. Ford and Couzens hated each other. Ford forgot his early concern for maintaining purchasing power and joined Couzens in maintaining the right of a rich man to do exactly what he pleased with any amount of money under any circumstances.

The storm broke on February 9, when the Guardian group asked the Reconstruction Finance Corporation for a loan. Ford agreed initially to let the new money go to small depositors first, but Couzens feared that the RFC loan would strengthen Ford and threatened to protest it in public. Ford became so angry he withdrew his offer to leave his money in the bank, instead of demanding payment like other depositors.

"No, no," Ford said, "there isn't any reason why I should tie up several million to keep Senator Couzens from shouting from the housetops. And there isn't any reason why I, the largest individual taxpayer in the country, should bail the Government out of its loans to banks."

The Reverend Charles Coughlin, a Detroit Catholic priest, drew big radio audiences denouncing "banksters" who, he implied, were as bad as "gangsters." Thousands drew their money out of banks. Walter Reuther, then an unemployed automobile worker, cleaned out his bank account and went to Europe with his brother Victor. The Reuthers got their money just in time. Banks all over Michigan tottered and failed while waiting for the giants to slug it out in Detroit. Out-of-town bankers would not help.

Hoover had William Moran, chief of the U.S. Secret Service, dispatch 350 men to keep a watch on scandalmongers guilty of spreading "unfounded rumors" about Michigan banks. Meanwhile he kept working on the two ringleaders. He sent emissary after emissary to plead for a truce. He had the Treasury, the Federal Reserve Bank, the RFC, and the Secretary of Commerce working at it. On Monday, February 13, the banks were closed in honor of Lincoln's birthday the Sunday before. *The Detroit Free Press* quoted Senator Couzens as saying that the weak banks should not be allowed to open.

"For once in his life, Jim Couzens is right," Henry Ford replied. "Let the crash come!" According to Jesse Jones, RFC Administrator, the banks in Michigan went under because these two proud men would not get together on any plan, and no plan for Michigan would work without their help.

On February 14, St. Valentine's Day, Michigan Governor William A. Comstock proclaimed a bank holiday commemorating nothing but the necessity for it.

On Wednesday, an assassin barely missed the President-elect in Miami.

On Thursday, a plan to merge all the Detroit banks into a new one based on capital from New York was rejected.

On Friday, Senator Bankhead introduced a bill for stamp scrip, a system of dated money that became worthless if it was not spent. The same day, Hoover wrote Roosevelt begging him to bolster confidence by a "prompt assurance that there will be no tampering or inflation of the currency; that the budget will be unquestionably balanced, even if further taxation is necessary; that the Government credit will be maintained by refusal to exhaust it in the issue of securities." Hoover was so agitated that he misspelled Roosevelt's name on the envelope he personally penned and handed to a Secret Service agent for delivery to the President-elect.

On Saturday, pulse-takers noticed with disapproval that Senator Clarence Dill used the word "panic" four times in a radio talk on "The Enlarged Use of Silver and Inflation."

Hoover waited impatiently for Roosevelt's reply, but it did not arrive for ten days. Roosevelt had dashed off a polite refusal and forgotten to send it off. By this time, half a dozen states had proclaimed bank holidays. In the three weeks following St. Valentine's Day, a billion dollars in new currency was issued, and a billion dollars in gold dropped out of sight.

New money was needed, and instantly. Bankers feverishly devised systems for issuing some sort of paper that would circulate in place of cash. In the Bronx, the American Bank Note Company, the private manufacturer of paper money for South American countries, was printing millions of dollars of clearinghouse certificates that bankers thought might be used in a pinch. In Rochester, New York, the Todd Company, now a division of the Burroughs Company, turned out $40 million of a special safety scrip that blushed the word VOID if doctored. These activities were kept secret for fear of stimulating further demands for gold.

Undaunted by Roosevelt's cool and delayed reply, Hoover begged him to join in approving an Executive order controlling bank withdrawals. Constitutionally there was doubt that the Federal Government could close the banks, but Congress had passed a bill proposed by Senator Couzens permitting the Comptroller of the Currency to apply to national banks whatever measures states had taken to relieve state banks. The President had wide powers to act in time of war, but there was no precedent for him to impair private contracts in peace. Lawyers hunted for a basis, but Roosevelt refused to join any move to close banks before his inauguration.

On March 1, the banks were closed in 12 states.

106

On March 3, seven more announced holidays.

Both Hoover and Roosevelt were stubborn men, and each believed he was right. The supporters of each accused the other of "playing politics with the country." Neither appeared to distinguish between his own political stake and the fate of the country. Roosevelt could remark, with some dispassion and not a little satisfaction, that it looked as if the bank crisis was due to culminate on Inauguration Day. The timing would give him the free hand he wanted to launch his New Deal. Hoover was just as candid about getting Roosevelt to cooperate. "I realize that if these declarations be made by the President-elect, he will have ratified the whole major program of the Republican Administration," he told his advisers. Agnes Meyer, wife of the Governor of the Federal Reserve Board, likened the end of the Hoover Administration to the end of a Greek tragedy. As in a symmetrical plot by Aeschylus or Racine, two protagonists brought ruin by steadfastly holding to opposing views of what was right.

Hoover went out in the closest thing to a national breakdown the United States has ever experienced. Food supplies were failing. In Detroit, where there had been no money for three weeks, municipal laborers fainted from hunger on the job, with uncashable paychecks in their pockets. Milk flowing into Detroit on temporary credit was drying up at the cow because farmers could no longer buy feed on credit. So many egg orders were canceled that unexpected baby chicks yellowed Michigan farmyards. In Clear Lake, Iowa, farmers burned their corn for fuel, rather than take scrip for it. Fresh produce rotted on freight cars in Baltimore. Food moves on cash, and the key island of Manhattan could not live very long without it. Immigrants on the lower East Side who remembered the collapse of the German mark hoarded groceries as well as cash.

The United States of America was technically bankrupt. An incredible $250 million worth of gold had been withdrawn from

107

its reserve during Hoover's last week. There was not enough gold left in the Federal Reserve Bank to back the currency. There was not enough cash in the United States Treasury to meet the Government's payroll, let alone the $700 million in short-term certificates redeemable in cash or gold on March 15. J. K. Galbraith, then an instructor in economics, publicly recommended drawing money out of private banks and depositing it in Postal Savings, the banking system run by the Post Office, on the theory that the Government would make good if no one else would.

In Detroit and many other places, relief had simply stopped. Where banks were closed, relief checks could not be cashed. In Kenosha, Wisconsin, the unemployed besieged the city hall demanding relief, while inside the city council stayed in session for 48 hours. Police would not let the unemployed meet in St. Louis. The Communists organized "hunger marches" on city halls and on the legislatures of half a dozen states. They had committees agitating for the immediate payment of all bank deposits in full and all wages and relief checks in cash.

Secretary of War Patrick J. Hurley admitted that he was concentrating troops around the big cities because of what "Reds and possible Communists" might do. Relatives of Henry Wallace's wife told him about a secret clique of Army Reserve officers mobilizing in different parts of the country in case Roosevelt was not able to maintain order. People working in downtown Chicago and New York considered how best to get out of these cities if railroads were unable to operate and the unemployed should barricade the highways.

Local government, the first line of political authority, was paralyzed for lack of cash. Boston had not paid its police for months. Boston banks had their employees deputized to guard what cash and gold remained when they were forced to close. Police never had been needed so badly. Crazed and restless people were attacking banks and trying to rob them. Millions of

108

dollars of insecurely hidden cash tempted thieves. Storekeepers who had been quietly accumulating cash left their cashboxes at police stations for safekeeping over weekends.

Some of the crimes were bizarre. Friday morning, for instance, Mrs. Martha Lauchran, thrifty Brooklyn wife of a shipyard worker, woke up worrying about the banks. She took the $80 she had in the house to the South Brooklyn Savings Bank and exchanged it for gold. The gold must have been heavier than she expected, because the $1000 she had on deposit there she drew out in bills. Her next stop was another bank, where she took out $1200. Last stop was The Dime Savings Bank, where she withdrew $7300.

On her way home, she passed a butcher shop and suddenly remembered she didn't have a thing in the house to eat. She started to go in, but two men grabbed her loaded pocketbook and made off in a small coupe. Someone got the license number.

One of them took the pocketbook home, put $7500 in a paper bag, and stuffed the paper bag in a chair. He then went to the poolroom where he spent most of his time and tried to burn up the handbag. The gold was awkward and of no use to him, so he threw it into an ashcan. The other one's wife was on relief. He went home and gave her $10.

Then the two men drove to Atlantic City. They bought themselves new clothes from the skin out. They ate as much as they could and drank as much as they could and slept in the most expensive bed they could rent for the night. Next morning, they drove on to Washington for the Inaugural festivities. They mingled with dignitaries packing the town. They bought themselves tuxedos and went to the Inaugural Ball. Sunday morning, they headed for Florida, where the millionaires were. When they were finally caught, they had managed to spend less than $2000. The gold had been carted away to the dump and lost, but the folding money in the chair was recovered.

Meanwhile, behind closed doors at the Federal Reserve, Government officials worked to save the banks in Chicago and New York, the strongest institutions in the country. On Friday, groups of sleepless bankers in both cities gathered around telephone wires to Washington where Treasury and Federal Reserve officials sat checking the disappearance of reserves. Some New York bankers were for going down with the ship. Others believed the Government should close the banks. Finally, late at night, while Hoover's party sat in the White House and Roosevelt and his advisers in Washington's Mayflower Hotel, Governor Herbert Lehman proclaimed a bank holiday in New York State.

The morning of March 4, Inauguration Day, bank holidays were proclaimed in the states where banks still were open. With every state out, Federal Reserve banks closed too. Trading was suspended on all the stock and commodity exchanges.

Roosevelt had a clean slate. As protocol demanded, the incoming and outgoing Presidents rode down Pennsylvania Avenue together in an open car. Roosevelt tried to make small talk, but Hoover would not speak.

6

$ $ $ $ $

RESCUE

INSTEAD of merely saying "I do," Roosevelt repeated every word of the oath of office after bewhiskered Chief Justice Charles Evans Hughes. Then he turned to the rostrum, cocked his Dutch chin in the drizzle, and proceeded with finality to break with the past. "I am certain," he said, in the voice that was to become a part of our life, "that my fellow Americans expect that on my induction into the Presidency I will address myself with a candor and a decision which the present situation of our Nation impels."

It was the first Inauguration to be widely broadcast. In stores, in homes, in hotel lobbies, people gathered around radios, quiet with the sense of history. Parents told their children to listen so that one day they would be able to tell their children what they had heard.

"Only a foolish optimist can deny the dark realities of the moment.... Values have shrunken to fantastic levels ... the means of exchange are frozen in the currents of trade; the withered leaves of industrial enterprise lie on every side; farmers find no markets for their produce; the savings of many years

111

in thousands of families are gone ... a host of unemployed citizens face the grim problem of existence, and an equally great number toil with little return. ...

"Rulers of the exchange of mankind's goods have failed, through their own stubbornness and their own incompetence, have admitted their failure, and abdicated. ... The money changers have fled.

"This Nation asks for action, and action now. Our greatest primary task is to put people to work. ... I shall ask the Congress for the one remaining instrument to meet the crisis—broad Executive power to wage a war against the emergency, as great as the power that would be given to me if we were in fact invaded by a foreign foe. ...

"The only thing we have to fear is fear itself—nameless, unreasoning, unjustified terror." Roosevelt had charm, an intuitive sense of timing, and he radiated confidence. He was a born showman, and history had given him, as playwright Robert Sherwood observed, "the advantage of a good act to follow."

The famous speech was so effective in rallying people from their despair that its psychology is worth analysis. He admitted that things were bad. He affixed blame. He was confident things could be fixed. He offered action and "action now." He called for sacrifice. He asked for unprecedented powers. He promised to do his best. He prayed God for help.

But his success was too simple for art. As the Quakers would say, he really "spoke to the condition of men." In 1933 that condition was desperate, and Americans thrilled as if to a trumpet call. In relatively affluent 1960, some people sneered when Kennedy urged his inaugural audience to "ask what you can do for your country." Roosevelt put the thought less gracefully 37 years earlier when he said, "Our true destiny is not to be ministered unto, but to minister to ourselves and to our fellow men." But he inspired the whole country.

Many simply wept. Others took action. Louis Brownlow, pio-

112

neer public administrator, was in Florida convalescing from an unshakable cold acquired during Chicago's municipal crisis. His nose instantly dried up, and he headed for Washington to offer his services, "no longer afraid that there might be too much centralization of government." "Tommy" Corcoran, a smart young lawyer, clever enough to become one of Roosevelt's most brilliant political aides, was so moved that he left half of his money in the bank instead of drawing it all out as he had planned.

Austrian currency speculator Franz Pick was in Paris on his honeymoon. When he caught the phrase "sound and adequate currency" over the scratchy shortwave radio, he figured Roosevelt was preparing to go off gold and instantly contracted to exchange 250,000 dollars in American money for a foreign currency. So many of the international "money changers" came to the same conclusion a few hours later that Pick was able to turn the foreign currency back into dollars and deliver them under his contract at a profit.

The American "money changers" excoriated by Roosevelt swallowed their pride and hailed him as a champion against the easy money party in Congress. Henry Hazlitt, the columnist who later denounced "Big Government," urged a dictatorship that would bypass Congress and "get things done." The well-to-do who admired Mussolini for getting Italian trains to run on time hoped Roosevelt would be equally effective, and the highbrows among them quoted Pareto, the Italian philosopher who questioned the value of democracy to civilization.

Democracy was on everyone's mind. The week the banks closed, I was on the Vassar debating team that prevented a visiting debating team from Smith College from proving *"Resolved:* That Democracy is an outworn form of government." I took the rebuttal, and we won strictly on points; Smith had the popular side. Vassar had laid in three weeks' supply of food, and a good thing, too. The crisis made us think, and thinking made us hungry. A girl would talk herself around in a circle

113

and then drop out to join another bull session and talk herself around again.

We would not have felt any more confident about the future of democracy if we could have known that much the same kind of discussion was going on behind armed guards at the U.S. Treasury in Washington and in the principal Federal Reserve banks. Federal Reserve bankers were getting groggy from lack of sleep. Vice-Chairman Randolph Burgess was lying exhausted on the cot in the first-aid room of the New York Federal Reserve Bank, checking and rechecking his assets against new developments.

At the Treasury in Washington, Republican and Democratic opposite numbers stayed awake together for days. Their discussions had the theoretical flavor of college bull sessions: how define solvency so that at least one bank in every state could pass the test and open its doors?

Roosevelt's Secretary of the Treasury, Will Woodin, was for giving the President a blank check. Senator Carter Glass did not think the Senate would go along. "Have him do what's necessary and get authorization afterwards," it was suggested. But the real problem was what he should do. Some kind of scrip or clearing-house certificate issued by associations of banks in each city seemed the only currency on which banks could reopen. The Government would either have to back the banks or else take them over, it seemed; but it would take time to separate the sound from the unsound. One group of leaders was for closing the weakest banks forever and funneling assets to the stronger ones. Another contended that it was not legal to open some banks and keep others closed; better pay an across-the-board percentage so that every depositor could get 25 percent of his money. If you do, objected others, you'll simply lose 25 percent the first day. Everyone conceded banks could no longer pay out gold, but there was disagreement about whether this meant that the country was "off the gold standard."

Mel Traylor of Chicago's First National Bank was for liquidating doubtful assets and getting down to brass tacks, no matter how much it hurt. Make bank stockholders pay. Suspend bank dividends. "I am not willing to go on being a member of a banking structure which is a stench in the nostrils of the world," he shrilled. Then he broke down and wept. George Harrison of the New York Federal Reserve doodled ladies in crescent moons. A. A. Berle, Jr., the youngest brain truster, amused himself by taking notes on how the wise men acted. The meeting in the Treasury was inconclusive.

Banks would have to be restored, if only to refinance Government obligations falling due the next week, but what would they pay out to depositors? Government bonds were no longer liquid enough to serve as assets against which currency could be issued. "Put the Government on a cash basis!" Traylor cried. "On that basis, I'd buy governments."

Raymond Moley, Roosevelt's chief economic adviser, coolly suggested that the President did not need to bother with the banks at all in order to meet the March 15 refinancing. He could just appeal to the people on the radio, and they would take the money out of their socks. There were loud boos of disbelief.

"I vote we do something," someone said, and everyone voted yes.

"Every once in a while I'd look out the window and pinch myself," Berle recalls. "This sort of thing happened in South American countries, but not in the U.S.A." Margaret Mead was in the wilds of New Guinea. When a South Seas trader told her that all the banks in her country were closed, she simply did not believe him. The sense of unreality even touched Roosevelt himself.

After the inaugural, he had sworn in his Cabinet, given a family party, and gone to bed. Sunday morning, while the haggard men argued in the Treasury, he decided to take possession

115

of his official desk. He had himself wheeled into the great oval office of the President of the United States and dismissed his attendants, so that he could sit in the historic place by himself.

The big room was empty and quiet. The huge desk was bare. President Hoover, at that moment window-shopping unnoticed on Fifth Avenue, had taken everything movable but the flag and the Great Seal. There were no documents. No scratch paper. No pencil. No telephone. Not even a buzzer. A cripple, the President of the United States sat alone at the controls of a paralyzed country. Roosevelt shouted for help, and his secretaries, aides, and Secret Service men came running.

The rest of the day was busy. The group at the Treasury pulled itself together and drafted a Presidential order stopping the export of gold, closing banks, and giving the Secretary of the Treasury power to issue scrip and set the terms on which banks would open. Toward midnight, the new President called Congress into session for the following Thursday, March 9; he proclaimed the Bank Holiday order under the authority to regulate foreign exchange and prevent hoarding granted the President by the Trading-with-the-Enemy Act of 1917. Roosevelt sounded unshaken, but the bankers waited apprehensively for dawn. Some of them had predicted riot and revolution.

"Do you think that when the banks all close people will climb trees and throw coconuts at each other?" Yale Professor of Psychology Edward S. Robinson asked worried friends. "I will venture a prediction as to exactly what will happen. When the banks close, everyone will feel relieved. It will be a sort of national holiday. There will be general excitement and a feeling of great interest. Travel will not stop; hotels will not close; everyone will have a lot of fun, although they will not admit that it's fun at the time."

Monday morning, March 6, almost everyone, including many of the affected bankers, heard the news over the radio, or read it in the paper at breakfast, and wondered whether to go to

116

work. A few old-fashioned bankers blustered that the Government had no right to close the banks. On Saturday, the ultra-conservative Mellon National Bank of Pittsburgh had defied the state holiday order, but by Monday morning even the Mellons were not willing to "liquidate everything." From coast to coast, banks stayed shut, but almost everything else opened up in one way or another.

The first problem was getting to work. Many people who had some big bills hidden away couldn't find a nickel for the streetcar. Post Offices and railroad stations normally made change for the public, but they soon had to stop. Storekeepers spent the morning trying to distinguish between legitimate customers and customers making a small purchase just to break a big bill. In New York a well-heeled gentleman caught with nothing but one $500 bill and three $100 ones, spied a nickel under the grating over a subway station and managed to snag his fare with chewing gum on the end of a stick. In Chicago, where the fare was seven cents, people raided piggy banks. In smaller places, people simply hopped on the regular bus and the driver let them ride free.

Berle had spent a sleepless night devising a "habit basis" instead of a gold basis for the currency. Everybody would get up in the morning and do what he normally did, giving or taking IOUs whenever payment had to be made. At the end of the day, the chits would be deposited in a bank, and currency would be issued against them. To a surprising degree, this is just what people did spontaneously. Goods moved whether there was money to move them or not.

Neighborhood grocers took care of regular customers, but rationed them to no more than their usual purchases, at least until the grocers could be sure that suppliers would treat them the same way.

Absolute strangers trusted each other. A lawyer with an honest face rode across the continent giving railroad conductors his IOUs. When a Detroit friend called Berle to beg enough money for coal for the local hospital, the young brain truster called the president of the North American Coal Company, who started a bargeload moving right away. "If you fellows get things fixed up, we'll get paid, I expect," the coal man said, "and if you don't, that coal won't do anybody any good on the dock at Ashtabula."

People thought up novel ways of doing business as usual. A Flatbush husband gave his wife her regular Monday morning household allowance in 35 one-dollar checks. A New York hotel sent around to ministers to exchange bills for the silver on collection plates, only to find that many churches had taken the Sunday offerings in checks. In Atlanta, a taxi driver accepted his fare in postage stamps. In Boston, a hardware store took "el" tickets. In Buffalo, two prizefighters slugged each other for a prize of potatoes and tomatoes. Massachusetts state institutions prepared to pay wages in fuel and food. The madam of a high-class brothel in Providence, Rhode Island, who was doing her place over, passed the word that she would accept books with fine bindings instead of the traditional cash. Macy's broke its rule against credit for regular customers, but paid wages in cash. Mayor James Michael Curley of Boston forgot about collecting taxes and rushed food and fuel to the cashless. "Lay aside the shutoff wrench!" he ordered the Water Department.

Roosevelt had resolved to keep a diary as President. Luckily, the resolve lasted through Monday, because aside from the cook's daybook of who ate what, Roosevelt's own account is the only official one we have of what went on that day in the White House. Everyone else in the place was too new or too confused to write anything down.

Roosevelt had the first-class temperament that lets a man always sleep soundly. Monday morning he had breakfast in bed

118

and read what the papers printed about the Bank Holiday and gold embargo he had proclaimed just before turning in at 1 A.M., the night before. By 10 o'clock he was in the Senate chamber for the funeral observance of the death of his Attorney General, Senator Thomas J. Walsh of Montana, who had died of a heart attack on a Pullman on his honeymoon. After the ceremony, Congressmen pressed in on Roosevelt to assure him that anything he wanted would be rushed into law, sight unseen.

Back at the White House, Roosevelt seems to have been surprised to find a score of governors waiting for him in the East Room. He had invited them weeks before to discuss unemployment. Gifford Pinchot of Pennsylvania had closed his banks in such a hurry he had only 95¢ on him for the trip. Allen of Louisiana had forehandedly drawn his expense money before shutting off the supply. Roosevelt was unprepared to deal with unemployment and didn't know yet what he was going to do about the banks, but the governors were so enchanted with him personally that they were for giving him virtual wartime powers to do anything he wanted. They all stayed on for lunch, but afterwards some of them recovered sufficiently from his spell to try to get RFC loans for their pet banks before going home.

Just before lunch, Roosevelt left the governors long enough to fire off a statement regretting the death early that morning of Mayor Anton J. Cermak of Chicago, who had stopped the assassin's bullet intended for the President-elect, in Florida. The President also promised to see two Communist petitioners who were waiting outside. During the morning, Washington police had jailed a score of Communist demonstrators who were demanding $5 a week relief for Negroes, equal to that given to whites, and sent some of the demonstrators to the hospital with cracked skulls. Roosevelt left orders to permit orderly Communist parades in the future. Next day's *Daily Worker* tactfully downplayed the demonstration. Meanwhile, Mrs. Roosevelt was telling reporters at the first First Lady press conference ever held that she planned to greet White House guests herself at the door and let newspapers quote her directly.

After lunch came assorted visitors: Jim Farley on postponing appointments for the duration of the crisis; Lew Douglas, Budget Director, on announcing a drive for economy in government to improve the business climate; farm leaders urging currency inflation; Will Woodin, Secretary of the Treasury, to report no progress on a plan for the banks; the Kaiser's grandson, a chum from student days, to exchange personal photographs.

Roosevelt probably also saw Harvard classmate James H. Perkins, the little-known new chairman of the scandal-ridden National City Bank. (Next day, this bank announced that it was splitting into two, so that its investment operations could be entirely separate from its deposit accounts. The move was one jump ahead of the Glass-Steagall Act that required banks to engage in one or the other activity so as to avoid tempting bank officers to speculate with depositors' money. Charles E. Mitchell had resigned as president of the National City Bank after testifying to the Pecora Committee that he had evaded income tax and had been buying the stock of his own bank to push up its price. Exactly two weeks later, Mitchell was arrested on the income-tax charge.)

At the Treasury, the bankers were coping with a flood of queries on the loosely worded proclamation closing the banks: Can I legally give up $25,000 in gold held in trust for my grandchildren? Can I get enough cash to move my pigs to market? During the day, the Secretary of the Treasury had ruled on emergencies. Banks could make change, grant access to safe-deposit boxes, and pay out money for emergency food and medicine, but there was no decision yet on a basis for reopening the banks.

All day long, everyone had expected scrip to be issued.

120

Woodin himself had so advised reporters. With encouragement from Roosevelt himself, Amos 'n Andy built their Tuesday radio show around scrip ("New money? I can't even git a-hold of none o' de *old* money."). Will Rogers came out for it, too. "The psychology of the stuff not being actual money is going to make everybody want to buy something." To bankers, scrip was the honest solution. It was phony money that looked like phony money.

"I'll be damned if I go back into those meetings until I get my head cleared," Secretary of the Treasury Woodin told Raymond Moley. Woodin was no banker. Roosevelt had appointed him because he was one of the few manufacturers who had supported his campaign. He didn't look the part. He was slight and offhand, composed music, and made notorious puns. "I'm going to be more concerned with Federal Reserve notes than with musical notes for a while," he told reporters when he was appointed. "I must saw wood and keep quiet." They called him "elfin," "Peter Pan," "child-faced," "Wee Willie Woodin." He literally worked himself to his death the next year.

Monday night, composer Woodin took to his guitar. "I played some. Then I slept some. Then I thought some. And then it came to me. We don't have to issue scrip at all. We can issue currency against the sound assets of the banks. It will be real money that looks like money." The plan required examining all the banks, to decide how many loans and mortgages were good, and then issuing currency based on these alone. On Tuesday, Roosevelt was delighted with the idea and ordered it carried out.

As Robinson had predicted, the holiday made people feel like kids let loose because the schoolhouse had burned down. Will Rogers found the nation "united and happy, tickled with poverty." Anthropologist Ruth Benedict reported "a good deal of cheerfulness." Journalist Mary Heaton Vorse ascribed the euphoria to a sense of relief that the worst had come. "We're

121

on the bottom," Woodin told reporters. "We aren't going any lower."

The good humor was something more than the rise of spirits that goes with dramatic disaster. For four dreary years, the trouble had been money. Now that it was gone, everyone was in the same boat. "A great many people's checks are now as good as those of a great many others," cracked impostor "Prince" Michael Romanoff. Rich and poor faced the world with an equally uncertain future beyond the cash they happened to have on hand. One survey averaged it at just $18.23 a family, after the piggy banks were robbed. Twenty dollars was a lot of money in 1933: a month's rent for a flat over a store, an overcoat, a dinette set, a month's wages for a live-in maid.

Very few people took advantage of the holiday. Insurance companies arranged to continue honoring policies that had lapsed for nonpayment of premiums. Many organizations paid employees in cash or part cash instead of by check. A notable exception was the United Press Association, fondly remembered by correspondents for its favorite cablese instructions, "downhold expenses." When the banks closed, the UP limited all its employees to $50—by check.

A few worked the crisis for publicity. Southern California orange growers gave the unemployed 2,000 carloads of oranges they could not sell. Film stars volunteered to take pay cuts they expected anyway. But most people tried to help, and some made real sacrifices. Officials of American Express rushed cash from city to city, transferred funds by traveler's checks, and rescued Americans stranded abroad. The Corn Products Company advanced funds to the Argo State Bank in their plant town outside of Chicago so that their employees would not lose money deposited in it. The Marshall & Isley Bank of Milwaukee, which had managed to turn almost all its assets into cash, sent a man down to the post office on Monday to return a box containing the last few million dollars they had received from the Chicago Federal Reserve Bank. They figured it would do more good in some weaker bank.

The day generated paradoxes. John D. Rockefeller, Sr., ran out of change and had to give his caddy a dollar. In Chicago, Cook County took in $3 million by getting permission for banks to release deposits for the payment of taxes only. The biggest headline in the Communist newspaper, *The Daily Worker,* was an appeal for funds: UNCASHABLE CHECKS MENACE 'DAILY.'

Courts took the law into their own hands. They gave bootleggers heavier fines than usual, because it seemed wrong for them to be better off than honest citizens just because they did a cash business. A Federal Judge excused Senator James Davis from trial on a lottery charge because "his detention in New York at this time would deprive the State of Pennsylvania of representation during a national crisis." The Governor of California reprieved a condemned murderer because he was not sure whether a hanging was legal on a "holiday," but men scheduled for release from the New York State Reformatory had to stay over because they couldn't cash the checks the state gives prisoners when they leave. The stories delighted people, because they felt that things were upside down anyway.

On Thursday, the new Congress did not even try to think what should be done. There was no playing to the galleries. There were no partisan ploys. The Emergency Banking Act was whooped through so fast that Congressmen did not have copies before them. When the Clerk had trouble making out the marked-up copy he read to the house, he was interrupted by shouts of "Vote! Vote!" It gave the President power—never since repealed—to close the banks, expand the currency, and invade the "sanctity" of private contract when he deemed it necessary. That very day, he used the new power to stop payments in gold and keep it in the country.

In the next few days, banks were allowed to pay out funds for freight and feed, to move foodstuffs, to make change, and to take deposits. Depositors had no "confidence" in bankers, but they believed Roosevelt. On March 12 he told them over the radio that "it is safer to keep your money in a reopened bank than under the mattress." Next morning the people who had lined up in front of banks to take their money out lined up to put it back again. Within two weeks, three fourths of the banks were back in business. The new Federal Reserve notes authorized for emergency currency did not have to be used.

There was no time to check the assets of each bank properly and no real yardstick against which to measure which ones should open and which should remain closed. One Treasury official snatched sleep in his office, waking whenever a banker phoned in for a decision. RFC Administrator Jesse Jones persuaded both General Motors and Ford to found new banks for Detroit to replace the banks that Ford and Couzens had allowed to crash. All banks in California were so shaky that the banking officials could not see how any of them could open. "Are you willing to take the responsibility for leaving them closed?" Woodin retorted. He ordered some opened on the general principle that California had to have banks. Renewed confidence kept them going. One bank given up by its own directors was reopened by clerical error and weathered the storm.

Roosevelt could have nationalized the banks. A great many depositors probably thought he had nationalized them. All that concerned them was that something was being done. "If he had burned down the house," Will Rogers quipped, "people would say, 'Well, at least he got a fire started.' " Instead, Roosevelt used the first hundred days of his Administration to rescue the country by sweeping emergency measures that permanently broadened the franchise of Government.

There was major action almost every day:

- On March 9, the Emergency Banking Act and the embargo

124

on gold exports put the country off the gold standard in practice.

- On March 20, the Economy Act enabled Roosevelt to cut some veterans' pensions 10 percent and the salaries of Senators and Representatives 15 percent.

- On March 31, the Civilian Conservation Corps (CCC) authorized the Labor Department to choose unemployed men 18 to 25 years old, pay them the traditional hired man's wage of a dollar a day plus keep, and put them to work fighting dust storms, restocking streams, and saving forests.

- On May 12, the Federal Emergency Relief Administration (FERA) was authorized to spend $500 million of Federal money in grants to state and local relief programs. The same day the Agricultural Adjustment Act (AAA) undertook to raise farm prices by buying up the crops of farmers who limited acreage and rescue small farmers from foreclosure, and empowered the President to inflate the currency by cutting the gold content of the dollar, coining silver, or issuing new currency (the "Thomas Amendment").

- On May 18, the Tennessee Valley Authority (TVA) started the Federal Government developing power, making fertilizer, damming streams, conserving natural resources, and relocating the marginal farmers of a seven-state pocket of poverty.

- On May 27, the Securities Act charged underwriters with full and fair disclosure of the character of the securities offered.

- On June 5, Roosevelt signed a joint resolution of Congress abrogating the gold clause in public and private debts.

- On June 13, a Home Owners Loan Act set up a Government corporation (HOLC) to take over the mortgages of small homeowners threatened with eviction.

- On June 16, Congress passed three revolutionary measures:

1. The Banking Act of 1933 divorced commercial from investment banking, so that bank officers could not float securities with depositors' money, and through a Federal Deposit Insur-

ance Corporation (FDIC), insured deposits up to $5,000 against failure. This was the Glass-Steagall Act.

2. The Railroad Coordination Act appointed a Federal Coordinator of Transportation to consolidate duplicating railroads and do whatever was necessary to make them pay.

3. The National Industrial Recovery Act appropriated $3.3 billion for public works and established a National Recovery Administration (NRA) to get industries and their workers to write their own codes of fair competition, with minimum wages and prices. The public works appropriation supported both the Public Works Administration (PWA) under Harold Ickes, which tried to get the most value for its money, and the Federal Emergency Relief Administration (FERA) under Harry Hopkins, which tried to make the most jobs for its money.

There was something for everybody. For farmers, price support. For the unemployed, Federal relief. For bank depositors, Federal insurance against bank failure. For investors who had bought worthless securities, Federal policing of security issuance and trading. Debtors took heart because the President was given power to inflate the currency, and mortgages were extended. Creditors were reassured by the pay and pension cuts. Business got protection from price and wage chiselers. Labor got protection for unions. In a crisis, mortgages could be stayed, gold impounded, banks closed, veterans deprived of their pensions and private parties of their property.

No one really worried about whether all this was constitutional. Lawyers knew the powers were far too vague and broad to stand up in court, but no one had the heart to push the point. When someone asked Fiorello LaGuardia, the dynamic Representative from New York City, whether it was constitutional to prevent foreclosure of a mortgage, he pointed to my father, who was serving on a citizens' committee drafting a mortgage moratorium law, "Ask Mr. Bird, he's the lawyer here." Father and

126

the other lawyers just laughed. The idea was to get something going and get it going fast.

AAA was debated during the spring planting season. Every day the bill was discussed, farmers jumped the gun by planting more cotton and breeding more pigs than they had planned. AAA's first act was to clear away this excess. In 1933, the new agency spent $100 million plowing up ten million acres of cotton and slaughtered six million little pigs, most of them too small to eat.

This destruction shocked the country. The red tape seemed intolerable. According to one of the many stories circulated, Federal agents fined a widow in Maine $18 for slaughtering one of her pigs and curing it against the winter without paying the AAA processing tax. In 1935, AAA was declared unconstitutional, but the principle of subsidizing farmers by paying them for what they did not produce was retained, under the guise of conservation, and has been the basis of Federal support for agriculture ever since.

To get NRA moving, Roosevelt appointed General Hugh S. Johnson, who had organized voluntary registration for the draft in World War I by appeals to patriotism. General Johnson used the same methods to persuade manufacturers to agree on NRA codes. He locked into a room men who had competed with each other for years and exhorted them to agree. Cheers broke out when the cotton textile industry agreed to abolish child labor.

The oil industry could not agree. Desperate wildcatters were ignoring existing production restrictions and bringing in so many new wells that in East Texas oil was literally cheaper than water. Johnson impatiently drew up a code himself and told the industry that it would have 24 hours to approve it. Veterans of foreign oil explorations who had virtually ruled whole nations fought each other for mimeographed copies of the proposed code that Johnson held in his hand.

The codes came through, but not fast enough for Johnson. He called on every enterprise in the country for voluntary compliance with a blanket code putting a temporary floor on wages and hours. Postmen distributed the "Reemployment Agreement" forms to every employer on their routes. "Cooperators" paraded to brass bands and displayed the Blue Eagle to show "We Do Our Part."

Chiselers were ostentatiously exposed. Some restaurants got around the minimum wages by charging employees for meals that were formerly on the house. Rebels challenged the law. A restaurant in the Middle West refused to sign and inspired a story that some newspapers headed "CHICKEN ON THE MENU BUT NO BLUE EAGLE ON THE WALL." Henry Ford, author of the New Era concept of high wages and low prices, denounced the auto code as a conspiracy between his competitors and the international bankers, while the publicity-conscious burlesque "industry" virtuously did its part by limiting production to four strips a show. Johnson soon had codes for cotton textiles, shipbuilding, woolens, electricals, garments, oil, steel, lumber, automobiles, and soft coal.

The hoopla stimulated stories. People told each other about the Chinese laundryman who protested that he was doing the shirts just as cheap as he possibly could. He thought the Government investigator was going to put him in jail for charging too much rather than too little. A bootblack in St. Louis cannily signed the Reemployment Agreement, cut his hours to 40, and demanded that the NRA make up his loss of income. Johnson was well aware that the codes were full of loopholes, but he hoped the experiment would last long enough to give business a shot in the arm. It came to an end in 1935, when the Supreme Court declared NRA unconstitutional.

CCC was Roosevelt's pet project, and he cut red tape to get the boys into the woods. Six weeks after he was inaugurated, the first flabby, listless city boys were getting acquainted with

128

camp life and learning to attack conservation chores the Forestry Service had long hoped to do. CCC was immensely popular. The money sent home from the boys' pay saved thousands of families from relief. Their work literally saved several Plains States from blowing off the map in dusty years. All told, they put in a billion trees, half of all the trees ever planted in the United States. They saved the forests from fire and flood, restocked streams, protected wildlife.

Most important, they saved themselves. In nine years CCC took 2.5 million boys, many of them from slums, and made men of them. They had educational adventures. One crew spent a summer protecting the last two trumpeter swans in Yellowstone Park. Another literally fired the last shot of the Civil War—an unexploded shell unearthed during work on the national park at Gettysburg. World War II officers prized the CCC veterans as noncommissioned officers. They had learned how to live in a camp and under discipline, half the battle in any war.

The most urgent need was relief. To get FERA aid to the unemployed in a hurry, Roosevelt appointed Harry Hopkins, an intense social worker from New York City. The new FERA chief was not a man to waste time.

"People don't eat in the long run," Hopkins said. "They eat every day." A half hour after he was appointed, he found a desk in the hall and started firing telegrams off to states before workmen could move him into his office. During the first two hours he spent $5 million. Hoover's POUR and PECE organizations had studied and exhorted. Hopkins spent first and studied afterwards. "I'm not going to last six months," he explained, "so I'll do as I please."

Hopkins had no organization chart. He wanted nothing for himself. On a salary of $8,000 a year, he was taking care of children by a former wife and one winter could not afford to buy his new wife a coat. He liked race tracks and racy people. He was not discreet in his speech, manner, or dress. But he got

129

things done. An observer from the Army Corps of Engineers, a crack mover of men, credited Relief Administrator Harry Hopkins and his "able young assistants" with putting more men to work faster than the Army was able to draft them in World War I. "These assistants address Mr. Hopkins fondly as Harry," the military man noted, "yet he holds their respect, confidence, and seemingly whole-souled cooperation."

Hopkins was one of the few New Dealers who really knew something about the poor before the Depression drew attention to them. He enlisted other social workers as his eyes and ears. Every day their reports poured in to him from all parts of the country. Ace journalists Lorena Hickock and Martha Gellhorn worked on his staff. They ferreted out the human side of relief, and their reports contributed anecdotes and telling phrases to the President's fireside chats.

"Let's try it!" Roosevelt would say when someone had a bright idea. Hopkins encouraged local administrators to experiment. Camps were set up for boys on the road. So many who were suffering from tuberculosis had managed to get to the Southwest that a special work camp was organized there to treat them. In West Virginia, where children were starving, a relief administrator who happened to be in the National Guard borrowed a camp to feed them up. They gained an average of five pounds during their two weeks' stay. "Do we get three meals tomorrow, too?" one boy asked after his first night.

Hopkins and his spies discovered a class of farmer the American public did not realize existed—farmers too far gone for AAA crop payments, too far away for city relief, and sometimes literally starving for lack of seeds or a plow. For them, FERA's Rural Rehabilitation Administration worked out individual programs of loans and moves to better land. Relief offices sometimes got their first repayment in cans of fruit and vegetables.

Emergency was the key word in FERA. Relief was supposed

130

to be local, minimal, and temporary. Most localities getting the Federal grants supplied food only, many by making the unemployed lug home a set order of groceries from a warehouse. Hopkins used his granting powers to stimulate more work relief projects that gave families cash they could spend as they pleased. By fall it was clear that relief families were going to have to be carried over the 1933–34 winter.

Appalled at the prospect of a permanent relief class, Congress set up the Civilian Works Administration (CWA) to put the unemployed to work on projects suggested by local authorities. CWA took men from relief rolls, but required no means test and paid prevailing rates or NRA minimums. Hopkins and his crew exerted themselves to get the projects going before winter closed in. "A wonder they're still alive," gruffed General Hugh Johnson, a legendary worker himself and no particular friend to Hopkins. Two weeks after the money was voted, CWA distributed 800,000 paychecks. In some depressed towns, newly paid workers cleared the shelves of retail stores. New paint brightened towns literally grown gray. Hope and pride revived. "We're not on relief any more," a woman could say. "My husband is working for the Government."

Within two months, CWA was paying four million men. They could be seen almost everywhere, standing around outdoors doing as little as possible and often in a deliberately inefficient way. Rather than spend money on wheelbarrows, for instance, one project had men carrying dirt 50 feet by the shovelful. Hastily improvised projects intended to be temporary were often just silly. A FERA director in New York City told a reporter he was teaching men to make "boondoggles"—linoleum-block prints, leather belts, and such. The word was needed for the new phenomenon of made work, and it stuck.

If some of the work relief projects were unimaginative—and these the most visible to passersby in the street—FERA and

CWA made thousands of thrilling improvements many of which are in use today. Miles of rides are smoother for the work done by relief projects on roads. Relief workers built playgrounds, picnic grounds, parks. They cleaned up dilapidated schools, fixing desks, washing walls, painting, wiring, and repairing. Sometimes they tore an old schoolhouse down and built a new one out of the wreckage to save on materials.

When Key West could not pay for garbage collection, an FERA project cleaned up the mess and cleared the littered beaches. In Detroit, CWA workers relaid the trolley tracks, painted and modernized the cars. Unemployed teachers taught over a million and a half adults to read and write, and kept many rural schools going. Unemployed rabbis compiled a Jewish dictionary. Doctors immunized a million children. Public health projects laid miles of sewer and rooted out countless disease-bearing mosquitos. In Syracuse, N.Y., relief workers dug up thousands of poplar trees whose roots were strangling the city's sewers.

In the spring of 1934, Roosevelt hoped that work relief could be cut back because, "after all, no one starves in warm weather." Business revived a little, but unemployment stayed high. On April 8, 1935, the Emergency Relief Appropriation Act authorized $4.8 billion to continue PWA and CCC and to launch the Works Progress Administration, the biggest and best-known work relief project. Between 1933 and 1938, WPA put five million individuals (including a cousin of Nazi leader Hermann Goering) to work at prevailing wages doing a dazzling variety of jobs that neither private enterprise nor local taxpayers would tackle.

The hunt for noncompetitive work that took a lot of labor and not much in materials uncovered important needs. WPA workers served hot school lunches to hungry youngsters, gave beauty treatments to hospital patients, fought mosquitos, took

132

care of nursery-school children, repaired library books, taught Southern Negro girls how to do housework, cleaned teeth, and drew snickers for building 100,000 privies that helped to save West Virginia babies dying from diarrhea ("their little stomachs busted open"). One of the projects that qualified for WPA because it took a lot of labor for the materials was the extinction of a fire that had been raging underground near Columbus, Ohio, since 1885, when coal miners set a seam of unmined coal on fire to get even with the bosses. *Time* giggled at a work relief project for developing a "learning machine" that was reported on respectfully in the 1960s as a smart way around the shortage of teachers.

Most WPA projects were public works that states and local governments would have undertaken if they had had money. A third of all the money WPA spent went for roads and bridges, 10 percent more for public buildings, another 10 percent for parks and playgrounds. But WPA also pioneered worthwhile improvements in the quality of American life that local taxpayers never would have authorized. Harry Hopkins put professional and white-collar people to work showing what Federal aid to education, science, and the arts could do. Unemployed teachers taught unemployed workers. Unemployed artists, actors, and writers were given work in their fields. Some of the WPA projects made permanent contributions in results as well as in the salvage of talent:

• NYA (National Youth Administration) helped 600,000 young people pay their way through college, and a million and a half others stay in high school, by employing them to improve their own communities and often their own schools. NYA tried experiments that foreshadowed the 1964 poverty program. One was a rehabilitation camp for girls. Another was a camp at Quoddy, Maine, where young people could work at three different trades during their stay, to see which one they wanted to follow.

• FTP (Federal Theatre Project) brought social protest plays and a version of *It Can't Happen Here* in Yiddish and Spanish, and in English with an all-Negro cast, to people who had never been to the theatre before.

• FWP (Federal Writers Project) produced state guides in use to this day.

• FAP (Federal Art Project) put unemployed artists to work decorating hospitals and post offices, and sponsored thousands of projects that kept teachers, librarians, historians, draftsmen, musicians, and even scientists working at their professions. Federal patronage of the arts proved so successful, and from that time on, gained such wide acceptance, that in 1965 President Johnson proposed a National Foundation on the Arts and Humanities to spend $10 million a year subsidizing artists and intellectuals of all kinds.

• WPA started the Rural Electrification Administration (REA), which lighted up the farms the power companies had never seen a potential profit in serving. When Wall Street laid off 1,400 clerks in the Recession of 1937, a Financial Employees Organizing Committee seriously petitioned WPA to create a project that would put them to work investigating corporations. As a rescue operation, WPA could try social reforms that would have aroused immediate opposition if initiated on their merits alone.

Ideas were popular in 1933. As Governor, Roosevelt had recruited Columbia's Professor Raymond Moley to invite selected professors up to Hyde Park for long bull sessions out of which the campaign line was built. Rexford Tugwell and young A. A. Berle, Jr., were members of this "brains trust," or "brain trust," as it later was called. They floated from assignment to assignment in Washington, recruiting others. Professors took leave from their universities to serve in Washington or commuted between campus and Federal agency. Law students went to

134

work in the agencies and stayed on to become political legmen or aides to Congressional committees.

Government attracted the brightest young men who formerly would have gone into business or the professions. Like Brownlow, some simply headed for Washington when they heard Roosevelt's Inaugural Address and offered their services. Hubert Humphrey abandoned his pharmaceutical studies, took up political science, and became a work relief administrator. James W. Fulbright, later a brilliant Senator, went straight from law school to work in the Anti-Trust Division of the Attorney General's office. Of Roosevelt's "Young Turk" lawyer troubleshooters, Benjamin V. Cohen, Thomas G. Corcoran, and Abe Fortas stayed on in Washington and in 1965 were trusted confidants of President Johnson. To John Maynard Keynes, accustomed to the restrained if dedicated British public service, the New Dealers were refreshingly young and bouncy. A surprising number were women.

No intellectual himself, Roosevelt was a good listener and open-minded about queer notions. "We must lay hold of the fact that economic laws are not made by nature," Roosevelt once explained. "They are made by men." He left the door wide open to suggestions.

All over Washington, in the little red-brick houses in Georgetown where the New Dealers found quarters, there was infectious gaiety and endless talk. "Night after night we talked about wheat futures, the Roosevelt program in reference to market speculation, the commodity dollar, the compensated dollar— and, just to get away from it all, the cheese dollar," William Harlan Hale said. "And when the ladies retired to the salon after dinner for coffee, what did they discuss? Once I overheard a particularly charming one holding forth on the price of hogs."

The early New Deal days were like the start of a war. Self-interest, politics, and criticism were subordinated to the drive for "action now." "President Roosevelt has done his part,"

135

Charles Edison, son of the inventor of electric lighting, wrote for his office wall, "now you do something. Buy something—buy anything, anywhere; paint your kitchen, send a telegram, give a party, get a car, pay a bill, rent a flat, fix your roof, get a haircut, see a show, build a house, take a trip, sing a song, get married. It does not matter what you do—but get going and keep going."

If confidence alone could have ended the Depression, then the Hundred Days would have done it. People felt better. Beer was legal again. Manufacturers raced to build inventory ahead of the NRA codes and the inflation that Roosevelt threatened. Prices rose. So did the stock market. And in the absence of any real boost to purchasing power—even relief didn't get going until midsummer—so did inventories.

On July 19 the stock market broke under the weight of commodity speculations by "New Deal plungers." The drop broke the spell. Nothing, it seemed, had really changed. It was summer, and people were tired of the pace. Lorena Hickock began reporting complaints to Hopkins. AAA and NRA pushed food costs up faster and higher than wages could follow, leaving consumers and relief clients worse off than before. When roads were repaired by work relief, subsistence farmers who depended on road work for cash had to go on relief themselves. Farmers could not get pickers because relief workers were afraid that if they went off relief for a few days they'd never get back on.

Roosevelt had given the people "action, and action now," but he had not attacked the fundamental causes of the crisis. Instead of going off gold in such a way that the currency would be expanded, he took the power to create inflation into his own hands where he could control it. Instead of taking over the banks and the stock exchanges, he regulated them. Instead of permitting the liquidation of private debts, he organized Government support to help the debtors pay them. Instead of the simple guarantee of prices that would cover their costs, farmers got the restrictions and red tape of AAA. Instead of the universal 30-hour week proposed by some Congressmen, labor got minimum wages and hours under the business-dominated NRA.

People felt as if they had been rescued. The emergency should have been over. Yet the year ended with millions of men, women, and children dependent on Federal relief.

7

$ $ $ $ $

SOCIAL SIGNIFICANCE

"HOW can I explain the position of organized labor to Father
when you keep passing me the chocolate sauce?" The earnest college girl in the cartoon is arousing the social conscience of her
well-off father while her embarrassed mother vainly tries to
stanch the flow of ideology with rich food. Anne Cleveland,
Vassar '36, drew the scene, and everyone who went to a liberal
arts college in her time recognizes the mood of social protest.

We felt that the New Deal would never get to the bottom of
the trouble. We felt that something basic was wrong with the
setup and it was up to us to find out what was wrong and do
something about it. We enjoyed a pleasurable sense of millen-
nium. Things could not go on as they had. We felt injustice
as personal guilt. "If you give your coat to the first man shivering on the street," we used to say, "then what are you going
to do for the next one?" It worried us that we had a coat. A
girl who was on the Daisy Chain tied her hair back with heavy
brown twine. We were ashamed that our parents had sent us
to snobby private schools. We imagined that the unemployed
looked hungrily over our shoulders, just as we had imagined

that the starving Chinese suffered when we refused to eat our spinach.

Intellectuals who had wallowed in Freudian self-analysis during the rebellion of the individual in the Twenties now took an almost masochistic delight in denying the dark underside of life. "There is no longer I," exulted humorist Dorothy Parker. "There is WE. The day of the individual is dead." We did not think we had a right to a private life until we first had straightened out society. One of the heroines of our campus was a girl who made the ultimate personal sacrifice for the cause: she married—and I am sure in name only—a political refugee and left him after getting him safely across the Mexican border into the United States.

The college students who felt this way were not, of course, a majority. There were as many politically apathetic girls at Vassar in 1935 as there are now, but the active ones were more active then. The articulate young men and women who have made careers out of their talent for communication shared a sense of political commitment in the French sense of the word. For a time they were united as intellectuals seldom have been. Whatever has happened to them since—and few are as committed today—they still dominate the publishing houses, universities, Government agencies, and the arts. Until they grow too old, the intellectual institutions of the country will be run by what Richard Rovere, the *New Yorker* writer, calls "the liberal establishment."

Being a liberal is now time-bound and specific. My daughter, Vassar '57, does not see the point of Anne Cleveland's cartoon. One reason is that she took mathematics and art at college; I took economics. Art was popular in her day, but very few took economics. In my class of 1935 it was the other way around. More of my classmates majored in economics than in any other subject except English. Sylvia Porter, Hunter '32, says that she switched from English to economics because of "an overwhelming curiosity to know why everything was crashing around me and why people were losing their jobs." College professors recall the Depression as a wonderful time to be teaching, because students really questioned the world and really wanted to find out about it.

The interest was general. More sharply than ever before or since in peacetime, people realized that their dearest personal hopes depended on what happened in the impersonal world the newspapers reported. They read avidly for clues. Public libraries reported nearly four million new borrowers between 1929 and 1933, and the business of circulating libraries, operated by bookstores as commercial ventures, rose so spectacularly that publishers complained they were ruining the book business. Books were a dispensable luxury, so their sales dropped, but nonfiction suffered less than fiction, and books on economics sold almost as well as before the Crash.

More people wanted information instead of entertainment from their reading. *Time* did well. *Fortune* survived, although it was brought out in 1930 at the unheard-of price of a dollar a copy. But the star gainer of the decade was *Reader's Digest,* then a modest reprint of factual pieces without fiction, pictures, or advertising.

It was a time for economic speculation. Politics and economics drew lecture audiences that formerly had turned out for talks on psychology and sex. The week after Roosevelt's inauguration, nearly half a million Americans wrote him with suggestions of one sort or another for beating the Depression. But the only alternative to capitalism in existence was the Communist "experiment" in Russia.

It is hard for people born into a world in which Russia holds the atom bomb to understand how harmlessly academic the Soviet Union looked before World War II. To many, "Red" was just another word for rebellious. In 1932 the president of the Farmers Union in Wisconsin, the state that was later to

140

produce Joe McCarthy, could tell a Congressional committee "there are more actual Reds among the farmers of Wisconsin than you could dream about." The year before, when Governor Theodore C. Bilbo of Mississippi warned that dispossessed farmers were ready to lead a mob, he could add, "And I'm getting a little pink myself."

The Crash widened the little circle of Americans watching the Russian experiment. *Humanity Uprooted*, a book on Russia by Maurice Hindus, did not do well when it first came out, but gathered sales as the crisis deepened. To many, Russia was the other place to go if you did not like the way things were being run here. Many did go. Author Vincent Sheean made a heroine of the American girl he found in the Hotel Metropole who talked five straight days explaining why the only honest thing to do was to join the Communist Party there. At one point during the worst of the Depression, Amtorg, the Russian trading office in New York, was getting 350 applications a day from Americans who wanted to settle in Russia. Some went to work as engineers, others to observe and write books.

Interest in Russia was not held to be evidence of disloyalty to the United States, and in the early Depression at least, non-Marxists tolerated members of the Party as misguided but not necessarily sinister people to have around. Mrs. Roosevelt put up leaders of the Communist-led American Youth Congress in the White House. A scientist in the General Electric laboratory at Schenectady ran for Attorney General on the Communist Party ticket and kept his job. On March 7, 1932, seventy Soviet engineers watched 3,000 unemployed attack the Ford plant in Dearborn in the nearest thing to revolution ever abetted by the Communist Party, U.S.A. They were *inside* the plant, invited there from Russia by Henry Ford to learn mass-production methods.

Early in the decade, Protestant preachers of the social gospel looked to Russia for lessons in the brotherhood of man and

141

sometimes equated the materialism of the comfortable middle class with the capitalist system. Some were drawn to the movement against capitalism by what they saw as pastors of labor congregations. Professor Reinhold Niebuhr of Union Theological Seminary started his career preaching to and for labor in Detroit, and United Auto Workers organizer Homer Martin first became interested in labor because of what he saw as a Baptist preacher in the neighborhood of Chevrolet's plant in Kansas City. Catholic labor priests called capitalism as godless as Communism. When Hitler and Stalin declared their alliance in August 1939, Dr. John Haynes Holmes confessed from the pulpit of New York's Community Church that he had deceived himself in excusing the Soviet regime. "I am sick over this business as though I saw my father drunk and my daughter in the street."

When the Depression jolted American intellectuals into looking at society instead of inside themselves, they saw it was in need of reform. Most of them would have been more comfortable with traditional American reformers and radicals like Jacob Riis, the housing reformer, William Jennings Bryan, the free-silver man, Progressive agrarian Robert M. La Follette, or Woodrow Wilson, the good government man. But when they turned left to protest their disgust with business, they found the ground occupied by Communists.

Communism provided an irresistible explanation for the Depression. It certainly looked as if capitalism carried the seeds of its own destruction, that the people or the workers or somebody else would have to seize the "means of production" if there was to be any production at all, and that there would have to be some better way to distribute the goods than business had so far devised. Stuart Chase's book, *A New Deal*, which gave Roosevelt's program its name, proposed a mixed economy, but it ended by asking, "Why should the Russians have all the fun of remaking the world?"

142

In September of that election year, *The New Masses* ran a symposium under the general title "How I Came to Communism," in which a number of writers who were not members of the Communist Party stated their belief that only socialism could save the country. Included were the world-famous novelists Waldo Frank and Sherwood Anderson; our most honored literary critic, Edmund Wilson, author of *Memoirs of Hecate County* and *To the Finland Station,* who once wrote that the Soviet Union was "the top of the world where the light never really goes out"; the genial editor, lecturer, and critic Clifton Fadiman, then a deeply conscientious, thoughtful, and aspiring novelist. Other contributors to the symposium were Upton Sinclair, an old-fashioned native American radical who wrote the "Lanny Budd" series and some powerful novels of social protest, and Mike Gold who was, of course, a Communist in the literal sense.

Marxists who hoped the revolution could be effected at the ballot box rolled up a record 885,000 votes in 1932 for Norman Thomas, the Socialist candidate. Those who publicly endorsed what Dos Passos derided as the "near beer" of Socialism included such future pillars of the established order as Henry Hazlitt, who in 1963 opposed the minimum wage and urged old-fashioned budget-balancing in his *Newsweek* column; Elmer Davis, Rhodes Scholar, who later interpreted America to the free world as Director of the Office of War Information; poet Stephen Vincent Benét; theologian Reinhold Niebuhr; playwright George Kaufman; social worker and later Senator Paul Douglas; civil liberties lawyer Morris Ernst; the philosopher John Dewey; and the economist Stuart Chase.

It seemed as though everyone was getting on the bandwagon. "Marxism was for Jim's generation what an actress had been for youths of a gilded age," Mary McCarthy wrote wickedly of the hero of *Portrait of an Intellectual as a Yale Man.* In 1932, F. Scott Fitzgerald put aside his gilded companions long

143

enough to wonder whether it would be necessary to work inside the Communist Party to bring on the revolution. Lewis Mumford said that if he voted at all, it would be for the Communists.

The Party never had so many glittering admirers again. The New Deal won some. Visits to Russia alienated others.

In 1934, John Dewey found it necessary to write an article explaining "Why I Am Not a Communist." His objections turned out to be to "official Communism, spelled with a capital C." He was interested enough in the idea of Communism to lead a commission of inquiry into the Moscow trial charging Trotsky with treason. Those who couldn't hold with the Russians invented their own forms of Marxism: Lewis Mumford was for "basic communism"; Max Lerner for "planned collectivism"; Alfred Bingham for a "cooperative commonwealth."

The Partisan Review disengaged itself. Young intellectuals of the mid-Sixties who follow its clues to what is intellectually "in" may be surprised to learn that it started as the organ of the John Reed Club of New York, an organization directed from the Soviet Union by the International Union of Revolutionary Writers "to recruit writers to the cause of revolution." According to co-founder Philip Rahv, *The Partisan Review* "emerged from the womb of the depression crying for a proletarian literature and a Socialist America" in the spring of 1934. The December 1937 editorial announcing its break with the Party reaffirmed the magazine's "responsibility to the revolutionary movement in general."

The revolutionary movement was more influential than the Party. It may have enlisted as many as a million strategically placed Americans. Few of these actually joined the Party, and those who did usually departed in disillusionment or became lifelong anti-Communists. But the strength of the revolutionary movement was that it was more than a political party. It was a total world that had an answer for every headline: a program, friends, a style, a language, causes, a guide to action, even a defense against loneliness.

The watchword was "social significance." In the Depression, this boiled down to a few very simple notions: the rich are corrupt and doomed; the poor are exploited and probably noble; business is founded on fraud; the revolution is sure to come; individual virtue is useless because the system itself is wrong. Baldly stated this way, the Marxist origins of the notions are clear, and all of them sound questionable. In the world of social significance, however, they were never baldly stated. They were merely demonstrated and propagated. They became the rationale for judgment and action of people who did not realize that they were following a Marxist "line." To take them one by one:

The rich are corrupt. There was ample evidence for this notion. The bad behavior of the rich was the commonest non-Marxist explanation for the Crash. J. David Stern made the point by running two items side by side in his *Philadelphia Record:* PAINT MAKER GIVES 76 EMPLOYEES $100,000 SO THEY CAN START THE YEAR FREE FROM DEBT, CALLS IT HIS CONTRIBUTION TO NEW DEAL and WIDENERS' $100,000 PARTY RIVALS GLITTER OF GILDED AGE: MUSIC ALONE COSTS $10,000. Six months later, when the Recession of 1937 struck, Roosevelt attacked rich men who incorporated their yachts or gave up their American citizenship to avoid income taxes.

Publication of the names of the highest-income-tax payers stimulated discussion about how much a man could legitimately earn in a year. In 1937, Chairman Alfred P. Sloan, Jr., and William S. Knudsen of General Motors headed the list with incomes of more than half a million dollars a year. That year a book by Ferdinand Lundberg, *America's Sixty Families,* made a sensation by documenting from public records that control of

145

the "means of production" in the United States was held in the hands of a few.

The idea that the rich were bad was not exactly new. The Bible makes it hard for a rich man to get into Heaven, and the old Progressives of the nineteenth century had at least as much to say about the dishonesty of the rich as was generally said during the Depression. But to these familiar pronouncements the Marxists brought something new and hair-raising: the rich were doomed to evil by class membership. Neither honorable behavior nor concern for his fellow man could save a Christian gentleman from exploiting the workers, nor could he change his class membership by taking thought.

"Why are you rich and exquisite?" the psychiatrist in S. N. Behrman's 1936 play *End of Summer* asks the socially conscious rich woman of the play. "Because your forebears were not moralistic, but ruthless. Had they been moralistic, had they been concerned, as you pretend to be, with the 'predatory system'—this awful terminology—you'd be working in a store somewhere wrapping packages or waiting on querulous housewives with bad skins or teaching school."

The socially conscious among the well-off accepted their fate. "Everything considered, he preaches a remarkably good sermon," a well-heeled lady in a *New Yorker* cartoon of the time says. "It's so hard to avoid offending people like us."

So many intellectuals were leftist during the early thirties that foundations bearing the names of the great American capitalists often patronized their class enemies. Party member Granville Hicks financed his Marxist *The Great Tradition* with funds provided by the estate of John Simon Guggenheim, who made a fortune by robber-baron methods in mining. Talented but impecunious left-wing artists and writers accepted grants from such capitalist foundations without demur.

146

"Donate his socks to the Guggenheim Fund," Guggenheimer Kenneth Fearing once wrote in a poem about a poor man run over by a truck.

Diego Rivera, the Mexican muralist whom the socially significant artists had made popular, dramatically attacked the nation's leading capitalists with their own money. In 1932, the lowest point of the Depression, he was in the United States with contracts to paint frescoes for Edsel Ford in Detroit and for John D. Rockefeller, Jr., in New York. On the walls of the Detroit Art Institute he painted his Marxist's-eye view of the toil inside automobile factories. When a clergyman complained that a fat, ugly baby being vaccinated was a blasphemous reference to the Christ Child, Detroiters mobbed the Art Institute to see for themselves. Mexican enemies of Rivera publicly warned Edsel Ford of a mural Rivera had done in Mexico showing Henry Ford as a leering stockbroker fondling ticker tape with one hand while he raised a glass of champagne to a female companion with the other. The Fords did nothing, but when Rivera painted a portrait of Lenin on the walls of Rockefeller Center, the Rockefellers had it taken down. The incident lived on in the title of the poem "Frescoes for Mr. Rockefeller's City," by Archibald MacLeish.

Painters of the Thirties put red, bulbous noses and hypocritical smiles on the faces of the rich. The then Marxist playwright Clifford Odets describes the businessman in his 1935 play *Awake and Sing* as one whom "the lives of others seldom touch deeply." Miriam Beard's 1938 *History of the Business Man* indicted American businessmen for failing to set themselves goals worthy of their efforts, and critic Edmund Wilson, economist Stuart Chase, and novelist John Dos Passos kept complaining that there was something more to life than making money or even making things. In Marc Blitzstein's play-with-music, *The Cradle Will Rock,* a painter and a musician kept by

147

the wife of the villainous millowner sing, "There's something so damned low about the rich."

The workers are noble victims. The austere Marxist theory that labor is the source of all value and will eventually "expropriate the expropriators" was translated into simple propositions: See how the common people suffer! Look, they've been robbed! Watch how they will triumph in the end! Novelists, playwrights, painters, photographers, journalists, and even social scientists devoted their talents to delivering these messages. The lot of workers was passionately described by the best talent in the country, so that we forget that the poor suffered almost as much in prosperity, when they were not news.

Literature discovered what the unconsciously snobbish called "the little people." Mill workers, strikers, migrant pickers, sharecroppers, soda jerkers, miners, the night shift, the unemployed—these are people too, like you and me. Walt Whitman's paeans to the common people were revived, and like Lincoln, he became a posthumous Communist saint. A Broadway hit of 1937 was *Pins and Needles,* a musical comedy about garment workers acted by garment workers. It was a good show, but theatergoers saw social significance in the talent it uncovered in ordinary workers.

According to Marx, workers were poor because they were paid only a pittance of the wealth they created. Capitalists were portrayed as ever on the alert for ways to get more out of them. Left-wing writers publicized instances of short pay, the fraudulent scale used by mine operators and milk buyers, the extra hours textile workers were sometimes forced to put in on pain of dismissal, the high prices miners were charged when they had to buy at company stores, the refusal of doctors to testify against big companies in compensation cases, the police brutality mobilized against strikers, the activities of finks, scabs, labor spies. Sociologists began to notice that the working classes

148

get more satisfaction out of cooperating with each other than in competing for personal advantage as the capitalist ethic prescribed.

Artists and writers glorified the migrant wanderers. Artists on WPA put them on post-office walls they were commissioned to decorate. John Steinbeck made a hero of Joad, the migrant in *The Grapes of Wrath,* who keeps the jalopy running. At the end of *U.S.A.,* Dos Passos has his migrant hero Vag tighten his belt and watch an airplane fly across the night sky carrying "big men with bank accounts, highly paid jobs, who are saluted by doormen; telephone girls say good morning to them." Marxist writers championed the Negroes. Novelists analyzed the psychology of lynching; painters were fascinated with the scene, sometimes making the victim look as if he had been crucified.

Desperation made dramatic short stories. In Steinbeck's "Daughter," a sharecropper shoots his daughter because he does not have anything to give her to eat. The painters documented the unemployed scrounging for food in ashcans, along railroad tracks, in breadlines. Descriptive painting titles from the collection made for the New York World's Fair of 1939 include "Sharecropper," "Lodging House," "Not Wanted," "Bureau of Relief," "The Hungry," "Last Cow," "Driven Away," "Seeking Work."

Consumers are systematically cheated. The Marxist principle of production for use rather than profit revived medieval objections to all interest as usury and all commerce as fraud.

In 1932 Stuart Chase listed 16 ways business makes money. All of them were immoral, but six consisted of hoodwinking, overcharging, or underserving the consumer. Before the Depression, Chase had joined with F. J. Schlink in a book, *Your Money's Worth,* that alerted consumers to the dangers and deceptions of advertised products. In 1932, Schlink and Arthur Kallet wrote *100,000,000 Guinea Pigs,* warning of the hazards of foods, drugs, and cosmetics. During his Marxist period, Edmund Wilson wrote:

"It is a formidable undertaking to persuade people to invest at high prices in a great variety of valueless breakfast foods and toothpastes; in cosmetics that poison the face, lubricants that corrode your car, insecticides that kill your trees; in health builders made of cheese, fat reducers made of cascara, coffee made of dried peas, gelatine made of glue, olive oil made of cotton-seed, straw hats made of wood shavings, sterling silver made of lead and cement, woolen blankets, silk stockings and linen sheets all made out of cotton, sealskin coats made out of muskrat, and mink and sable out of woodchuck hides, mahogany furniture made out of gumwood which will splinter into bits under use; in foods that do not nourish, disinfectants that do not disinfect, electric irons that burn out in one brief burst as soon as they have been attached to the plug, shock-absorbers that cause you to ride more roughly and gas-logs that asphyxiate—(all articles which have actually been put over with more or less success)."

The humor magazine *Ballyhoo* gained circulation when the regular periodicals were losing, in part because it lived up to its name by satirizing advertising.

It became fashionable to brush your teeth with salt, grease your face with pure lanolin, and buy a new car just after the model year had turned, to prove your emancipation from the fairy tales of advertising and "planned obsolescence." The really "in" often insisted on patronizing cooperative food shops or restaurants as a protest against business. Although no cheaper, cooperatives were held nobler because none of the money went for profit.

Rumors charged manufacturers with shortchanging consumers. According to one story, an automobile company was feverishly trying to find and buy back an experimental car that had been sold by mistake—it had a carburetor that stretched gas 50 miles to the gallon. Other stories insisted that electric light

150

bulbs, silk stockings, and appliances were deliberately made to wear out quickly so that the consumer would have to replace them, a motive that manufacturers deny.

Everyone was a consumer, and everyone stood to gain by such left-wing campaigns as the fight to force Government grade labeling of canned goods, truth in advertising, and effective Pure Food and Drug Laws. Yet these immediately practical objectives were never popular. Consumer cooperatives grew, but they were never a real threat to retail trade. People did not really object to the way business treated them as customers. They seemed to resent business because they could not get jobs.

Enterprises for checking advertising claims started out as weapons of social protest. Early in the decade, Kallet and Schlink founded Consumers Research, Inc., to test products and inform subscribing consumers of the true value of products. The two fell out, and Kallet charged Schlink with "capitalist exploitation" of labor in an article in *The New Masses* and left to form Consumers Union. For a time, Consumers Union was more liberal politically than Consumers Research, but in the 1960s both publish advice to consumers without ideological connotations.

It's the system. Marxists believe that individuals are helpless to save themselves by their own efforts. They exist only as members of their class. Everything strictly personal is decadent or meaningless. People are valuable only for their roles in history. The view encouraged people who might in other times have been novelists to think of human relations in the abstract. The Lynds could have stated their insights into Middletown in a novel, and the same can be said of the most striking concepts of W. Lloyd Warner's analyses of the classes in Yankee City. Subjective impressions, which had no place in the popular fiction of social significance in the Thirties, migrated to sociology.

Interest in persons as objects viewed from the outside made

151

fiction read like nonfiction and reduced character to caricature or allegory. Granville Hicks, a Party member who taught English literature, once apologized for the crime of having liked Proust in his youth. Novels drew more heavily than before on actual news events. The big novel *U.S.A.*, by Dos Passos, had sections of facts about real people. No fewer than six novels and two plays were based on the 1929 strike of $9-a-week workers in Gastonia, North Carolina, during which Ella May Wiggins, 20-year-old working mother of nine children, was shot to death. Novelists and playwrights went to see how the poor lived and wrote brilliant factual reports for magazines. Even comic strips began to build plots from events in the news.

Painters abandoned concern with style and concentrated on representing ideas, like cartoonists. American artists adopted the style of Diego Rivera and other Mexican muralists who painted great allegorical essays on human justice, on war and peace, on capital and labor. When abstract painting later became popular, Communists and matter-of-fact Americans alike faulted its lack of social message. In 1965, artists are again interested in the human figure and in ideas. A school of "pop" artists is using the straightforward folk art of advertising and propaganda to make statements of their own about contemporary life. The garish, deliberately crude paintings of artists on WPA are being unearthed from Government warehouses and admired for their very crudity. Art critic Emily Genauer pronounced a cache of Depression paintings turned up in 1965 distinctive for their "informative, nostalgic record of a city of elevated structures, pushcarts, old neighborhoods, today gone or rapidly disappearing."

The purely objective view is, of course, a photograph. During the Depression, sensitive men and women began using the camera to document the sordid facts of poverty. *Life* photographer Margaret Bourke-White and her novelist husband, Erskine Caldwell, discovered the common people of America in

152

their book of captioned photographs, *Say, Is This the U.S.A.?*
For the Farm Security Agency, Dorothea Lange produced a
classic set of photographs demonstrating the human havoc created by dust storms, and Pare Lorentz made a classic documentary movie, *The River,* with a Whitmanesque text celebrating the Mississippi River and the cause of conservation. Many
of the photographers of social significance were Party-liners.
By 1942, members of the Photo League of New York City
were active in Party work.

In 1936, *Life Magazine* launched a new style of "photographic
journalism." It was so successful that *Look* and other competitors soon appeared. "The March of Time" made the news-
reel a major feature instead of a filler. The artistic flowering
of photography set ordinary people with the price of a Brownie
to snapping the American scene, as well as each other, all over
the country. Cameras and film were one of the growth industries of the Depression.

Hallie Flanagan put facts on the stage. In order to give jobs
to as many unemployed actors as possible, she invented the
"living newspaper." With the help of The Newspaper Guild,
she dramatized such unlikely subjects as the AAA, the history
of the Negro, flood control, and the sugar beet industry, in
some cases by having actors read whole paragraphs from *The
New York Times,* statistics and all. Characters were either
actual people in the news, such as Milo Reno, the farm leader,
and Earl Browder, the Communist candidate for President, or
allegorical figures. Some of the devices were unexpectedly efficient presentations of abstract relationships. In "Triple-A
Plowed Under," four actors explained how low farm prices
spread Depression and brought it back again to the farm:

Farmer to Dealer: I can't buy that auto.
Dealer to Manufacturer: I can't take that shipment.
Manufacturer to Worker: I can't use you any more.
Worker: I can't eat.

153

Concern for "reality" figured in architecture and design. When the George Washington Bridge across the Hudson River was under construction in the early 1930s, the chief engineer wanted to leave out the masonry facing originally planned for the towers so that the steel that actually supported the bridge would show. The change was made in part because it saved money.

Economy was usually given as the reason for bare stages, functional architecture, and chunky "modernistic" furniture, some of it aggressively utilitarian (like beds with built-in radios and lights), which is being revived today. In retrospect, what seemed the deliberate ugliness of the first "modern" furniture was in keeping with a general fear of sentiment. Instead of pleading for the unemployed, New Deal social workers concealed their altruism behind a barrage of statistics.

Life on the left would have been much grimmer if intellectuals had not been imaginative enough to find that social significance, like the Boston matron's God, was everywhere. A woman could prove that her heart was with the common people by calling her domestic helper the cleaning "lady" instead of the cleaning "woman," or choosing a coat without a fur collar when everyone else in her set had a fur coat. She could gossip her fill without seeming to be merely personal by describing as "middle-class" the clothing, interior decoration, or amusements of people she disliked. If necessary she could display her social conscience by inviting Negroes to her parties. During the Depression, Communists ostentatiously treated Negroes as social equals when few others did, and they were not usually sensitive enough to personal feelings to avoid insulting Negroes by singling them out for special courtesies.

The posture of social significance could be maintained by using Marxist terms: "apparatus" for organization; "opportunistic" for hypocritical; "cadres" for personnel; "propagandize" for enlighten; "chauvinism" for irrelevant loyalty, as to

154

race in "white chauvinism"; "progressive" for Communist sympathizing; "bureaucratic" for arbitrary; "self-criticism" for earnestness; "formalism" instead of "art for art's sake"; "reportage" for journalism.

The terms were sometimes tossed into conversations as a test of the other fellow's "political awareness," or they slipped out unawares and alerted veterans of the ideological wars to the speaker's Marxist experience. Non-Communist organizations were controlled by the (Communist) "fraction." Propaganda on the other side was "tendentious." Those who "deviated" were "confused," a word that has survived, especially with theater people, as a euphemism for "neurotic."

The intensity with which abstract concepts were discussed is one of the hallmarks of the movement. Like the "masses" in the paintings of the time, abstractions were allegorized into isms. When people "escaped" from the class struggle, or obstructed it, or were neutral or divided into factions, they entered the movements of escapism, obstructionism, neutralism, or factionalism. Disliked people were identified with isms. No word in the Communist language was more fraught with hate than "Trotskyism." There was even "Hooverism." The most important thing about anybody was his ideology, and if it did not show, it had to be "unmasked." When Archibald MacLeish "deviated," critic Michael Gold discovered the "Fascist unconscious" in his "Frescoes for Mr. Rockefeller's City."

Social significance was an obsession. It is hard to imagine anyone in the 1960s maintaining, as Mary McCarthy did once, that Wilder's play, *The Skin of Our Teeth,* affirmed the eternity of capitalism (Wilder was confused), or as Robert Forsythe (magazine writer Kyle Crichton) did in *Redder than the Rose,* that capitalism drove men to crime. The politically enlightened could resent the Christian burial Shakespeare allowed Ophelia as an example of privilege, and applaud Brutus as the Soviet champion of the people against Julius Caesar, the Fascist

155

enemy. Communist critics described Vivien Leigh, who played Scarlett O'Hara, heroine of the movie *Gone With the Wind,* as the "serpent of white supremacy."

For a time during the 1930s, American intellectuals involved themselves in politics, as European intellectuals have always done. In 1932, 53 well-known writers signed their names to an open letter urging the "Writers, Artists, Teachers, Physicians, Engineers, Scientists and Other Professional Workers" to vote for Foster and Ford, the Communist candidates for President and Vice President. Rejecting the "lunacy spawned by grabbers, advertisers, traders, speculators, salesmen, the much-adulated, immensely stupid and irresponsible 'business men'," they announced that they had aligned themselves with the "frankly revolutionary Communist Party, the party of the workers." Among the signers were Sherwood Anderson (*Winesburg, Ohio*), Lincoln Steffens, whose *Autobiography* was a 1931 bestseller, Erskine Caldwell (*Tobacco Road*), Matthew Josephson (*The Robber Barons*), John Dos Passos (*The Big Money* and *U.S.A.*), and the critic Malcolm Cowley.

That same year, Theodore Dreiser headed a distinguished delegation of writers, journalists, and educators who went to Harlan County, Kentucky, to report conditions there. They rather enjoyed the risks they ran. When mine operators tried to discredit their reports by charging him with adultery, Dreiser called a press conference to announce that he was impotent. The sensation helped to put the cause of the miners into newspapers across the country. Eighty students from Northeastern colleges set out in a chartered bus to make a "sociological investigation" of Harlan County and almost were lynched on the way. They made more news for the cause of the miners.

College radicals became noisier and aroused more sympathy than in the past. Under Communist leadership, they grew politically sophisticated. Where they controlled student publications, they often printed material that precipitated the touchy issue

156

of college controls over student freedom of speech. In 1936, the American Student "Union" threatened to "strike" Columbia University classes for the reinstatement of Bob Burke, President-elect of the junior class. Burke had been expelled for picketing the home of Columbia's President Nicholas Murray Butler in protest against an invitation from Heidelberg University in Germany, then in Nazi hands.

Words were weapons, but action was better. Intellectuals dreamed of becoming tough, amoral Hemingway characters. Membership in the Communist Party promised association with self-contained, impenetrable, leather-jacketed, black-hatted men and plain, hard women indefatigably dedicated to a cause beyond themselves, people who loved the human race in the abstract but no individual in particular, who knew *Robert's Rules of Order* backwards, who calculated every word and deed, listening hard and weighing the words of others against some inner standard. Those who joined found the revolutionary life considerably less exciting, but the dream persisted.

The Party offered glorious opportunities for dangerous action. In 1935, the manager of a ten-cent store in Harlem's black ghetto caught a boy stealing a knife. A few minutes later, a black hearse drew up. Word spread that the white storekeeper had beaten the Negro child to death. More than a thousand men and women broke into the store and surged down 125th Street. While the riot was still in progress, the Young Communist League prepared leaflets denouncing the police and scattered them from housetops.

Lawyers for the Party's International Labor Defense risked their own liberty in Southern courtrooms defending Negroes who were at the mercy of biased white courts and juries. In 1931, eight illiterate under-age Negro boys were sentenced to death in Scottsboro, Alabama, for the alleged rape of two white mill girls of uncertain virtue, one of whom had previously been

157

convicted of "hugging a nigger." The boys had obviously been railroaded. Scores of committees, delegations, and civil liberties organizations crowded into the backward little Southern town to report the trial and defend the boys. Communist-organized rallies for the "Scottsboro boys" were held on almost every American campus, as well as in Harlem, the Bronx, Brooklyn, Chicago, Philadelphia, Dresden, Berlin, Cologne, Paris, Rome, and cities in Latin America. The effort saved the boys from execution and kept the injustice of discrimination before the conscience of America, but at the time it seemed as if the men of good will were almost helpless.

College girls tried to "do something" personally by working with the exploited. Some of the missionaries were incredibly naive. I will never forget the shock on the face of a classmate of mine when she reported, of a summer spent working with Kentucky mountaineers, that "love does not exist among the lower classes." Coal miners could not understand why an upper-class girl would want so desperately to share their lot. They were naturally suspicious. "They don't hate you," a miner friend consoled Laura Gilfillan, a college girl who wrote a book about her efforts to join the working class. "They hate what you stand for—and you do stand for it, and you can't get away from it, no matter what your material condition. . . . You'll go back to civilization and a bath every day."

Intellectuals chided each other for being soft and ineffectual. Professor Granville Hicks, who joined the Party in an effort to demonstrate sincerity, warned his students that an intellectual had to study hard to raise himself to the level of the proletariat. A *New Yorker* cartoon of the early Thirties poked fun at the impractical revolutionary talk in Greenwich Village studios. "Oh, it's all very simple," a girl at an arty party is saying to a not very muscular young man. "Our little group simply seizes the powerhouses and the radio station." Stuart

158

Chase vividly warned what would come of such an amateur revolt:

> The railroads struggle with volunteer crews for a few days, but bookkeepers make poor firemen ... Central power stations bank their fires ... With coal, oil, railroads and electric power out of the picture, no factory wheel can turn ... Minneapolis and Chicago with wheat in storage will not be so fortunate as one might suppose. The wheat must first be milled, and second rationed among a frenzied mob mad with hunger. All ventilating systems will, of course, collapse, well-nigh finishing the Grand Central area ... Garbage collection will stop, sewers may be dynamited, hospitals must cease to function as suddenly as factories; ambulances will be without motive power. Lethal epidemics, those great scourges which medical science has steadily been forcing back for a hundred years, will break their fetters overnight and fall like avenging demons on a population weak with hunger and thirst.

The most ardent reformers could support themselves modestly by writing. Serious reporting and critical writing was in keen demand and carried high prestige. Established craftsmen in fiction and nonfiction sold well and some did not feel the Depression personally because their expenses fell along with the prices they were paid for contributions to magazines. Social workers were in demand, as Mr. Roosevelt's war on poverty gathered power, and many of them wrote movingly about the conditions they saw. When relief funds failed, they were as badly off as their clients and became the natural champions of the poor. Some of the settlement houses opened their doors to groups that were picketing relief stations to demand bigger payments.

The intellectuals who were leaders of progressive education turned from self-expression to social significance. They recommended that teachers make children aware of what was going on in the world and prepare them to change it for the better. Instead of Harold Rugg's *The Child Centered School* (1928),

159

students at Teachers College, Columbia, the source of most public-school administrators, were reading George S. Counts's *Dare the School Build a New Social Order?* In 1934, John Dewey and his disciples at Teachers College launched a journal of ideology, *Social Frontier,* that urged teachers to find ways to advance "the welfare and interests of the great masses of the people who do the work of society—those who labor on farms and ships and in the mines, shops, and factories of the world." As intellectuals they were keenly interested in Marxist ideas and invited leaders of the Marxist movement to write for them. Counts, Goodwin Watson, and others at Teachers College went to Russia to see what the great social experiment was doing in education. At their 1936 convention in St. Louis, school superintendents applauded Norman Thomas and passed around a jingle composed by William Andrew McAndrew, progressive educator who had been ousted as superintendent of the Chicago system:

> My board is bored
> And so am I.
> I'd like to kiss
> My board goodbye.

Educators tried to develop the social consciences of pupils. *Building America,* a *Life*-style periodical for high schools on current problems, delivered a vivid issue on "Steel" to high-school classes just as the CIO was signing its first steel-industry labor contract. At the time, some advanced high schools were teaching students how to detect and analyze propaganda so that they could make sense out of public affairs. Harold Sloan, brother of Alfred Sloan of General Motors, staked the 47 seniors at Lincoln School, the obstreperous experimental arm of Columbia's Teachers College, to study Government planning in the Tennessee Valley. The youngsters learned by doing. They rebuilt and whitewashed a rundown farmhouse.

160

The rank and file were more cautious. Most professional people were living precariously themselves. Writers like Stuart Chase could make money interpreting the Depression, but no other profession was as lucky. Actors need plays; in 1933, eight of the ten new ones on Broadway lost money. Newspapers merged and folded, so the slots for experienced reporters did not keep pace with the rise in population, much less with the young students of society who wanted jobs on newspapers. In 1933, there were 15,000 fewer teachers than in 1930, but one million more pupils.

Fear of reprisal restrained many teachers, lawyers, and preachers from social protest. Teachers who once feared they would be fired for being caught smoking now became careful about talking politics. Nobody with any money to pay a fee wanted to hire a radical lawyer.

Churches were broke, and parishioners who regularly made up ministers' salaries were by definition the capitalist sinners of the social gospel. When the Rev. Robert Elliott Burns called his Union, N.Y., congregation "cutthroats, skunks, snobs, greedy aristocrats," they stopped paying him. "It's hard to get bread and meat in this section," a Tennessee preacher told *Time*, when asked why he married a 13-year-old girl to a 37-year-old paralytic, "so I thought as long as some other one was going to marry them, I might as well do it ... but they gave me a dollar, which was all right, considering they got value received, I guess."

People without money could not always get medical care. In West Virginia, hospitals refused to take patients unless the bill was guaranteed; local authorities had no funds for hospital care; and the Federal Government had no authority to spend money for it. In the country, doctors sometimes tried to collect from relief authorities and also make the patient's family work out the bill, while competition was so keen among doctors in New York City that a majority of specialists had to kick back

161

fees to the family doctors who alone could bring them patients. Dr. Harold M. Hays, the surgeon brother of Arthur Garfield Hays, disclosed that a referring doctor once suggested that he hold off operating on a child with a fever of 103° until the family agreed to pay $1,000.

There is another side to these stories. Doctors and nurses were badly exploited. Hospitals would have had to close if they had not been able to get the free labor of student nurses and internes. One third of the hospitals of the U.S.A. paid internes nothing but room and board. In some hospitals they were not even allowed to marry girls with jobs who would have been glad to help them through school. In New York City, the Commissioner of Health urged the city to pay internes a pocket-money salary of $3.46 a week to keep them from accepting bribes from patients.

The capitalistic theory of medical training, of course, was that the long apprenticeship at low pay was an investment to be recouped from paying patients. Depression graduates could not recoup. Spending on medical care and death expenses fell one third per capita between 1929 and 1933, in spite of the fact that charges were less. The doctor was the first expense to be avoided, the last creditor to be paid. To protect their "investment," doctors and nurses supported their associations in limiting admissions to medical and nursing schools, tightening up on licensing provisions, and restricting public health services that might provide free care to people who could conceivably pay a fee for it.

Depression hastened the spread of plans for pooling the risk of hospital bills. In 1929, Dr. Justin Ford Kimball, of Baylor University, organized the first Blue Cross Plan to help Dallas schoolteachers and newspapermen save up together for hospital care. Each member paid 50¢ a month into a common "prepayment fund" on which subscribing hospitals drew to compensate them for an agreed number of days of care. In 1933, the Ameri-

162

can Medical Association approved of Blue Cross. It was non-profit, it was not insurance, and it did not compete with doctors.

Opinion polls showed that most people believed that the Federal Government should provide medical care for those unable to pay, but organized medicine resolutely fought the first moves to group practice, medical insurance, or "socialized medicine." In 1935, the Attorney General of New York State moved to dissolve the Life Extension Institute (where salaried physicians gave health checkups to candidates for insurance, and others, at $15 a head) under the rule that a corporation cannot practice medicine.

A Group Health Association was started in Washington, D.C., to make medical services available at lower cost, but the American Medical Association scared off doctors who might have made out better in group practice by warning that they would lose "status." Proposals to make medical service available on the basis of need would have helped many doctors struggling to get established, but only doctors with prestige to spare, like Hugh and Edward Cabot, of the old Boston family, dared risk the tarnish by publicly supporting such plans.

The phoniness of the issue is more apparent now that "socialized medicine" has been operating for some time in other advanced countries of the world without impairing the responsibility of physicians. The real question of conscience for doctors must always be the other way around: How to square refusing medical care to a patient who cannot pay with the Oath of Hippocrates, which requires the physician to put the welfare of the patient ahead of his own?

The tension created by the Oath of Hippocrates and the uncollected bills may explain, in part at least, the tenacity with which physicians cling for support to "medical ethics," which seem increasingly aimed at protecting the doctor, rather than the patient. It is hard for anyone trained as a physician to turn

163

down demands for help from the sick, and yet that is exactly what many doctors had to do during the Depression.

In Royse City, Texas, two doctors placed the following ad in the local newspaper:

TO WHOM THIS MAY CONCERN: If you are expecting the stork to visit your home this year and he has to come by way of Royse City, he will have to bring a checkbook to pay his bill before delivery.

In 1934, the Nassau County Medical Society suggested that any code of medical ethics should provide that "free medical care is a charity which it is the privilege of the physician to bestow ... it is not a commodity which can be demanded." They also set the public straight on clinics: "Clinics were developed for the [education of the] doctor, not the doctor for the clinics."

Critics of capitalism enjoyed popular support from people who were not remotely radical. Those who tried to debunk "social significance" risked painful investigation themselves. A frequent target was William Randolph Hearst, who paid the highest income tax of 1935 (on $500,000 income). When Teachers College Professor Counts lectured on "economic democracy" at Stanford University, Hearst banned mention of that institution from all Hearst newspapers. He sent investigators posing as students to expose "Red" professors at Columbia, Syracuse, and Chicago universities. When one of these was himself exposed, he confessed that he was doing it to hold his job. "I wouldn't like working in a slaughter-house either, but if that was the only work open, I would probably do it."

Taxpayers and their organizations called the social workers who wanted higher relief payments "Red." Merchants called managers of competing farm cooperatives "Red"—and sometimes roughed them up for good measure. Utilities called TVA "Red," because it set a yardstick for their profits. The Pinker-

164

ton Detective Service called "Red" activities in labor unions to the attention of employers they hoped to get as clients, although the La Follette Civil Liberties Committee got a crack Pinkerton operative to admit under oath that he had never found any. Grade labeling of canned goods and informative food and drug labeling were stigmatized as "Red."

"Red-baiting" was usually easy to discredit, not only because the motives of the baiters were so transparent, but because they were almost invariably nonintellectuals who were so ill at ease with ideas that they threw haymaker punches that their agile victims could make ridiculous. State laws requiring teachers to swear allegiance to the Constitution united the academic community in anger. A proposed law against inciting members of the armed forces to disobedience antagonized the Army and Navy. Hearst was laughed out of court when his supporters tried to boycott the Columbia Broadcasting System for giving Communist Earl Browder 15 minutes of time, and when they proposed in Washington and other cities that textbooks be reviewed for subversive material and teachers be forbidden to mention Communism in the classroom at all.

Fun was poked at attempts to show how Communists were spreading Red propaganda through the movies. The investigating committee headed by Congressman Dies was told that Shirley Temple, the child star, was a "stooge of the Reds." The committee cited *Juarez*, a movie about the revolutionary overthrow of Mexican Emperor Maximilian, without realizing that the Communist Party had denounced the movie for its sympathetic treatment of Maximilian.

Later, in wartime, the snobbish equation "anti-Red equals anti-intellectual" boomeranged tragically against the intellectual community during the uneasy years when some people thought that the all-destroying bomb could be kept a national secret and a bowing acquaintance with Communists or Communism raised suspicions of treason. At the very kindest, the

165

snobbees could now retort, "All right, you're not Red now, but if you're so smart, how come you didn't see through these friends of yours back when?"

The question is legitimate, but embarrassing. The equation "anti-Red equals anti-intellectual" discouraged competent inquiry into the impact of Marxist thinking. Then, a curious law governs American fear of Communism; it says that the perceived size of the Red menace varies inversely with the number of Reds with whom the viewer is acquainted and the distance from Moscow. Thus Communism is held a dreadful menace in Wisconsin and Georgia, states that have few Communists; less of a menace on the East and West coasts, where most of them are; more of a menace in American Legion posts, which do not attract them; less of a menace in Ivy League colleges, or England, where they circulate more or less openly.

Every position on the spectrum from right to left moved a little leftward under their pushing. In 1933, bankers talked of boycotting Government bonds, in 1936 they had accepted the indignity of Federal deposit insurance, by the time of World War II they scarcely blinked at wartime credit regulations. Businessmen who originally had praised Roosevelt for cutting the budget were fearful of the budget cuts of 1937. As late as 1932, the American Federation of Labor opposed Government unemployment insurance, but by 1940, all unions were deep in politics, supporting Roosevelt, demanding Government protection for labor and consumers. The most forlorn figures of the decade were probably the Socialists, many of whose programs were enacted into law, leaving them no place to go but to their ancient enemies, the Communists. As for the Communist Party, it accumulated members by virtue of its location at the end of the line.

Historians like Charles and Mary Beard were according more weight to economic factors in history, economists like F. W. Taussig turned away from the staunch doctrines of classical laissez-faire, and some who were less articulate were thinking their way left, too. The Republican platform of 1936 was more "socialistic" than the Democratic platform of 1932: Alf Landon, Republican candidate for the Presidency, undertook not to repeal Social Security, but to administer it better.

Just as the young usually recover from a college dose of Communism, so did the whole country. In the 1930s, nearly everyone who was intellectually alert was a Red, or at least flirting with the pink. After the explosion of the atomic bomb, however, the context changed unalterably. "Hell, I was no Communist as we know them today," James Horan quotes a gray-haired suburban grandfather on his Depression politics. "There was just a lot of excitement around in those days and I wanted to be part of it."

The reading matter of the 1960s would be quite different if everyone who had admired Soviet Communism and despaired of American capitalism had been struck by avenging lightning in the act. Recent bestseller lists would be without Mary McCarthy's *The Group,* Edmund Wilson's *The Cold War and the Income Tax,* and Vincent Sheean's *Dorothy and Red. The New York Post* would be without writers Langston Hughes and Max Lerner; the New York *World Telegram & Sun* without Murray Kempton. *The New Yorker* would not have had Richard Rovere, Lewis Mumford, S. J. Perelman, Muriel Rukeyser, Edmund Wilson, Dwight MacDonald, and James Thurber, while *Esquire* would not have inherited Dorothy Parker. There would have been no Heywood Broun, no Robert and Helen Lynd to write *Middletown.* Some would find life duller without Ruth McKenney to write *My Sister Eileen;* others, without Gypsy Rose Lee.

And it is not too much to say that the prevailing view of the Depression was formed by two novelists who self-consciously worked for revolution "outside the Party" until both deserted Marx. One was James Farrell, who reported the exploitation of

167

city workers in *Studs Lonigan* and other novels of proletarian life. The other was John Steinbeck, whose novel *The Grapes of Wrath* established the refugees from the Oklahoma dust bowl as the symbol of Depression and capitalist exploitation. In 1940 Steinbeck won the Pulitzer Prize for *The Grapes of Wrath,* and in 1962 he received The Nobel Award for Literature for the body of his work, of which *The Grapes of Wrath* remains his most admired book.

The Marxist intellectuals were more powerful than they knew. They scared business, conditioned the voters to extensive Government intervention, channeled normal, human compassion into political expression, and inadvertently helped save capitalism by moving everyone from Mr. Roosevelt to the bankers just enough to the left for them to see the social significance of decisions traditionally regarded as purely private.

8

$ $ $ $ $

BUT NO REVOLUTION

THERE was a day in Detroit when it looked as if the much promised revolution had actually come. On March 7, 1932, workers, bosses, police, and Communist Party members acted as if they were characters in a proletarian novel.

It was down around zero in Detroit, and windy, but nearly 3,000 men and some women bundled up to go on the two-mile Hunger March. Some of them had been among the 7,000 people who had crowded into Danceland the night before to hear Communist leader William Z. Foster. The Unemployed Council of Detroit and the Auto Workers Union were going out to the employment office of the River Rouge plant at Dearborn to ask Henry Ford to take back some of the men he had laid off.

The Communists were behind both sponsors. They had organized Unemployed Councils to call Hunger Marches demanding relief, unemployment insurance, and "defense of the Soviet Union" in every city, including Washington. Two years before, *The Daily Worker* claimed 100,000 demonstrators had turned out in Detroit for International Unemployment Day. Back in 1930, witnesses told a Congressional investigating committee there were between 1,500 and 5,000 Communists in Detroit. The Party had grown since then, recruiting working-class members from foreign-born mechanics attracted to Detroit factories and native-born Scandinavians from the north woods traditionally sympathetic to socialism. The Unemployed Council had a good name. It was so effective in helping unemployed tenants resist eviction that once 100 Detroit policemen were needed to dispossess a Polish family.

They had drawn up 14 demands to make of Henry Ford:

1. Goods for all laid-off Ford workers.
2. Immediate payment of 50 percent of full wages to all laid-off Ford workers.
3. A six-hour day without reduction in pay.
4. Slowing down of deadly speed-up.
5. Two 15-minute rest periods daily.
6. Free medical aid in the Ford hospital for employed and unemployed Ford workers.
7. No discrimination against Negroes as to jobs, relief, medical service, etc.
8. Five tons of coke or coal for the winter.
9. Abolition of service men (spies, police, etc.).
10. No foreclosures of homes of former Ford workers.
11. Immediate payment of a lump sum of $50 winter relief.
12. Full wages for part-time workers.
13. Abolition of graft system in hiring workers.
14. The right to organize.

There was something to be said for the general idea. More than 50,000 auto workers had been thrown out of work during the year. Henry Ford had employed about a third of the idle, but he had moved his plant outside the city limits, so he paid no taxes toward the $2 million a month the City of Detroit was spending on relief that winter.

The March started out good-humoredly. Marchers poured in to the assembly point in downtown Detroit. They stood around singing, stamping their feet, and greeting new arrivals. They carried banners:

"Come on Workers, Don't Be Afraid!"
"We Want Jobs!"
"We Want Bread, Not Crumbs"
"Tax the Rich and Feed the Poor"
"Open Rooms of the Y's for the Homeless Youth"
"Fight Against Dumping of Milk While Babies Starve"

Marchers jammed streetcars. Catching the spirit of the protest, some of them tried to rush past the conductors without paying their fares, but a Detroit police detail of 70 uniformed patrolmen had that situation well in hand. The marchers had a Detroit police permit. Mayor Frank Murphy was proud of his record of permitting Communist demonstrations. Around two o'clock, when the parade started, the Detroit police escorted the marchers to the Dearborn line.

The Dearborn police were not so tolerant, and the Unemployed Council had not asked them for a parade permit. The little town was supported by Ford's property taxes and its mayor happened to be Clyde M. Ford, owner of a Ford agency and a distant relative of Henry. A block before the Dearborn line, Communist leader Al Goetz halted the march and warned that the Dearborn police would try to stop them. "We will try to get through somehow," he said, "but remember, no trouble."

The whole Dearborn police force of 40 men was waiting at the line with $1,000 worth of tear gas. "Where are your leaders?" Acting Chief of Police Charles W. Slamer asked.

"They haven't come back yet," those in front evaded. The crowd murmured. "We are all leaders!" others shouted.

"Where is your permit?" Slamer asked.

"We don't need one," the crowd shouted. They kept on marching.

The police discharged their tear gas. Some of the marchers

171

answered with rocks, sticks, and clumps of frozen mud. Others fell back, choking. "Come on, you cowards!" a Russian-born girl shouted, and her boy friend, Joe York, rallied the stragglers.

The wind blew the gas away. Thoroughly aroused, the marchers stoned the police down the road toward the employment-office gate. A rock knocked out Chief Slamer. The Dearborn fire department tried to get hoses connected to spray the rioters with water, but the marchers stopped them. Policemen had been badly beaten up, but they had held their fire as they had been ordered to do, and there had been no shooting.

Harry Bennett, Ford's sinister bodyguard and chief "service man," was entertaining Governor Fred Green inside the Rouge plant at a private showing of a movie when the scuffle started. As soon as he was informed, he headed for the scene, waving a white handkerchief from his car. According to his own account, he was going to tell employees in the crowd that they would all be back at work within two weeks, when the new models would be ready for production. Over the protests of his clerk and the police, he insisted on getting out of the car and was instantly mowed down by a volley of bricks and rocks.

The police opened fire. The crowd broke and ran. The Detroit police detail that had escorted the marchers to the line came to the rescue of the outnumbered Dearborn police. Nearly 60 marchers were caught and arrested. Those who were too badly hurt to be sent to jail were handcuffed to their hospital beds. Four were dead, 50 were hospitalized, and another 50 wounded marchers refused hospitalization to avoid police interrogation.

Each side said the others shot first, but no guns were found on the marchers. The dozen or more police who were hospitalized, as well as Harry Bennett, suffered blows from sticks and stones. Except for a news photographer whose camera was shot out of his hand, all the wounded were shot in the back, side, or legs. All accounts agree that the police ended by firing point-blank into the crowd.

172

"Responsibility is not difficult to fix," *The Detroit Free Press* editorialized. "The inciters were William Z. Foster and the other Red agitators." The Communist leaders who spoke on Sunday had ducked, but Dearborn authorities talked of arraigning them for criminal syndicalism, or even murder, if they could find a legal way to do it. Detroit agents of the Immigration Service raided known Reds to see if they were illegally in the country and deportable.

"Responsibility for the tragedy obviously rests squarely upon the shoulders of Henry Ford," the American Civil Liberties Union announced. Roger Baldwin, veteran civil liberties lawyer, threatened to sue Ford, defend anyone indicted for speech alone, and contest the constitutionality of a 1931 Michigan law allowing police to determine when an assembly is unlawful so that they could escape criminal liability for the death of anyone killed in breaking it up.

"The company feels no responsibility, since none of its men were involved," a Ford statement read. "The plan was hatched by Communists in Detroit." Ford spokesmen were among the few in Detroit who could not see why the unemployed should attack the company that employed the most men at highest wages. The march aroused so much sympathy that the Communists were proud to accept the blame for it. After the first day, Ford played down the Communist angle. On Wednesday, *The Detroit News* blamed the riot on the failure of the marchers to get a permit from the City of Dearborn. A grand jury investigation later blamed the Dearborn police but exonerated Ford.

The Communists saw their opening, and they pressed it. One of the dead was a 16-year-old newsboy slated to go to Russia for Party training. Another was a young district organizer. No one seemed to claim or care much about the other two. The Party took charge of its martyrs.

The whole funeral was red from start to finish. The four

173

coffins were red. Thousands packed into Workers Hall to see them. Loyal Party members and sympathizers came from Ohio, from Chicago, from Grand Rapids. Instead of prayers, there were speeches. Leaders pledged to avenge the dead by organizing the auto workers. Fists waved in the air in Communist salute. The hunted Communist leaders were saluted. Witnesses to the riot spoke.

Outside, a parade of 15,000 people formed to escort the hearse to the cemetery. A 28-piece band played what the newspapers called "Communist hymns." Twelve violinists wailed the Russian funeral march of 1905, the year of the uprising the Czar had bloodily repressed. There were signs: "Ford Gave Bullets for Bread"; "Slow Down the Daily Speed of the Ford Plant."

The parade was so orderly that the police and the Party later disputed credit. According to the Communists, the police didn't dare come within miles of the parade. All the Communist organizations marched under their own banners, as in a St. Patrick's Day parade. Spectators showed the red in neckties, scarves, and bows on cars, the way the non-Irish show the green out of courtesy on St. Patrick's Day. Several hundred children in red berets with hammer-and-sickle insignia were members of the "Young Pioneers of America of Foster Troop." Forty men followed with wreaths of red flowers.

The hearse and official cars—mostly Lincolns and Fords—were draped in red. At the cemetery, the four red coffins were lowered into a common grave to the singing of "The Internationale," and the red flowers were thrown in after them. A man watched with his five-year-old son. "I want him to see what is class struggle," he said. Meanwhile, back at the Ford plant, the Dearborn police, reinforced by deputy sheriffs and state troopers, stood waiting, machine guns mounted on the factory walls. No one came. The crowd drifted away from the speeches at the grave and went home.

It was the best chance the Communists ever had in the

174

United States. The automobile industry was almost shut down. Regular Ford workers were standing by for the new V-8 model, and the rest of the industry was waiting to see it before going ahead with production. The City of Detroit was so broke that the day after the Hunger March the Police Commissioner had to lay off 162 policemen. Yet nothing happened.

"There is something wrong with the Reds in this country if they can't do better in a Depression like this," said a man who was laying in supplies against riot.

Stalin agreed. In 1934 he rebuked comrades who thought that the Depression would pull down capitalism right away without any effort on their part. "The victory of revolution never comes by itself," he warned. "It has to be prepared for and won. And only a strong proletarian revolutionary party can prepare for and win victory." Like Presbyterian salvation, the dictatorship of the proletariat was inevitable, but not automatic. The elect had to work for it.

The Communist Party, U.S.A., worked hard to win workers, Negroes, and the unemployed. It sent labor organizers to the coal miners and the textile workers whose condition most closely approximated the plight of those victims of early industrialization that Marx and Engels had thought would revolt. They sniffed the country for smouldering tinder that could be fanned to revolutionary flame. Their Trade Union Unity League promoted strikes among the exploited Mexican field hands of California and the cigar makers of Florida. The strikes all failed, but they publicized poverty and injustice.

The Communists defended Negro rights when almost nobody else did. The Party crusaded against lynching and against discrimination in relief. Party workers explained Marx to farmers who were spilling milk and threatening mortgagors. They did some of the most effective social work among the city unemployed, investigating cases of neglect and organizing neighbors to resist evictions for nonpayment of rent. The Communists or-

175

ganized Hunger Marches on the Detroit style all over the country. They showed the unemployed how to demand relief outside city halls and relief stations. They organized strikes on work relief projects.

All three targets failed to respond. Workers shunned the Communists. In 1931, the Party had 75 "shop nuclei" compared with 652 "street nuclei," as they called nonindustrial groups. After five years of Depression, the Communists could claim to lead only one percent of the mine strikes and two percent of the automobile strikes. Educated Negroes sometimes joined the Party for the intellectual companionship they could get nowhere else, but the really depressed Negroes were repelled. "It's bad enough to be black," one Negro explained, "without being Red, too." And while the unemployed willingly demonstrated —most of them, after all, had nothing better to do—they would not stay to do the Party's hackwork. Men who talked like radicals when they lost their jobs quickly reverted to their normal politics when they found work. An unemployed worker who denounced capitalism said he was going to vote for the Republicans because "they have the money and if we put them back they will start the factories going."

The Communists were the merest handful. When asked how many Communists there were in the United States, most people grossly overestimated the membership the Party boasted of having. In 1930, the Communist Party, U.S.A., reported 7,500 members to the Communist International (Comintern); in 1932, 12,000 to 14,000. In 1939, when the Party had been cooperating broadly with liberals and supporting Roosevelt in an effort to arouse sentiment against Russia's enemy, Hitler, the Party may have had 90,000. In spite of the noise Communists made on campus, only one half of one percent of American college and high-school students were involved in the student protests and petitions they organized.

176

But the small size of the Party was not the full measure of its failure. Lenin advocated a small elite rather than an unwieldy mass movement. The real failure of the Communists was that they could not channel or sustain the interest they aroused. They could not keep the few they recruited. During the first few years of the decade, the Party recruited 49,000 new members and lost 33,000.

The Comintern ordered the American Party to recruit workers who could paralyze the country by refusing to work, but whenever it tried, intellectuals came instead. The Party did better among the Jews—who would have climbed faster up the middle-class ladder to success without it—than with the uneducated Negroes, who really needed a revolution. The Party did not do as well with the blue-collar unions as it did with unions newly formed among white-collar and professional workers in the big cities.

The hardships of teachers vulnerable to pay cuts and layoffs helped the American Federation of Teachers (AFL) to grow. More effective in influencing working conditions was the Newspaper Guild. Columnist Heywood Broun organized it in 1933 to protect editorial workers from layoffs and pay cuts that had many reporters borrowing lunch money from the better-paid and tightly unionized Linotype operators in the plant. Hollywood bristled with unions organizing screen writers, actors, hairdressers, painters, scene designers, and makeup artists. All of these unions had important and at times controlling Communist "fractions."

Intellectual protest groups borrowed trade-union terminology to emphasize their sympathy for labor and to establish themselves as brain workers, rather than exploiting capitalists. The American Student "Union" encouraged student "strikes" against attending class, in protest against university policies. Liberal lawyers in Government, labor, or politics named their organization the Lawyers Guild for its laboristic flavor. In 1935, thirty New York ministers qualified for admission to the AFL as Ministers Union of America, Local 1, in order to express their faith in "the right and necessity of organization on the part of those who labor with hand and brain."

Those who labored with their hands were less enthusiastic. They did not want a revolution. They did not want to control the "means of production." What they wanted was steady work, and neither the union nor the Communist Party was handing it out. However mean the boss, he was the only hope for a job. Clannish themselves, working-class people thought it only natural that the boss discriminated against workers who talked of organizing against him. "I don't blame Mr. Pugh a bit the way he feels about the unions," a textile worker said of his employer.

Under Harry Bennett, Ford's "service men" were supposed to ferret out the union-minded and get them fired. Whether some of the stories told about the company spies were true or not, they were implicitly believed, and that is what is needed to maintain a rule by terror. The company statement that few Ford men joined the Hunger March of March 7, 1932, was probably true. Most people in Detroit believed that the company had cameras trained on crowds of demonstrators so that they could identify any of their own workers and cross them off the rolls. Since most of the men were waiting for a call back to work, they had every reason to keep in the good graces of the personnel authorities. Ford agents had been going from house to house warning the unemployed to keep away from the Communists if they wanted to work for Ford. Many of the marchers picked up by the police insisted they were looking for work at the employment office and had nothing to do with the demonstration.

Terror paid off for employers. In December 1934, the La Follette Civil Liberties Committee listed 2,500 American companies whom it had found employing detective agencies to combat unions. A sales brochure of Bergoff, Inc., professional strikebreakers, described its services as follows:

The Strike Prevention Department. This department is composed of men possessing natural leadership qualifications. Men of intelligence, men of great persuasive powers, to counteract the evil influence of agitators and the radical element.

The Undercover Department. Our undercover department is composed of carefully selected male and female mechanics and workpeople. They furnish accurate information on the movements and contemplated actions of their fellow employees—"forewarned is forearmed."

The Open-shop Department. This department is composed of an organization equipped to supply all classes of competent mechanics and workpeople to keep the wheels of industry moving during a strike.

The Protection Department. This department is composed of big, disciplined men with military or police experience, for the protection of life and property.

The Investigation Department. Our investigation department is international in scope and embraces all branches. The personnel is composed of male and female operators of the highest caliber.

Outlawed outside the United States, strikebreaking had flowered into a profession with its own methods and its own language. Terms defined by the La Follette Committee give some idea of strikebreaking methods:

fink: a strikebreaker
noble: commander of a strikebreaking squad
missionary: spreader of anti-union propaganda, especially among workers' wives
hooker: spy who tempts workers to spy

Operatives in the "Undercover Departments" of automobile companies had cunning ways to trap unwary workers into admissions of discontent. Once identified, the malcontent might be transferred to a "killer" machine or framed in an infraction of the rules so that he could be fired without exposing the spy. Spies watched from behind posts. They hung around toilets and bars. They egged the rebellious on to talk. A dictator is not essential to the barbarities of a totalitarian police state. In an industrial city like Detroit, an easy labor market sufficed to maintain a reign of terror under the Constitution of the United States.

When jobs were scarce, employers could violate labor laws and work women and sometimes children into the night without fear that they would complain. Pennsylvania Governor Pinchot's investigating commission found an employer in Allentown checking off 33 cents from the pay of each child to reimburse himself for a $100 fine imposed on him for working the children 50 to 90 hours a week and failing to carry workmen's compensation. In April, children under 16 struck a Pennsylvania shirt and pajama shop because half of them were working all week for less than $7.40. To protests like this, employers had a short answer: "Quit, if you don't like it."

The quit rate is a measure of what people will endure to hold a job. In prosperous 1929, more than three workers out of every 100 gave up their jobs each month. In 1945, when women were leaving jobs to rejoin returning servicemen, the quit rate was more than five per 100. In February 1933, it dropped to one out of every 200, just about the minimum to allow for people who faint on the job. Among those who didn't quit were mill girls in New England working for $4 and $5 a week, store clerks in Chicago working for a nickel an hour, and men earning 10¢ an hour at Briggs Manufacturing in Detroit.

Sam Insull, the utility-stock promoter, is supposed to have declared that "the surest guarantee of a contented working

180

force is a long line at the employment-office window." Employers did not have to pit one straight-time worker against another. When a layoff impended—and that was most of the time—the workers eagerly sought new grounds on which to compete. Stenographers practiced their smiles as well as their shorthand. By selecting the very fastest and fittest, "efficiency" experts could speed up the line and cut the piece rate. Sometimes the men themselves lowered "labor costs."

"The other day I answered an ad," an unemployed factory worker told a reporter. "When I got there, there were 40 applying. The man looked us over, picked out one, and said, 'I'll take you and pay you $15 a week.' Another fellow in the crowd called out, 'I'll work for $10,' and got the job."

Unions could not remedy these conditions, because they could not make a strike stick. During the first Depression years, Bergoff's "Open Shop Department" could whistle up a large if not necessarily very competent work force in a few hours by passing the word about available jobs to hack drivers, flophouse desk clerks, charity employment services, barkeepers, and jobless men congregating on street corners. During 1917, a year of war boom, there had been 3,600 strikes. In 1932, only 841.

Unions had actually been losing ground ever since World War I. As late as 1932, the American Federation of Labor opposed Government "intervention" in labor relations as strenuously as did the National Association of Manufacturers. The idea of both was that working conditions were issues for "voluntary" agreement between employers and employees. Unions, not Government, should safeguard the workingman, said the Federation.

Under this voluntary regime, only the railroads, the building trades, and a few crafts like those of the printers and the garment workers had been organized. These workers had skills that they could withhold effectively in bargaining. Increasingly,

181

however, mass-production methods took the skilled operations out of the worker's hands and built them into the machines, leaving him only a simple repetitive task that anyone could learn in a few hours.

Unions had not gained during the boom. Depression all but wrecked them. In 1932 less than 12 percent of nonfarm workers belonged to unions, down from 19 percent in 1920. Depression weakened the declining traditional unions. When their members lost jobs, they stopped paying dues, and young people saw no reason to join when they did land a job.

Job terms were so generally regarded an employer's private affair that the first draft of the NRA law gave labor no voice in the codes of fair competition that industries were to hammer out for their own regulation under Government guidance. When Federation President William Green complained that industrywide agreements might be used to put labor unions out of business, General Johnson impulsively wrote in a proviso he thought would put these fears at rest:

"Employees shall have the right to organize and bargain collectively through representatives of their own choosing, and shall be free from the interference, restraint, or coercion of employers of labor, or their agents, in the designation of such representatives." The write-in was Section 7A.

John L. Lewis, president of the United Mine Workers in the bloody coal fields, saw possibilities in the sentence that Johnson had not intended. He compared Section 7A with the Emancipation Proclamation that freed the sleves. "Forget about injunctions, blacklists, and the fear of dismissal," he told miners. "The President Wants You to Organize!" Within a few months the UMW membership doubled, and was back to 1920 strength.

Union organizers rushed in to emulate Lewis, and General Johnson had to help them. The NRA law required that the workers of an industry approve its code. Where no union existed, the Government encouraged one. Where several unions

182

claimed jurisdiction, NRA had to decide which should approve the code. When the mayor of a steel town refused to allow radical workers to attend a meeting called by Frances Perkins, Secretary of Labor, she walked into a post office, grabbed a chair, and invited the workers to state their grievances under the protection of the United States flag. A few weeks later, she invited the presidents of the major steel companies to her office to find some way to make a joint statement with labor approving the hours and wages of the NRA steel code. To the disgust of Miss Perkins, they backed away into a corner "like a bunch of 11-year-old boys at their first party" for fear that a social introduction to William Green might be construed as acceptance of unionism.

The protection offered by Section 7A shattered the illusion of a contented labor force. Unions sprang up and struck for recognition. The silk workers struck in Paterson, tool and die makers in Detroit, miners in southern Illinois. Boot and shoe makers, steelworkers, shipyard workers, even airline pilots struck. By midsummer 1933, there had been 1,000 strikes. To keep strikes from stalling the progress of NRA, General Johnson set up a National Labor Board under Senator Robert Wagner of New York. General Electric president Gerard Swope, an early advocate of NRA codes, helped the Board by persuading fellow employers to recognize unions so that the codes could be written. One employer he tackled was a hosiery-mill owner who would not meet with the union being organized in his mill. He insisted his workers did not want a union. "Let them vote on it and we'll see!" Swope suggested. The millowner objected that it was his plant, not theirs. He was born in Germany, and in his anger he stuttered.

"But vy, vy should they vote?"

"Because this is America," snapped Swope, "and that's the way we do things here." Against the owner's wishes, the Conciliation Board of the Department of Labor held an election in the plant, by secret ballot, that returned a majority for the union. There was no legal basis for such a forced election, but it worked, and others followed.

John L. Lewis readily agreed to an election, but he wanted it held at union headquarters. "What do you think would happen to nonunion miners if they came in to vote there?" Swope asked.

"Well, I guess they would have their heads bashed in," Lewis replied with a broad smile, conceding the point.

Employers fought back. One way was to take their jobs away from a union town and move the plant to a place where labor was more docile. The threat usually secured the cooperation of local authorities. In Cleveland, the A & P actually closed its 300 stores for a few days and laid off all its employees there to warn them of what would happen if they organized a union. Citizens of Muncie, Indiana, told the Lynds that General Motors was paying the salaries of extra policemen on the city force in order to keep the union out of town.

Section 7A opened a Pandora's box by exposing secret union-busting tactics. The La Follette Civil Liberties Committee publicized the criminal measures employers were able to take against unions in towns where they could intimidate the local law. In 1935, New York Senator Robert Wagner was able to muster support for a law defining some of the grosser union-busting tactics as "unfair labor practices." The National Labor Relations Act put the Federal Government officially into the business of holding union elections and outlawing intimidation and fraud in labor negotiations. Slipped through Congress without strong Administration support, the Wagner Act perpetuated the machinery General Johnson had improvised to implement Section 7A when the Supreme Court declared the whole NRA unconstitutional.

When crude tactics were outlawed and exposed, employers tried to combat the unions by subtler means. James H. Rand

184

of Remington Rand devised a "Mohawk Valley Formula" for breaking strikes that he offered to other industrialists through the NAM. It proposed to demoralize strikers and win public sympathy by a back-to-work movement operated by a puppet organization; by vigorous attack on labor leaders as "agitators"; by threats to close or move plants; and by "missionary" visits to strikers to persuade them to give up the fight. But these milder efforts were outlawed, too. When a citizens' committee in Johnstown, N.Y., called in fund-raiser John Price Jones for advice, he suggested that they back a national "right-to-work" movement striking at union coercion.

John L. Lewis had been the first to see the organizing possibilities in Section 7A. In 1935, he was the first to see that permanent Government protection for unions made possible an entirely different kind of labor movement. At the AFL convention of 1935 in Atlantic City he urged that the time was ripe for big, all-inclusive "industrial" unions that would represent every worker in an entire industry and confront each employer with the union's power to pull out his entire force, while permitting a competitor to operate. Lewis frankly welcomed Government support. Old-fashioned "voluntarists" in the AFL opposed the abolition of craft lines. The dispute was hot. At one point Lewis hauled off and smacked craft union leader "Big Bill" Hutcheson. Lewis pulled the militant new leaders out of the AFL and formed the Congress of Industrial Organizations (CIO).

Shielded by the Wagner Act, the CIO set out to organize the big, mass-production industries that had kept unions out. For a brief springtime, American labor was evangelical in the tradition of European labor movements. There was singing:

> Rush, says the boss,
> Work like a hoss.
> I'll take the profits,
> And you take the loss.

185

Strikers and organizers sang "Solidarity Forever," the labor hymn that explained the Marxist theory of labor as the only value:

They have taken untold millions that they never toiled to earn,
But without our brain and muscle, not a single wheel would turn

Intellectuals and college students helped organize unions and volunteered to go south and help the textile workers. They organized publicity support for labor. Ivy League colleges had units of the League for Industrial Democracy on campus. Both Yale and Harvard negotiated contracts with their scrubwomen, AFL and CIO respectively. Middle-class ladies organized the League of Women Shoppers to investigate stores that paid substandard wages and boycott them. In this atmosphere, mayors, governors, and police were no longer willing to side automatically with employers when violence threatened.

The first reaction was more violence. Wildcat strikes burst out all over. In November 1935, the workers in Akron's Goodyear Tire factory simply stopped the production line at 2 A.M. and refused to move out of the plant. It was the first "sitdown" strike, and it captured the public imagination. Employers could not evict the sitdowners by force without endangering their property, and any efforts of the police were open to public scrutiny. The sitdown strike was supposed to have been invented by Communists in France. It suggested seizing the means of production, and it dramatized the fact that the workers in some cases were the only ones who understood how to operate the machinery. In the United States, the sitdowns were less ideological. They merely released animal spirits and called attention to grievances.

The sitdowns seemed spontaneous. General Motors workers sat down in an Atlanta Fisher Body plant when they were not allowed to wear their union buttons. In South Bend, Bendix

186

Products automobile-accessory workers—800 men, 300 women —resorted to bundling, when the company tried to freeze them out. When the company turned the heat on and off alternately, the sitdowners danced, roller-skated, and sang. In Detroit, bakery workers threw loaves of bread at police trying to dislodge them with tear gas. A motion-picture projection machine operator in a Manhattan theater stopped the film to protest to the audience about his low wages. Striking waitresses "packed" restaurants, or got their friends to order coffee and occupy all available seats. Gravediggers sat down in Kansas City, and in Chicago, Negro wet nurses "sat down" for a higher rate per ounce for their milk.

The movement was contagious. There was a time in the spring of 1937 when Chrysler and Hudson automobile plants, packing plants, hotels, cigar factories, laundries, bus companies, steel mills, aluminum mills, and drug, shoe, and department stores were all occupied by sitdowners. Strikers inside the Exide Battery plant in Philadelphia whiled away their six-week stay in making a movie that showed how to run a well-ordered sitdown. In most places, sitdowners organized meals, exercise, and entertainment, and were careful of company property.

Law-abiding citizens, including President Roosevelt, deplored the illegality of the sitdowns, but regarded them with sympathy in view of the justice of the workers' cause. With police support for employers withdrawn, sitdowners could not be evicted. In December 1936, John L. Lewis opened attack on General Motors. Sitdowners occupied the Fisher Body plant in Flint, Michigan, for the first six weeks of 1937. The Chevrolet plant in that city was occupied, too. Some workers wanted to settle and go back to work. Union men fought nonunion men. A group of employers urged the Governor to send in troops. John L. Lewis countered with a threat:

187

"I shall personally enter General Motors' Chevrolet Plant Number Four. I shall order the men to disregard your order, to stand fast. I shall then walk up to the largest window in the plant, open it, divest myself of my outer raiment, remove my shirt and bare my bosom. Then-n-n, when you order your troops to fire, mine will be the first breast that those bullets will strike. And, as my body falls from the window to the ground, you will listen to the voice of your grandfather as he whispers in your ear, 'Frank, are you sure you are doing the right thing?' "

Governor Frank Murphy delayed sending in troops. "You must remember that the men on strike are as sincere and as earnest as you," he told the employers. But after a riot broke out in the plant, Murphy sent the troops.

In February, General Motors capitulated. President Roosevelt helped GM President William Knudsen save face. He personally telephoned Knudsen and asked him to meet with the union. In that way, Knudsen could explain his change of heart by saying, "The President wants me to settle." Chrysler fell into line.

Ford held out. Henry Ford could not believe that his men wanted a union. He insisted that they were misled by agitators. Walter Reuther, then a young man of 30, and his union chief, Dick Frankensteen, a former football player, handed out handbills across the way from Ford's River Rouge plant urging "Unionism not Fordism." When the two organizers mounted the overpass on which workers crossed the road to the plant, Ford service men seized them and pulled their coats over their heads so that they couldn't talk to the men. Harry Bennett tried to claim that the assailants of Reuther and Frankensteen were ordinary Ford workers who resented attempts to unionize them, but photographers, clergymen, and representatives of the La Follette Civil Liberties Committee were on hand to confirm the union story. According to Frankensteen:

188

"They knocked me down again, turned me over on my side, and began to kick me in the stomach. When I would protect my side they would kick my head. One of the attackers would say, 'That is enough, let him go.' Then they would pick me up and stand me on my feet, but I was no sooner on my feet than they would knock me down again. This went on about five times. They let me lie there for a while. Every once in awhile someone would grind his heel into me. They pulled my legs apart and kicked me in the scrotum."

Like the white people of the South who are honestly convinced that their "Nigras" love them, Ford thought he was a hero to his workers. Later, in 1941, he was genuinely crushed when a strike-won Government-supervised election showed that less than three percent of "his" workers wanted to continue without a union.

Steel fell in 1937. Everyone expected the big battle would be with U.S. Steel, the longtime symbol of Wall Street and big business. But the Steel Corporation was already headed by a professional manager up from the ranks. President Benjamin Fairless did not shy away from the union as the steel leaders had done in the office of Miss Perkins a few years earlier. He received Philip Murray, chairman of the Steel Workers Organizing Committee, and politely pointed out that his father had been a miner.

"Call me Ben," he urged.

"Yes, Mr. Fairless," Philip Murray replied.

U.S. Steel signed without a fight. Smaller steel companies held the fort. Tom Girdler, president of Republic Steel, was a belligerent tycoon of the old school. He refused to have anything to do with the union. He locked strikers out of his plants. Tension mounted. When pickets at the Republic plant in Chicago taunted them, the police fired point-blank into the crowd, killing ten—seven with bullets in the back—and leaving scores of wounded without medical attention. The La Follette Civil

189

Liberties Committee had movies of the massacre that showed that the Chicago police had started it. The movies were banned in Chicago. The City of Chicago tried to remove 1,000 strike-breakers, who were living in the Republic plant, claiming that the health code was being violated. Girdler sent 21 Pullman cars inside the gate on the siding to house the Chicago strike-breakers and dropped food by airplane to others, who were be-sieged inside Republic's Warren and Youngstown plants, when the Post Office refused to deliver food by mail. In June, Gird-ler was willing to talk to the steelworkers but not to *sign* any agreement with them. The National Labor Relations Board found him guilty of unfair labor practices. Eventually he ca-pitulated.

By 1938, General Electric, American Woolen mills, and many other big employers had recognized unions. Four mil-lion workers had been unionized in two years. The mushroom growth strained the facilities of union organization. The early organizers were evangelists, rather than administrators. CIO leaders, including John L. Lewis, had no particular love for the Communists, but they found disciplined Party members in-dispensable helpers. Left-wingers were articulate. They were willing to do the dirty work. They had a superb grasp of parliamentary procedure. They had been working away at many of the industries that now recognized unions. They branched out inside unions to win militant young organizers who were not Communists, and they knew just how to help a leader rise.

By 1939, Communists controlled the Maritime Federation of the Pacific; United Electrical, Radio and Machinists; State, County, and Municipal Workers; International Longshoremen and Warehouse; Mine, Mill and Smelter; Fur Workers; Amer-ican Communications Association; United Cannery, Agricul-tural, Packing and Allied Workers. Communist fractions plus fellow travelers dominated Mike Quill's transport workers,

190

The Newspaper Guild, the teachers' union, and the furniture workers.

War swept new members into all the CIO unions, as employment on Government contracts mounted. At war's end, about a third of the blue-collar workers were paying union dues. Unions were in America to stay. Under Communist stimulation, the CIO tried hard to involve workers in politics, but without notable success; the Communists had irritated American labor leaders by switching from sacrificial militancy to abject renunciation of the bread-and-butter interests of American workmen when the workers began making armaments for the Soviet Union. By 1950, they had been cleaned out of every CIO union. Peace, plenty, and the political detachment of pre-Depression days returned to American labor. The growing numbers of clerical and salaried workers were not organized, and the labor force kept growing faster than unionized employment. In the 1960s, unions again faced the elimination of jobs that curbed their growth in the Thirties. Automation—featherbedding, or job security, depending on where you sit—is the only real issue.

Except for the brief New Deal period when Government and intellectuals from the middle classes took up labor as a cause, the American labor movement has been conservative, politically apathetic, and weak. Neither the fears of domination by foreign agitators expressed by Tom Girdler, nor the hopes of Edmund Wilson for a tough new totalitarian type of leader emerging from labor, were to come true. Neither the Communists with their abstractions, nor the labor unions with their demand for class solidarity, were able to make more than temporary capital out of the Depression.

The intellectuals and the Communists misinterpreted American labor. The revolution they loved to discuss was pure projection onto the workers of what the intellectuals and Party people thought they would have done in their place. When workers sat down or threw rocks, intellectual left-wingers supposed they had a plan. Usually they were just reacting. It is doubtful that the Akron rubber workers, for instance, thought they were taking over the means of production, as Marxist writer Ruth McKenney implied in her account of that sitdown, *Industrial Valley*. Frances Perkins, an acute observer, said she "heard no statement by them that a man had property rights in his job."

To some Europeans, as a matter of fact, Americans seemed to be taking the Depression rather too quietly. Mobs picketed Buckingham Palace in law-abiding England with much more vigor than any of our unemployed mustered in demonstrations before the White House. Our Depression was deeper than theirs, but their Communists were stronger among the workers. The phenomenon was puzzling. When working-class Americans talked of Reds and revolution, they seemed to mean violent protest in general, rather than a Marxist program in particular.

Most working-class people were against Communism and lukewarm about unions. On a 1940 poll, Earl Browder won most working-class votes for the title of labor's number one enemy, and John L. Lewis was second; after a decade of disillusion and "service men," a cross section of working-class people all over the country still voted Henry Ford labor's number one friend. Outside of Detroit, Ford was still the apostle of high wages. "Wall Street set some unions on Henry Ford and tried to put his back to the wall," a textile worker explained. To many workingmen, Henry Ford continued to be a champion against poverty.

The most militant protests came from the politically conservative miners and farmers who were used to taking matters into their own hands. The violence of the farm strikes and the mines was the violence of vigilante frontiersmen, who still fascinate the young of all ages in television shoot-'em-ups.

Mother Bloor, the Party's veteran agitator, reported that she "never saw anything like the militancy" of the farmers who defied mortgage foreclosures and dumped their milk because they did not like the price they were being paid for it. But these were not Parisian workmen. They were frontier traditionalists.

They were not overthrowing the Government. They *were* the Government. They gathered to save a neighbor's farm, to do justice as the community saw it. A judge was only their surrogate; he had no majesty of his own. When members of the Farm Holiday Assocation threatened to pull the judge out of his chair at Le Mars, Iowa, he ordered them to take off their hats out of respect for the court. "He had no right to ask that," one of the farmers said later. "We farmers paid for that courtroom with our taxes, and it was as much ours as his." At Pringhar, Iowa, the farmers leading a foreclosure riot made the sheriff kneel down and kiss the American flag.

Farmers who interfered with the foreclosure of mortgages could not see that they had done anything "wrong," or even rebellious. According to Karl Pretshold, reporter for the Socialist paper in Oklahoma City, the eight members of the nearby Custer County Protection Association who were arrested for obstructing the foreclosure of a mortgage on the farm of a 70-year-old neighbor had none of the sense of cause or the sophistication of labor demonstrators afoul of the law. They had never been arrested before. They did not know how they were going to pay for a lawyer. It never occurred to them that a collection could be taken up to defend them. They felt they had simply come to the aid of a friend. They did not object to foreclosure of the mortgage, only to "putting the old man out on the road." They had planned to arrange with the insurance company that held the mortgage to let him stay on, so that he would not lose the cattle and pasture he had acquired with his own labor.

Appalachian miners and textile workers—mountain people all—were violent by tradition. Miners were armed because they were dressed. They protested in the thundering cadences of John L. Lewis and Thomas Wolfe, because it was right for a man to protest. "God" put the coal in the hills, and the right of miners to make a living mining it was absolute and had nothing to do with any train of history. Textile workers did not begrudge the millowners their right of property. They struck only to defend their own dignity when it was threatened by humiliating efficiency methods that required a grown man to ask permission to go to the toilet.

The labor violence uncorked by the New Deal was, of course, an equal and opposite reaction to the violent repressive measures employers had long used to maintain an "easy labor supply." Steel mills preparing to cut wages mounted machine guns in the plant instead of leaving its protection to the police, so workers felt that they were engaged in private warfare. Fundamentally, labor violence was simply one aspect of the violence of American life in general. We prized personal freedom so highly that we curbed it only at the verge of chaos. The incidence of physical violence was so much higher in the 1930s than now seems compatible with an industrial society that the evidence is worth a quick look.

The World Almanac's Chronology of the year 1933 lists a score of suicides, murders, kidnappings, riots, lynchings, armed robberies, bomb scares, and jailbreaks. Thirty years later, the only comparable items were incidents involving Negro rights. In the Thirties, people acted as if they were lynching, bombing, strangling, and cutting each other up for the sheer hell of it. Newspapers covered murder trials day after day with loving attention to detail. The assassination of President Kennedy, surely the most spectacular incident of violence of the century, stimulated fewer column inches than the kidnapping of the Lindbergh baby.

The crimes of 1933 were violent and colorful, and they often aroused sympathy because the perpetrators took from the rich and gave to the poor. John Dillinger, the notorious bank robber who defied local police and escaped with ease from local jails, said that he took to bank robbing after his parents lost their money in a bank failure. In the "Union Station Massacre" of Kansas City in 1933, gangsters attempting to free a prisoner being taken to Leavenworth killed three officers and also the man they were trying to rescue. The same year, the kidnapper George "Machine Gun" Kelly collected a ransom of $200,000 for oilman Charles Urschel. The papers bristled with accounts of banks robbed and bankers murdered, rich kids kidnapped, mortgages forcibly burned. It was great to hear how the rich got hurt.

Through the bravado ran a fear—maybe a half-hope—that law and order would not prevail without extralegal assistance. When a lynch mob broke into the jail at San Jose, California, and strung up two kidnappers who had drowned their hostage, the Governor of the State of California commended the lynching as a "good job" and "lesson to every State of the Union."

Violence was, of course, nothing new in America. The kidnappers and racketeers were supposed to be the bootleggers turned out of a job by the repeal of Prohibition. The riots of the Depression—even the massacre that left the ten dead at Republic Steel—were tame compared with the draft riots of the Civil War that killed a thousand in New York City alone, July 13-16, 1863. The Harlem riot of 1964 was less bloody than its predecessors in 1943 and 1935.

Most people were puzzled rather than indignant when mindless rioting devastated the Negro area of Los Angeles and killed 36 people in August 1965. Newspapers asked sociologists why such a thing had happened, and Governor Pat Brown appointed a blue-ribbon committee of outsiders to investigate. News re-

195

ports neither moralized nor sensationalized the facts. Tolerance for violence has steadily declined since the Depression.

This is as it should be. A complex society as heavily populated as ours cannot let individuals fight it out among themselves. Private warfare of various kinds had to go, but it lasted long in America, the land of the free, in part because the Depression delayed industrial progress and all the social changes that go with it.

9

$ $ $ $ $

MR. ROOSEVELT'S WAR ON POVERTY

"I DON'T advocate taking everyone on relief rolls out and giving them a shot," Major Edward L. Dyer (U.S. Army, retired) told the Washington Society for Philosophical Research in 1936. "But euthanasia should be considered in cases of old age where the persons are of no use to themselves or anyone else."

Major Dyer's logic was inexorable. If meaningful work is a man's justification for living, then the superfluous people might just as well be dead. Clumps of silent, motionless men standing around waiting for work made up as an excuse to pay them wages were embarrassing to themselves and passersby. According to one crack, a WPA worker sued the Government because he hurt himself when the shovel he was leaning on broke. A farmer was supposed to have asked the druggist for "some of that WPA poison. It won't kill the squirrels, but it will make them so lazy I can just stamp them to death."

The jokes were few and in bad taste. A lot of people on relief were obviously too old or sick or ill-trained or discouraged to do a day's work. In 1935, one out of every six on relief was rated unemployable. Many more could do the WPA work, but they were too old or awkward or ill-favored to get jobs from a private employer as long as he could hire workers who were more pleasant to have around. In a loose labor market gray hairs, black skin, foreign accents, difficult names, or visible handicaps made a candidate "socially unemployable," even if he could do the job.

But the most troubling aspect of work relief was that it drew on a well of unemployed workers that never ran dry. In accordance with Parkinson's Law, the number of applicants grew directly with the number of jobs to be filled. No matter how many jobs the projects made, there were never enough to go around.

During the first three years of the New Deal, Federal, state and local governments spent more than $4 billion on relief of all sorts, most of it on work projects supported by the Federal Government. More than one of every five American earners was involved at some time or other, but the programs did not cut into the hard core of unemployment. Harry Hopkins calculated that the 3.5 million he had on WPA rolls at their peak just about equalled the new workers growing up between 1929 and 1936.

By 1935 it was clear that unemployment was not an accident that would go away. Anyone who paid attention to the people on work relief projects feared that a very large number of them were superfluous people who could never get any other kind of job. Yet Roosevelt and Hopkins talked in terms of tiding the unemployed over to better times. "It is perfectly crazy for you, Harry Hopkins, to let the public think you have any idea that private industry is going to put these relief clients to work before next election day—or any future election day," Lorena Hickock scolded her boss Harry Hopkins.

We now say that the labor force—the number of people willing and able to work—grew faster than new jobs, but no one wanted to come out and say it that way in 1935. Conservatives preferred to contend that relief demoralized workers who would otherwise have applied themselves to qualify for private employment. Liberals like Harry Hopkins, who knew better, did not want to suggest that we might have a permanent relief "class" on our hands. If the Government was going to provide a job for everyone who was unemployed, the Government obviously hoped that the unemployed would be few.

The Government avoided defining unemployment. The political battle over definition persists to this day. The history of the battle is instructive, because the stakes have always been the recognition of the extent of industrial distress and the Government's responsibility for it.

In January 1929, liberal New York Senator Robert Wagner introduced a bill to force the reluctant Bureau of the Census to count the jobless. When the Census of 1930 turned up 3,187,-947, President Hoover "corrected" the figure down to 1,900,000 by cutting out those he thought were not seriously looking for work or were merely "between jobs" in seasonal trades, while liberals objected that the Census had not found all the unemployed in the first place. Next, a law requiring the Bureau of Labor Statistics to measure unemployment on a regular basis was passed with no appropriation to make the count or even to study the technical problems that Hoover himself had "solved" arbitrarily. The United States had a better official count of its pigs than of its unemployed people. Politicians as well as economists had to use estimates of unemployment made by labor unions or the more conservative National Industrial Conference Board.

In 1934, Roosevelt got the House to appropriate $7.5 million to hire 105,000 canvassers to take a census of the unemployed around election time. Republican Senators killed the House bill because they feared it would be used to pay for Democratic campaign workers.

In the spring of 1935, Roosevelt talked about a special census of the unemployed, but he did not get around to taking it until a year after the election of 1936, when the Recession of 1937 was starting. During this time he preferred to leave the number of unemployed "untold . . . because of the impossibility of an exact definition of what constitutes unemployment." Republicans grumbled at voting the Administration a "blank check" for relief. Conservatives demanded a definition and a count that would, in George Sokolsky's words, show whether we were "helping men and women over a bad time" or "breeding a population that will not work for a living."

The Census of 1937 was taken by voluntary registration, like the World War I draft. Postmen distributed blanks for the unemployed to fill out, but Americans had been more willing to report themselves for the draft than to declare themselves unemployed. A door-to-door census check disclosed that only 72 percent of the unemployed returned questionnaires. Conservatives claimed that some people with jobs reported themselves jobless. Gallup found that 20 percent of those who turned in questionnaires thought they were job applications. The count did not distinguish between regular members of the labor force and people who would work if they got a chance but could get along without it. Worse, a business downturn made the census obsolete before the totals were compiled. Its volunteer head, President John D. Biggers, of Libbey-Owens-Ford Glass Co., had to discharge 4,000 of his firm's 5,000 Toledo workers right after the count.

In 1940, the Government needed a better estimate of the money required for work relief, so the Bureau of the Budget called in the professional statisticians. They recommended periodic interview by trained census enumerators of 35,000 households chosen as a true cross section of the U.S. population to find out who was working, who had been looking for work in the past week, and who had been neither working nor looking

200

for work. The probability sample was technically elegant. Academic sniping ceased.

Political sniping resumed in 1945 over plans to take care of the unemployment expected at the end of the war. What was full employment? Some planners figured we needed 60 million jobs. "If you estimate 60 million jobs," objected Conservative Senator Robert A. Taft, "that means two jobs for 18 million families. Those second people in the family that work do not have to work, perhaps. They will if they get a good job, and if they don't they may not work. Are those people unemployed, or how are you going to count them? Should we insure two jobs for 18 million families in the United States? Wouldn't it perhaps represent a higher standard of living to have fewer families in which two people have to work?"

During the 1960s the controversy has been more intense than ever. In September 1961, for instance, *Reader's Digest* published an article entitled "Let's Look at Those 'Alarming' Unemployment Figures—Are we Getting a True Statistical Picture? Here is an Eye-Opening Report on an All-Important Subject." The article contended that many people counted as unemployed did not really need to work and did not deserve Government action on their behalf. A Presidential fact-finding committee and hearings by the Joint Economic Committee's Subcommittee on Economic Statistics rejected this argument, but the author made no defense of his charges and did not appear when invited to state them before professional statisticians.

Liberals who want the Government to do more for poor people, and Conservatives who want the Government to do less, are both uncomfortable with unemployment as the measure of the kind of distress the Government should remedy. Liberals talk about the Harlem dishwasher with six children who is worse off than he would be on home relief, in which the size of his family is considered. They also contend that the unemployment figures leave out people who have given up looking for work, or who would work if they thought jobs were available.

Conservatives think that unemployment is none of the Government's business, particularly if the unemployed are people who "ought" to stay at home, such as working wives. They would apply a "means test" to unemployment. A college student who is not very keen on working over the summer and does not find a job he likes should not be counted the same way as a father supporting a family who really "needs" a job. Liberals retort that you have no right to delve into motives. Both aim at a society in which everyone earns his own keep. In the 1960s, guaranteed-income plans are discussed in abstract terms by intellectuals as a way of taking care of workers displaced by automation.

There was nothing academic about guaranteed-income schemes in 1935. For a brief period, millions of ordinary Americans supported political movements that frankly proposed to hand out a living to some people without making them work for it. When Roosevelt did not bring back jobs, the idea caught on like the old-time religion.

In California, Upton Sinclair campaigned for Governor in 1934 on a plan to End Poverty in California (EPIC) by turning empty factories and tax-delinquent land over to the unemployed to work "for use" rather than for profit. He sold 200,000 copies of a utopian account of what he intended to do, written in the past tense as if he had done it. "I, Governor of California —And How I Ended Poverty: A True Story of the Future."

California old folks rallied to Dr. Francis E. Townsend, a retired physician who proposed to give everyone over 60 who would quit working $200 a month if he promised to spend it all in the month. By 1935, at least 10 million had signed his petitions, and Upton Sinclair's opponent had to endorse the Townsend Plan in order to win.

In November 1934, Charles Coughlin, the Detroit "radio

priest," formed a National Union for Social Justice to end capitalism by monetizing silver and so "recapturing control over money," nationalizing industry, and protecting labor against "the vested interests of wealth and intellect." His scheme was so popular that he was getting more mail than President Roosevelt.

In Louisiana, Senator Huey S. Long proposed to "Share the Wealth" and "Make Every Man a King" by taxing the rich to give every family a homestead worth at least $5,000, an income of $2,000, with pensions for oldsters, free college for bright youngsters, and a radio, a washing machine, and a car for every home. In 1935, he was a power not only in Louisiana but also in Washington.

Upton Sinclair was a Socialist, but the others were radicals of the right who drew on the old Populist campaign for easy money, and their followers were as American as corn. Townsend and Long attracted old Americans of the small towns and farms who had suffered from the collapse of prices and the competition of the chain stores and mechanized farming. They were the little businessmen, the grocers and druggists and farmers who were always in debt. Fundamentalist in religion, anti-intellectual by tradition, they were the salt of the earth, the backbone of the country, the originals of Grant Wood's "American Gothic" pair standing with pitchfork in front of their farm, their faces set against progress, Jews, foreigners, Eastern bankers, newfangled nonsense, and, of course, sin.

Politically articulate, these dispossessed old-stock Americans were the people who later supported Senator McCarthy's investigations of Communism in Government. Senator Goldwater thought they were still around in sufficient force to elect him President in 1964. In the early 1930s, Dorothy Thompson, then a foreign correspondent, thought the American primitives of the small town looked ripe for a native Hitler. She was so disturbed about the prospect that she induced her then husband, Sinclair Lewis, to write *It Can't Happen Here*. The theme was timely enough to make the novel a bestseller of 1935.

"It" did not, of course, happen here. Coughlin, Townsend, Long, and Sinclair all started by supporting Roosevelt. They all broke with Roosevelt as their own ambitions and extremism grew. All four dropped out of political sight almost as suddenly as they rose. More writer than politician, Upton Sinclair cheerfully went to work serializing his "I, Governor?" pamphlet when he was defeated in the fall of 1934, and continued his career as a novelist. A year later, Huey Long was assassinated at the height of his popularity. In 1936, his lieutenant, Gerald F.K. Smith, joined Townsend and Coughlin in a "Union Party," which disappeared under the Roosevelt landslide. The Roman Catholic Church ordered Coughlin off the air. Townsend, the most pathetic figure of all, was sentenced for contempt of Congress because he refused to answer the questions of an investigating committee, and would have gone to jail if Roosevelt had not pardoned him.

The grassfires of popular demand for guaranteed income burned bright because people realized with a shock that a great many people on relief would never get jobs again. Like flares of distress, the schemes lit up the pasty, sullen faces of millions of Americans whom progress had literally passed by: Tennessee mountaineers, Kentucky coal miners, "Okies" fleeing dust storms like Arab nomads, back-country farmers on land that should never have been cleared, and other victims of our headlong exploitation of natural resources; young people denied a chance to learn a trade or forced to give up schooling for dead-end jobs; old people whose children had left to look for work in town and could not or would not support them. In 1934, the New Deal turned from measures to rescue people hit by Depression to measures that would rescue people doomed to poverty and to leave children doomed to poverty behind them. In January 1937, Roosevelt told the country that the millions
204

"ill-housed, ill-clad, ill-nourished . . . and denied the opportunity to better their lot and the lot of their children" added up to one third of the nation.

Roosevelt was, according to his wife, a "very simple Christian," and he had a very simple vision. "I see no reason why every child, from the day he is born, shouldn't be a member of a social security system," he told Frances Perkins. "When he begins to grow up, he should know he will have old-age benefits direct from the insurance system to which he will belong all his life. If he is out of work, he gets a benefit. If he is sick or crippled, he gets a benefit. . . . The rural free delivery carrier ought to give each child his social insurance number and his policy or whatever takes the place of a policy. The rural free delivery carrier ought to be the one who picks up the claim of the man who is unemployed, or of the old lady who wants old-age insurance benefits. Everybody ought to be in on it— the farmer and his wife and his family. I don't see why not. Cradle to the grave—from the cradle to the grave, they ought to be in a social insurance system." Sir William Beveridge, author of the British "cradle-to-the-grave" security system, got the benefit of Roosevelt's vision when he visited the President in 1934.

But in 1935, even Frances Perkins shook her head in dismay at the prospect of administering such a vision. Roosevelt had wanted medical insurance, but the American Medical Association was so implacably opposed that the Administration did not even make a try for it. On August 15, the Social Security Act created a compulsory Federal system of old-age and disability pensions financed by contributions from employer and employee, set up a system of Federally supported state unemployment insurance, and sent the unemployable old and sick and injured back to the states with Federal grants.

Conservatives were outraged. Insurance companies and savings banks claimed the Government was "competing" with them.

Security would take all the "romance out of life." Children would no longer support their parents. Americans would be as demoralized as workers in Germany, where children brought up to social insurance chanted, "One, two, three, four. Only fools work any more." The "payroll tax" would discourage employment.

In the election of 1936 employers bluntly threatened their workers. Ingersoll Rand, Johnson & Johnson, and other employers put slips in the pay envelopes they issued warning that workers would lose their jobs if Roosevelt were re-elected.

When Social Security was later extended to cover domestic servants, most women paid the contribution of the employee as well as their own, rather than hold out on the cook, but in 1936, some large-scale employers deliberately created the impression that the Government was forcing them to take the whole contribution out of paychecks. "Effective January 1937, we are compelled by a Roosevelt 'New Deal' law to make a 1 percent deduction from your wages and turn it over to the government," a pay envelope enclosure said. "You might get this money back ... but only if Congress decides to make the appropriation." Republicans warned workers they would be fingerprinted. One campaign orator suggested that the Government might make everyone wear a dog tag—stainless steel to avoid skin irritation.

Social Security was expanded over the years toward Roosevelt's original vision of a society that left nobody out. The millions of checks made out to individuals since 1935 have brought home the value of the system, yet every expansion has been fought with the "dog tag" argument. In 1965, for instance, the American Medical Association campaign against President Johnson's attempt to complete Roosevelt's dream by adding medical insurance was based on the patient's alleged loss of "freedom" to hire the physician of his choice. In the Presidential campaign of 1964, Senator Goldwater urged that Social Security be made voluntary.

Social Security protected individuals against accidents and old age that made earning a living impossible. Like the farm subsidies, it was in part a "transfer" of income from all taxpayers to some who needed it. Transfers divvy up the pie, but do not bake a bigger one. More American in style were the New Deal experiments that paid off by creating new wealth to get the country growing again.

The highest payoff is always on money invested in making people more productive, so it is possible that the country profited more from NYA and CCC than from any other New Deal antipoverty measure. Although they were popular and never ridiculed at the time, they were originally justified as conservation and relief measures. NYA was defended, for instance, primarily because it reduced unemployment among family heads by keeping young competitors for available jobs in school and off the labor market.

The real value of the training programs is better recognized now that thousands of the young people they helped develop have become important contributors to the national wealth as midcentury adults.

When President Johnson was 27, he headed NYA for the State of Texas and did so good a job of it that President Roosevelt tried to have him talked out of giving up the job to run for Congress. Johnson can reel off the names of important Texans who got through school on NYA jobs. He likes to recall how his close friend, Texas Governor John B. Connally, Jr., "came from Floresville without a dollar in his pocket and got an N.Y.A. job at 17 cents an hour." The job helped Connally work his way through the University of Texas. Lyndon Johnson has emphasized education and training, rather than conservation, as the goal of the Job Corps he has modeled on CCC.

207

In 1964 he greatly expanded the NYA experiment to create work-study and work-training programs for young people and special vocational training for the hard-core unemployed.

The most original and the most brilliant achievement of Mr. Roosevelt's war on poverty was development of the Tennessee Valley. President Johnson hopes to do the same for Appalachia, but the task he has set himself will be easier. In 1933, Tennessee Valley people had less than half the average income of all other Americans. In 1964, Appalachian families were getting nearly two-thirds of the national average.

In 1936, when poet Jim Agee explored the Tennessee mountains, he found whole families who talked Elizabethan English and who lived and died ten miles from town without ever having been there. Some had never seen an electric light, a water pipe, or a doctor. No tenant house had paint or more than a single layer of knotholed lumber against the winter weather. None had screens against the fever mosquitoes. Sharecroppers working cotton patches had to get through the winter on advances of as little as $10 a month for families of six or eight. Many were blotched and stupid with pellagra because of limited food. Most tenant families lacked not only privies but even newspaper for toilet paper; mountain people retired to bushes and cleaned themselves with twigs and leaves. Many could not read or write. The Tennessee Valley had more than its share of the millions Roosevelt saw "whose daily lives continue under conditions labeled indecent by a so-called polite society half a century ago."

TVA legislation was passed during the flush of Roosevelt's first months in office by an unlikely coalition of advocates of public power and cheap fertilizer, conservationists, agricultural reformers who wanted to get the South out of one-crop farming, and social planners who dreamed of revitalizing country life. "What we are doing here," Roosevelt explained with disarming simplicity, "is taking a watershed with about three and a half

208

million people in it, almost all of them rural, and we are trying to make a different type of citizen out of them." The law created a Tennessee Valley Authority "clothed with the power of the government but possessed of the flexibility and initiative of a private enterprise." The Authority was to develop flood control, navigation, waterpower, and the natural resources of the Tennessee River basin, including cheap fertilizer from phosphate deposits at Muscle Shoals (acquired by the Government for munitions making in World War I).

TVA attacked every aspect of poverty at once, developing new techniques of accounting, public administration, education, farm demonstration, and community relations to surmount one difficulty after another. TVA did more than dam streams and reforest eroded land; it put Valley people to work building these improvements and taught them how to live by putting them in model communities while they worked, instead of in construction camps. TVA did more than make cheap electricity and cheap fertilizer; it showed farmers how to use them, involving the whole community in demonstrations that changed the habits of the most conservative people in the United States.

People who had never been away from home were moved into new houses and taught how to live new lives. The Authority once delayed the flooding of a valley rather than move a sick man in his nineties. The old man found out what was going on and objected that he did not want to "hold up the Government." Respect for the dignity of the Tennessee Valley people helped them to change. TVA attracted so much new industry that the Tennessee Valley is no longer predominantly agricultural. In 1965, per capita income is nearly ten times what it was in 1933.

The return is beyond the wildest claims of stock promoters. TVA contributes the equivalent of taxes to local and state government and is paying back all of the $1.4 billion the Federal Government invested in power production. By demonstrating that low rates and high volume can make money in power, TVA has helped to reduce electrical rates all over the country. It has increased farm productivity in every state by teaching farmers to plant cover crops and use fertilizer. Forest management of the Tennessee Valley has saved hundreds of millions of dollars in flood and fire damage, created forest industries with sales of $500 million a year, and attracted millions of dollars a year in tourist trade, fishing, and boating.

Public utilities figured that the barefoot Valley farmers would not be able to use the power the river could generate for hundreds of years. But TVA's all-out approach lifted the economy so fast that neighboring private power companies have made more money by increased volume than before. Valley experiments pioneered new uses for electricity, such as home heating. The market for power eventually grew beyond the capacity of the river and supported the development of power facilities which encouraged the location of the Oak Ridge atomic facilities in the valley.

The Authority proved that Government can be dynamic and efficient. It pioneered methods of managing many related enterprises, better accounting methods, better personnel methods, and new ways of working with organizations, public and private, to mobilize existing talent for change. It trained scores of creative public servants. Johnson's Secretary of the Treasury Henry H. Fowler started his career as a lawyer for TVA.

Equally dramatic was the payoff on the New Deal investment in extending electric power to American farms. In 1933, nine out of ten farmers had no electricity. Power companies maintained that they did not need it or could not afford it. They could not see that extending electricity to outlying farms might raise their productivity to the point where the owners could become paying customers, and when they could see it they regarded such an investment as too long-term and too low in return to be attractive to private enterprise. Unwilling to invest in farm lines themselves, they bitterly opposed proposals that the Government put up the money for power systems that demonstrated how cheap electricity could be. Sympathetic to farmers, Roosevelt caught the vision of a countryside revolutionized by electricity. To get it going with as little opposition as possible, he included a Rural Electrification Administration in the work relief act of 1935 on the theory that the unemployed could be put to work extending power to farms.

REA was a fight from the start. It first tried to get power companies to build the lines with low-interest Government money. They refused. City-owned power plants were not allowed to go into the country. REA finally helped farmers organize cooperatives that borrowed REA money and built the lines. Power companies tried to stop them by running "spite lines" through a cooperative's territory, which made its system uneconomic. But the farmers cheered the REA lines stretching out to bring city lights to their homes.

Utilities did not seem to realize how unpopular they had become. Small investors hated them for the stock frauds the Crash had uncovered. Public opinion favored outlawing utility companies that existed only to hold operating companies, yet the utility lobby fought the Public Utility Holding Company Act of 1935 with the crude tactics used successfully on state legislatures in quieter times. When freshman Senator Harry S. Truman refused to change his stand in favor of the "death sentence" for holding companies, the power lobby stimulated a blizzard of 30,000 letters of protest from his Missouri constituents. Truman voted for the bill anyway, but he never forgave the utilities. A Senate committee exposed smears, bribes, forged telegrams, and threats of libel suit or withdrawal of advertising from publications attacking utilities.

The farmers' lines pushed on with New Deal support. In the Texas countryside where the LBJ Ranch is located, for instance, Lyndon B. Johnson's NYA boys built the headquarters

211

for the Pedernales Electric Cooperative. When an area was wired, farmers would gather in a field at night to watch the lights go on. During Roosevelt's first two terms, electricity rates fell and a million dark farms burst into light. President Johnson is proud of his part in helping the cooperatives. In 1965, he was pushing the Passamaquoddy tidal electric project, which would provide a yardstick for private power in New England, where rates are still higher than elsewhere in the country.

The Public Works Administration made it possible for the country to move ahead by providing the schools, hospitals, waterworks, sewers, dams, bridges, courthouses, city halls, power plants, jails, and railroad stations, without which industry could not have expanded very far in war or peace. At the time, PWA Administrator Harold Ickes seems to have been the only public figure who saw this vision. PWA was set up under the National Industrial Recovery Act to spark recovery by boosting industry dependent on construction. But "Honest Harold" Ickes was a cautious, slow-moving old Progressive less interested in stimulating the economy than in getting a dollar's worth of public works for every public dollar. One New Dealer dreamed that Hugh Johnson and Ickes changed jobs. As PWA chief, Johnson was pumping money into circulation; as NRA chief, Ickes was slowly building codes that would endure for generations.

PWA did exactly what Ickes intended. It built or helped finance four-fifths of the public works constructed in the United States between 1933 and 1937, $6 billion worth of Depression bargains that would cost twice as much to build now. Huge as the bill was, it was not enough to spark recovery, or even to compensate for the disappearance of state and local public works spending. As J.K. Galbraith once cracked, "State and local governments balanced their budgets with Federal aid." Even PWA could not push construction of all kinds back to
212

two-thirds the volume of pre-Depression years when state, local, and private investors were footing the bill.

At the time, PWA was ignored because it created disappointingly few jobs. Once described as unwilling "to set a grown man chasing tumbleweed on a windy day," Ickes did not indulge in the benevolent inefficiencies of made work. Hopkins boasted that he could keep a man working for a month on $88, almost all of it wages. Ickes had to spend $330, but he claimed that the materials, equipment, and planning PWA bought created two and a half jobs in private industry for every man on the payroll. Inevitably, PWA was too late as well as too little. The only heavy construction projects approved and ready to employ men on public works in 1933 were Navy ships. It was not until 1935, when PWA spending for armaments was stopped as a matter of policy, that a substantial volume of civilian projects was out of the planning stage.

The social inventions of Mr. Roosevelt's war on poverty were impressive. Social Security, CCC, NYA, PWA, TVA, REA, all were ingenious ways around political opposition, either to effect the transfer of income from rich to poor, or to achieve direct Government investment. Although businessmen feared Government "competition," the New Deal projects did not attract private capital because the risks were too high, the payoff too long, or the rate of return too low for the capital market as then constituted. The machinery for many of the New Deal programs broke new ground. TVA showed what a Government corporation could be made to do. PWA, NYA, and the work relief programs pioneered ways of pumping Federal money out to people through state and local auspices, which have made it possible to equalize wealth between rich and poor states without abandoning state sovereignty.

Mr. Johnson's war on poverty leans heavily on the political imagination of Mr. Roosevelt's war. Almost as significant for the new war are the failures of the first one: housing, rural

213

resettlement, self-help projects, surplus disposal, self-government of industry through Government sponsorship, consumer protection by law, and, of course, enforcement of civil rights to remove the disabilities of Negroes.

Public power overcame private power objections to TVA and extending electricity to the farms; public housing made hardly any headway against the same kind of opposition from private real-estate interests. Government guarantees of mortgages rescued homes and farms from foreclosure during the first Roosevelt years, but neither the Federal Housing Authority (FHA), set up to insure loans to modernize and build homes, nor the U.S. Housing Authority, later established to lend money at low interest for low-cost housing developments, got off the ground before the war.

FHA did not demonstrate its value to the ill-housed until it made possible the suburban developments after the war. During the Depression, housing projects were valued for the jobs they made, rather than for their contribution to the people who would live in them. Residential construction was not an efficient way to make jobs. Real-estate "interests" included an army of small investors in buildings and mortgages rather than a few big company targets for attack. Roosevelt was more interested in sending slum dwellers back to the land than in improving their quarters in the city.

Many idealistic Americans believed that a man could always scratch a living out of the land. The fact. was, of course, that the poorest poor were living on the subsistence farms. Some who went back to the country when they could not find work had to throw their seed on the bare ground because they did not have a plow. Others ate the animal feed given them. Yet the glamour of independence on the land died hard. In a hilarious series of short stories, Martha Gellhorn described the early attempts to send city relief families back to the land under FERA's Rural Rehabilitation, which she had observed while

214

working for Hopkins. Plagued by mosquitoes, unfamiliar problems, and loneliness, the settlers were glad to get back to the city, where misery at least had company. "It was such a stupendous and splendid idea," she wrote, "and when you got right down to it, it was a chance to live in an abandoned Negro shanty or a badly made, too small, new house; without adequate water, heat or light, with inadequate provision for staple groceries or clothes or medical care; and work until your back broke to raise a crop for which there might or might not be buyers."

Rural Rehabilitation tried moving industrial communities stranded by the working-out of mines, lumber, or oil to places where they could farm successfully. Families from worked-over lumber land in Wisconsin, Michigan, and Minnesota were resettled at Matanuska Valley in Alaska, where after a great deal of criticism and Federal expense they developed the fruit, vegetable, and dairy production that Alaska needed.

More ambitious, more mystical, and much less successful were the communities set up by the Subsistence Homestead Division under the National Industrial Recovery Act. Such diverse philosophers as Mrs. Roosevelt, the Irish agrarian poet A.E. Russell, financier Bernard Baruch, and Quaker relief worker Clarence Pickett hoped that the Federal Government could combat the materialism of industrial city life by resettling the unemployed in self-sufficient farming towns.

None of these utopias survived as communities set apart. War bailed them out, or they were abandoned as too expensive. Arthurdale, West Virginia, the first subsistence homestead town, now looks like any postwar suburb. In 1935 it had cost so much and run into so much bad publicity that even FDR lost faith. The colonists always thought of the projects as temporary relief. They wanted not a new way of life, but a place in the one they knew. "After five or six years here," one member of an Arkansas community confided, "a man could save

215

enough to buy a little farm for himself." In 1935, NIRA's Homestead Division and FERA's Rural Rehabilitation Division were both turned over to Rexford Tugwell, one of the original "brains trust." A political scientist, Tugwell wanted to reform Government so it could deal with modern technology. He briskly reorganized the subsistence communities toward the production of cash crops and planned to house slum dwellers in suburban communities. His model "Greenbelt," outside Washington, is strikingly similar to the "projects" that real-estate developers built after World War II.

Nothing sounded simpler than to buy up crops farmers could not sell and give them away to the needy, or get the unemployed to process them into the food and cloth they did not have money to buy. In 1933, FERA took over surplus crops AAA had acquired and tried to distribute them. Farmers selling for cash and merchants complained. Beef hurriedly processed to salvage drought-stricken cattle spoiled. Manufacturers protested against Government competition. Makers of shoe machinery refused to rent it to relief projects undertaking to make surplus hides into shoes for the unemployed. Relief clients were not enthusiastic about the free goods. One little boy told a reporter he did not want to go to school in pants made of ticking, because then everyone would know that his family was on relief.

In 1934, as many as 50,000 families were working in self-help groups, some 15 percent dependent on FERA. Some made furniture, stoves, and dresses, and even exchanged these products by barter with other relief work groups, much as the Seattle unemployed had organized to help themselves. But the only people who really liked surplus disposal were farmers. In 1935, the programs were turned over to AAA and continued as farm relief without serious attempt to get the products consumed.

In 1938, when farm surpluses threatened again, Agricul-

216

ture's Surplus Marketing Administration began giving surplus foods to school lunches and, through stamps redeemable at grocery stores, to families on relief. The Federal School Lunch program has been going ever since and the food-stamp plan was revived in 1964, but both are sharply focused on welfare targets.

Reforms that bypass normal competitive business channels seem to work in the United States only when there is an appealing reason for them, such as the nourishment of school children. Industrial self-government by cartel works well in Europe, but NRA was not a success in the United States. It disappeared unlamented, leaving behind it the five-day week and the union election.

Mr. Roosevelt's war on poverty seemed outrageous to those who felt, with John Jay, that "this country should be governed by the people who own it." The significant American freedom, in their view, was the freedom of a man to invest a dollar in whatever enterprise he pleased without "Government interference."

Conservatives talked of a capitalist revolt to "save our liberties." In November 1935, Norval W. Adams, the Mormon vice president of Salt Lake City's First National Bank, urged the annual meeting of the American Bankers Association to stop Government spending by refusing to buy any more Government securities. Arthur H. Young, vice president of U.S. Steel, told the American Management Association he was willing to "go to jail or be convicted as a felon" rather than recognize unions under the Wagner Act. The same month, William Randolph Hearst announced that he would have to move away from California to escape the income taxes the state had passed.

In March 1934, Jouett Shouse and the Conservative Democrats who had badgered Hoover organized the American Liberty League to waken America from "the dream of fancied security" and save the Constitution. John J. Raskob, the

217

du Ponts, and other conservative men of means, contributed a million dollars to spread the gospel of individual initiative, free enterprise, and limited Government. Some of them had contributed heavily to elect Roosevelt. A committee of Liberty League lawyers openly advised businessmen to disobey New Deal laws as unconstitutional. Liberty League writers urged recovery by saving rather than spending and depicted the rich as self-made.

The Liberty League said nothing that everyone had not been reared to believe, yet it stirred unexpectedly bitter resentment. Charles Michelson turned on the multimillionaires who had employed him to discredit Hoover and demolished their "dupontifical" attacks. The League became so unpopular that the Republican Party begged it please "not to help" in the campaign of 1936.

Deposed from power and respect, unable or unwilling or too frightened to fight back, the embittered *rentier* minority vented its frustration on Roosevelt, "traitor to his class." A popular cartoon showed well-dressed Bourbons inviting each other to "Come along! We're going to the Trans-Lux to hiss Roosevelt!" "And if Roosevelt is not re-elected," an aging, dinner-jacketed lecher promises in another cartoon, "perhaps even a villa in Newport, my dearest sweet."

People who now advertise their incomes by complaining about the income tax established their claim to capitalist status in the Thirties by hating Roosevelt. A lawyer attracted attention by proposing a purse of $5 million to bribe Roosevelt to resign. Roosevelt's voice, his manner, his cheerful assurance, his intimate appeal to "my friends" in the radio audience infuriated the rich. When he mocked them, he smiled knowingly, and the charge became personal.

Presumptive gentlemen attacked Roosevelt with astonishing ferocity and irrelevance to the issues. The McClure Syndicate circulated an "unchecked" f.y.i. to editors quoting an "official of American Cyanamid" as maintaining, at a private gathering, that "the paranoiac in the White House is destroying the nation," that "a couple of well-placed bullets would be the best thing for the country," and that he for one would buy a bottle of champagne as quick as he could get it "to celebrate the news." Others like him talked about Roosevelt's legs, his family, his "failure" in business, his supposed Negro and/or Jewish blood ("Roosevelt" was supposed to come from "Rosenfeld"), his Communist plots, his vanity, his vacillations, his mentality.

J. P. Morgan's family kept newspapers with pictures of Roosevelt out of his sight, and in one Connecticut country club cited by Heywood Broun, mention of his name was forbidden as a health measure against apoplexy. Like primitives who avoid naming the devil, Roosevelt-haters referred to him obliquely as "That Man," "Your *Friend*," "That Madman in the White House," or "That Cripple in the White House." Endicott Peabody, headmaster of Groton, warned alumni attending its fiftieth anniversary celebration not to come if they could not be polite to their fellow Grottie, the President of the United States. The Roosevelts did not retaliate as a matter of policy, but the 1937 Social Register disclosed that Franklin Delano Roosevelt no longer belonged to the Knickerbocker Club and his wife no longer belonged to the Colony Club.

The Roosevelt-haters had one thing in common: they identified with the industrial development of the United States. As a landed aristocrat, Roosevelt attracted all those who had been hurt in the headlong industrialization of the country. Starving miners pasted newspaper pictures of Roosevelt in their curtainless windows. Factory girls wore Roosevelt buttons for jewelry. Intellectuals, farmers, Negroes, hyphenated Americans in the big cities, Jews, and educated women responded to his defense of human values against property rights.

The Roosevelt-haters misunderstood the strength of this coalition. The anti-Roosevelt press called the Wealth Tax Act of

219

1935 a "Soak the Rich" measure without realizing that this was exactly what a great many people wanted done. When the phrase boomeranged, William Randolph Hearst ordered his editors to substitute "Soak the Successful." Newspapers attacking Roosevelt had a combined circulation of more than twice the readership of newspapers that favored him in the election of 1936. The Roosevelt-haters did not realize that they were a handful of people talking loudly to themselves. As the election of 1936 approached, *The Literary Digest* took a straw vote based on telephone listings and automobile registrations and elected Landon by a landslide of 32 states, but the majority with neither cars nor phones were almost solidly behind the President. Even the "New Deal pay cut" failed to move workers.

"How's the boss going to know how you vote?" a steelworker told a Democratic Party worker.

"The women who come in here to have their hair done knock Roosevelt," a Fifth Avenue hairdresser said. "That's because they've got money and they're afraid he's going to take some of it away from them. We let 'em talk and say nothing ourselves, but I'll bet every girl in this shop votes for Roosevelt." Even Roosevelt underestimated the tide in his favor. Old pro Jim Farley was the only one who hit it on the nose: every state except Maine and Vermont went to the Democrats.

A boomlet had helped Roosevelt win in 1936, but the flush was stimulated by Government spending he himself did not approve. The Supreme Court had ordered the Government to return $200 million of processing taxes collected under AAA. Over Roosevelt's veto, Congress had passed a bonus bill distributing $2 billion to veterans in 1936 instead of in 1945 as originally provided. In part to meet these drains on the Treasury without going into debt, Roosevelt had proposed a tax on undistributed corporate profits, which encouraged companies to pay out almost all their profits in dividends. Prices and production rose almost to 1929 levels. Early in 1937, Leon Henderson, WPA's consulting economist, warned that recovery was unstable, because prices had risen faster than wages.

Bankers feared the recovery would bring on a dangerous inflation. To reassure them, the Federal Reserve Board raised reserve requirements, and the Treasury agreed not to issue paper money against the gold that was being shipped into the United States for safekeeping because it looked as if there might be war in Europe.

Roosevelt believed in balancing the Federal budget, and 1937 looked like the year to do it. He cut back relief, ordered PWA to stop building and RFC to stop lending, and even talked about postponing new post offices and road building for which money had already been appropriated. He did exactly what conservative economists had been urging for years. During six months in 1937 and 1938, the Treasury actually showed a small cash surplus. But the result was disaster.

On October 19, 1937, "Black Tuesday," the stock market broke. During the next six months, production dropped off even faster than it had after the 1929 Crash. By midsummer 1938, five million people had lost their jobs, and 14 percent of all the people in the United States were getting public relief.

The break stunned everybody. "I don't think anyone in God's world could have told me that the outlook was going to drop 50 percent in two or three weeks," William Knudsen, the big, slow Dane who was president of General Motors, testified in January 1938. People said some of the things they had said in 1929. Henry Ford proposed a Model-T type of three-wheeled tractor to help farmers. ("I don't care if we can't make a cent of profit. The main thing is to get something started.") The Ritz Fur Shop, Manhattan's secondhand fur coat exchange, was attracting attention with a "one-man bull movement" to lift the market by accepting stock at ten points over the market in exchange for its merchandise.

221

But, by 1937, Roosevelt was surrounded by people who had read Keynes and were aware of the impact of Government spending: Marriner Eccles of the Federal Reserve; Leon Henderson and his boss Harry Hopkins; New Dealers Tommy Corcoran and Ben Cohen; and even the President's own son, James. They pointed out that Social Security deductions were aggravating the deflation caused by balancing the budget. During the first year, benefits were negligible compared with the two percent of wages withdrawn from circulation by payment of the tax. The first payment, to a Cleveland motorman who became 65 the day after Social Security took effect, was exactly 12 cents.

Roosevelt listened, but he still felt that balancing the budget was a moral duty. In February he asked WPA to make the money it had left go further by converting to direct relief. When Keynes himself wrote to Roosevelt, the President turned the letter over to Secretary of the Treasury Morgenthau, Jr. An advocate of budget-balancing, Morgenthau replied with a noncommittal thank-you. But Roosevelt's interest in balancing the budget was second always to his interest in saving people from distress. In April 1938, he reluctantly sacrificed the budget to relief and asked for money to restore the spending agencies he had cut. Under new leadership, FHA began to lend to small homeowners. A new Farm Security Agency (FSA) started lending marginal farmers a billion dollars over the next three years to buy places of their own.

Congress passed the new spending, but "confidence" did not return. When several new stock issues failed and plans for expansion were canceled, Roosevelt began to take the newspaper talk of a "capital strike" literally. He confided to Morgenthau that a "wise old bird" had told him that business leaders were determined to get him out so they could establish fascist control of the United States. Morgenthau was sure that the wise old bird was Roosevelt himself.

222

Keynes had urged Roosevelt to treat businessmen "not as wolves and tigers, but as domestic animals by nature, even though they have been badly brought up and not trained as you would wish." He explained their nature with a dispassionate snobbery impossible to the haughtiest American. "Businessmen have a different set of delusions from politicians; and need, therefore, different handling. They are, however, much milder than politicians, at the same time allured and terrified by the glare of publicity, easily persuaded to be 'patriots,' perplexed, bemused, indeed terrified, yet only too anxious to take a cheerful view, vain perhaps but very unsure of themselves, pathetically responsive to a kind word. It is a mistake to think that they are more *immoral* than politicians. If you work them into the surly, obstinate, terrified mood, of which domestic animals wrongly handled, are so capable, the nation's burdens will not get carried to market..."

Roosevelt ignored the advice. Two weeks after announcing his spending program in April, he attacked the concentration of economic control over "other people's money, other people's labor, other people's lives," and launched Congress on a searching investigation into some of the tenderest parts of the business anatomy: mergers; banks and holding companies; trade associations; patents; the marketing of new inventions; identical bids and price changes; the burden of proof in antitrust laws. Antitrusters frankly charged that monopolists had "priced the country into a slump" and undertook to prosecute the conspirators.

The Temporary National Economic Committee inquiry was precisely the kind of "wrong handling" that Keynes had warned would ruin the disposition of businessmen and domestic animals. Of all the methods for defining the boundaries of public and private power, the New Deal developed a brand of guerrilla warfare that has become routine ever since. The ritual whacks that Government and business deal each other baffle foreigners

223

accustomed to smoother and less public transactions between Government and business.

Business blamed the New Deal, for instance, for discouraging new investment. The discouragement boiled down to police measures to which it is hard to see an honest objection: competitive bidding for the flotation of new securities, and full disclosure to small investors of the facts that big investors obtained as a matter of course; public review of the rules made by the security exchanges for ordering trading; separation of investment and deposit banking to help bankers resist the temptation to speculate for their own accounts with other people's money; stricter outside supervision of bank investments; Federal insurance of small deposits against bank failure.

The New York Stock Exchange and the SEC blamed each other for the Crash of 1937. The Exchange fired the first shot, perhaps because they were in a better position to see the Crash coming. In August 1937, New York Stock Exchange President Charles R. Gay warned the SEC that regulations on trading by insiders were discouraging the market to the point where "abnormal market conditions" might develop.

Sure enough, the market went down. "I am not arguing for the elimination of the speculator," SEC Chairman James Landis retorted in September, "but he should not dominate the market." Bear traders were blamed in "rumors from Washington," inspired, perhaps, by the wise old bird.

The New York Stock Exchange took the rumors seriously enough to appoint a committee to study trading in U.S. Steel to see if there were any irregularities.

The SEC took up the challenge to its prerogative of investigation. William O. Douglas, the tough new Chairman whom Roosevelt had appointed to replace Landis, instantly dispatched his own investigators. On November 22, Douglas reported that specialists had not supported the prices of the stock they were supposed to stabilize. "The problem of the permissible field op-

224

eration of the professional member trading on the floor of the Exchange for his own account is one which has long awaited solution," he rumbled, adding that the Exchange could no longer regulate itself "like a private club."

Meanwhile, back at the Exchange, the most dogged defender of the "private club" theory of regulation was Richard Whitney, a former President and then Governor of the New York Stock Exchange. He had been the hero of the first day of the 1929 Crash, and in 1933 had coldly refused information to the Pecora investigating committee, giving the explanation that "The New York Stock Exchange is a perfect institution." Neither SEC nor the wise old bird in Washington knew that the very day that Douglas attacked the "private club" a clerk of the Exchange had made bold to point out that Governor Whitney had made off with $1,125,000 in securities belonging to the Stock Exchange Gratuity Fund. It was only one of many such "borrowings" without leave. On that day, while President Gay was telling the newspapers that Douglas was blaming the Exchange for the collapse and Douglas was telling them he was ready to take the Exchange over, Whitney was out on the "street" negotiating one of the 111 loans he managed to extract from loyal members. In March 1938, after lending him a total of $27 million, even the "private club" could see that Whitney had to go to prison, if only by the historical logic that made it necessary for Charles I to lóse his head as well as his throne.

In April, while Whitney was settling into Sing Sing for taking stock that didn't belong to him, the SEC was threatening to regulate over-the-counter trading, where unrecorded telephone bidding made rigging easy to conceal. So the expediencies of political battle, exposé, rumor, charge, and threat.

Nearly 30 years later, they were at it still. Wall Street was purer and tamer and the SEC more polite when the crash of Memorial Day, 1962, ended a long bull market, but charge and countercharge paralleled the dialogue of 1937. There were suggestions that brokers engineered the drop to spite President Kennedy, and there was talk about the need for Government to maintain business confidence. When the SEC looked into trading records of the 1962 Crash, Wall Streeters talked about the role of speculators in maintaining "liquidity." After a preliminary report praising the Exchange as generally fair, the SEC asked for an end to floor trading by members for their own accounts, authority to publish over-the-counter prices set by telephone, and drastic restrictions on the operations of specialists. Next month the market almost stopped for a few minutes on the news of Kennedy's assassination. On investigation, SEC found several specialists had sold for their own profit stocks for which they were responsible. All of these problems had been aired in 1938. In 1963 they were still, as Douglas had put it in 1938, "awaiting solution." The ploys of SEC's missionary youth had hardened into sedate ritual.

The Recession of 1937 ended the New Deal. Drug and cosmetic interests (the "pain and beauty lobby") allowed the Pure Food and Drug Act to pass after five years of delay during which they had built loopholes for patent-medicine advertisers into it. Patent-medicine interests spread the false notion that the bill's author, Rexford Tugwell, was a dangerous Communist. They had discouraged reporting of the bill by reminding newspapers of their stake in drug advertising. They even organized an anti-Tugwell club in Chicago. People who knew nothing of the bill knew about "Rex the Red."

Congress wrote so many exceptions into the Fair Labor Standards Act of 1938 that Representative Martin Dies suggested it should be amended to require a report within 30 days to see whether anyone at all was subject to the minimum wages and maximum hours it set. It was Roosevelt's pet measure, but his last New Deal reform.

Opinion polls showed that Roosevelt was losing popular support. On many of them, the New Deal itself was cited as the

226

biggest bar to recovery. The Government was too big and powerful, people said. Relief was too high, and it should be run by local governments. Even the unemployed voted two to one to balance the budget by cutting expenses rather than levying new taxes. Louis Bean, Agriculture's smart statistician, studied the business figures and voting records and predicted the Republicans would gain 80 seats in 1938. His forecast was more accurate than that of the professional politicians.

The popular judgment was harsh. The New Deal did not cause the Depression—after all, the Crash predated the Roosevelt Administration by almost four years—but the verdict has to be that the New Deal did not go far enough. It failed to reform the economy, and failed to make it grow.

It made a beginning on reform. It brought the United States into line with modern civilized countries in putting a floor under want and applying the simple laws of fraud to banking and business. It publicized some of the areas where reform was needed, and it developed techniques for Government action in new fields: the Government corporation; local administration of Federal appropriations for social welfare; regulation of business by publicity and Presidential persuasion.

The chief beneficiaries of the New Deal were farmers, union labor, homeowners, bank depositors, debtors—people who had money or jobs to lose. Most of the people who gained and who kept the Democrats in power until after World War II were politically organized so that they could deliver votes, and they were literate and aggressive enough to fill out a Government form. All but the most tentative and experimental New Deal projects discriminated against the following sizable classes of people:

• Migrants; itinerants; part-time, domestic, or seasonal workers who were not covered by Social Security, minimum wages, or unemployment insurance, and often did not stay long enough in one place to qualify for relief.

- People certified as "unemployable" because of physical, mental, or educational handicaps, who were turned over to state welfare programs.
- Farmers too sick, old, poor, or ignorant to be risks for loans of any kind, rather than farmers who were merely poor risks for loans at the rates charged by private country banks.
- Big families maintained on work relief wages for work done, rather than on welfare payments scaled to the number of children to be supported.
- Sharecroppers, tenants, farm laborers.
- "Unorganizable" labor.

It is no accident, of course, that every single one of these groups had more than its share of Negroes. The civil liberty that people meant when they invoked the Constitution in the 1930s was not the right to vote or speak, but the right to control property, usually capital. The groups left out had neither votes nor voice nor capital.

The New Deal dodged the Negro problem. In spite of Mrs. Roosevelt's genuine sympathies, the Administration made no official effort to expand equality of opportunity in the Federal establishment, and employment policies were left to each New Deal agency to work out for itself. TVA barred Negroes from its construction housing, as was customary in the Tennessee Valley. AAA hurt Negro sharecroppers when it permitted the owner to collect for not planting and let his tenants go, and Depression closed escape to the North. Fewer Negroes left every Deep Southern state except North Carolina in the Thirties than in the Twenties.

Wherever national standards were applied equally, Negroes gained, if only by the rise it took to bring them up to par. When CWA paid standard wages, some Negroes were paid more than they had ever been able to get in private employment. Social Security was color-blind, but in many Southern states, local

228

administrators of Federal funds followed local customs and discriminated against Negroes.

The list of groups left out has a familiar ring. It recalls the definition of the self-perpetuating poor whom President Johnson promised to help in 1964. They are now generally defined as the nonwhite minorities, the aged, the migrant workers, the industrial rejects, children, families with a female head, people of little education. Many of them are the children of the underprivileged one-third of a nation that President Roosevelt saw, but did not reach. President Johnson's poverty programs implement the casual suggestion made at the Temporary National Economic Committee hearings that the "lower one-third" be brought into the economy by "such efforts as the food-stamp plan, slum clearance and low-cost housing, the extension of hospital and medical facilities, and the development of vocational and cultural programs for the less privileged."

The New Deal never faced the problem or the opportunity of industrial productivity. It merely noted that capital had increased its power over labor and consumers. The results—"technological unemployment" and "administered pricing"—were discussed not as economic trends, but as social sins. Roosevelt often talked as if he wished laborsaving devices would stop taking jobs away from people. In this climate, union campaigns for severance pay, retraining of displaced workers, or their assignment to "other work," laid a moral foundation for the featherbedding of payrolls with useless jobs that has become the hardest-fought labor-management issue of the 1960s.

Much as Roosevelt admired the local and the personal, his New Deal did not break up the hold of big firms on farming, labor, and Government. In 1929, the top five percent of American corporations had 84.49 percent of corporate income, and ten years later, in 1939, the top five percent had 84.34 percent. The New Deal encouraged unions to grow big. Its farm subsi-

229

dies rewarded big farmers enough to enable them to mechanize and improve acreage yields, so that they grew bigger at the expense of small competitors. Many actually received Government checks in excess of $10,000 for crops they did not grow.

Roosevelt sincerely believed in simple Government, but the Federal Government had to grow muscle and some fat in order to do the new things he wanted it to do. The pace and size of the Federal establishment dismayed the very liberals who wanted the Government to have more power.

Whenever my father went to Washington during the New Deal days, he was reminded fondly of the time he dropped in on the Secretary of State in 1905 with nothing much more on his mind than he would have had dropping in at his home-town county courthouse. In those days, he recalled, the Secretary of State did not have pressing business every day, either. Father just walked through the door in the Old State Building which said "Secretary of State" and introduced himself to the man at the desk. It was the Secretary himself. "My name is John Hay," he said. "What can I do for you?" Hay was Lincoln's old private secretary, but the easygoing Government manner in which he was brought up lingered as an ideal almost until World War II.

The New Deal seemed to create Big Government because Government had not kept pace with the growth of the economy before the Crash and the collapse meant that the Federal Government had to take over the public works that bankrupt states and local authorities could no longer do. And Government loomed larger on the horizon because business stood still: almost half of the very modest rise in the Gross National Product during the Depression decade was in goods and services provided by Federal, state, and local governments. This phenomenon is not confined to Depression. In the affluent 1960s, jobs are being created much faster in Government service than in

230

manufacturing, and very few of them are designed as work relief "boondoggles."

The New Deal did not reform American society. It did not reach the poorest. It did not cut down the richest. All this would have been forgiven if it had restored the steady growth that Americans expected to make everyone richer every year. But for the first time in American memory, economic growth simply stopped. The economy teetered for ten years on dead center. Roosevelt tried almost everything suggested, although he did not stick to anything very long.

Roosevelt first tried a little inflation, but his manipulation of the gold content of the dollar in the fall of 1933 failed to price the dollar low enough for American farm products to compete in the foreign market. Going off gold did not solve the problems of a creditor in international balances. The Federal Reserve Board occasionally dropped the rediscount rate to almost nothing, but interest rates simply did not have the influence claimed for them by classical economic theory. Business prospects were so low that no one could be found to invest money even if it were to be had for the asking.

Government spending is the antipoverty measure most frequently ascribed to Roosevelt. Conservatives assailed him for falsely assuming that we could "spend our way to prosperity." Liberals credit him still with acting on the advice of British economist John Maynard Keynes, who made a technical case for Government ordering of the volume of investment in his 1936 book, *The General Theory of Employment, Interest, and Money*. But for all the contemporary talk of spending, taxing, and electing, the New Deal never intended to spend its way to prosperity and never spent enough to give pump priming a fair trial. Keynes himself said as much. The deficits that conservatives bemoaned were simply too small to get the economy moving.

Nothing Roosevelt or anyone else did could get the economy

231

moving ahead again. The statistics tell the story of standstill. Industrial production in 1939 was exactly the same as in 1929, but thanks to "progress," two million fewer workers were needed to make it, and there were ten million more consumers to share it than in 1929. After a decade that had added six million workers to the labor force, ten million people were still looking for work.

10

$ $ $ $ $

WELFARE CAPITALISM

THERE had been a time in America when a man could put his occupation down as "capitalist" as unaffectedly as Stalin's daughter once gave her father's occupation as "revolutionary." After the Crash of 1929, the word "capitalism" was used approvingly to describe the American system, but no one willingly described himself as a capitalist by occupation. Cartoonists made it clear that a capitalist was an overfed man in a high silk hat who lived luxuriously on his money.

There had never been very many capitalists. Historian Frederick Rudolph figures that the American Liberty League did well in attracting 75,000 members, because there were no more than 150,000 Americans who stood to gain more than they lost by its program of unrestricted "freedom" for capitalism. In 1936, SEC Chairman Joseph Kennedy, President Kennedy's father, figured that there were no more than 56,000 Americans who drew more than $10,000 a year in dividends, the income required for the lush living pictured in the cartoons. By Joseph Kennedy's definition, capitalists were no more numerous in the land of capitalism than members of the Communist Party,

233

U.S.A. Add 750,000 heads of firms employing more than three persons, and there were some 800,000 active capitalists who lived by risking their own money, although many of these smaller capitalists did not ordinarily wear high silk hats. In 1960 there were 60 million more people in the country, but hardly any more who could qualify as capitalists under this definition. The vast majority of the top-income people worked for a living.

What happened to the idle rich? The Andrew Freedman Home for "destitute millionaires" did not experience the avalanche of applications in the 1930s that my father had led me to imagine. The Crash wiped out the speculators and the new-rich, but it merely dented the book value of the old American fortunes. If anything, fewer genuine capitalists were bankrupted than in the short, sharp deflation following World War I, when W. C. Durant lost General Motors, and the Armours lost control of their meat-packing business and might even have had to reduce their scale of living if it had not been for the fluky success of a worthless oil stock that Ogden Armour had bought for fun.

Nor is it likely that many stopped risking their money and retired to Bermuda, where the tax rates were kinder, although some of them talked of quitting. Atwater Kent, mass producer and first impresario of radio, retired from business in June 1936, shortly after the society pages carried word that he and his family were headed for Bar Harbor for the summer. An individualist who refused to drive the same car two days running, Kent hated Roosevelt so much that some said he did not want to be in business while That Man was President. *Radio Weekly* speculated that he got out because profits would never again be as big, and "as the possessor of a large personal fortune he is believed to be preparing for a period of rest and recreation." *Time* thought he was just bored with the radio business and had not found another to his fancy. But Kent was an exception.

234

Disenchantment with business may have been the reason why many sons of enterprisers dropped out of business to pursue nonprofit careers. Millionaire liberals like Marshall Field and Corliss Lamont rebelled against their fathers by joining the ideological protest against the system that had made their fathers powerful. A larger number rebelled less noisily by identifying themselves with welfare, education, politics, science, or the arts. Nelson Rockefeller is self-made in politics, and one of his sons lost his life in the noncapitalist pursuit of collecting primitive art in New Guinea. Alfred Sloan's brother Harold took his share of the proceeds of the sale of the family business (to General Motors) and has worked ever since on research in education. Paul Mellon, the son of Andrew Mellon, is a philanthropist, and Dr. William L. Mellon, Jr., and his wife have spent their lives as medical missionaries in Haiti. (In 1965, *The Wall Street Journal* complained that few Ivy League college graduates were going into business, and college teachers had the impression that genuinely upper-class young men were more likely than formerly to choose unpublicized or unpopular work in churches, museums, archeological digs, scientific research, the American Friends Service Committee, labor unions, and most recently the Peace Corps and the Congress of Racial Equality.)

It seemed as though there were fewer capitalists than actually existed, because those who stayed in business laid aside their silk hats and tried hard to live down the stereotype of the "capitalist." The original empire builders talked—or refused to talk —depending on how they felt at the time. When Commodore Vanderbilt petulantly pushed aside a question about the public interest, saying, "The public be damned!" he had no intention of consigning the entire population to eternal hell. He simply did not realize that special art is required to say what you mean, or even to look natural in public, and special art is

235

probably required for people who wield power to get the message across straight, even when they speak in private.

The New Deal forced capitalists to listen. Burrelle's Press Clipping Service grew from a little business serving individuals who liked to see their names in print to a fat contractor with corporations. Industrial leaders who had never been criticized generally reacted to what they read about themselves with wounded rage, but a few learned the art of talking to the public.

Theodore Vail, the manager who created the Bell System, taught telephone operators to cultivate "the voice with the smile" to avoid attacks that could have led to "postalization" or Government operation of the phone service like the mails. Response to public opinion became a habit with the phone company. When The New York Telephone Company had to lay off employees in 1938, for instance, it offered them a bonus for retiring and saw to it that the offer was well publicized. In the 1960s, the phone company is not reproached for installing machinery to put people out of jobs, although it is the most widely automated industry in the country.

Some industries had made constructive responses to the muckrakers who attacked them around the turn of the century. Before World War I, a *Wall Street Journal* reporter by the name of Pendleton Dudley had persuaded the Chicago meat-packers to invite the public in to see the conditions surrounding the slaughterhouses that writer Upton Sinclair exposed in his novel titled *The Jungle*. Ivy Lee, a New York newspaper reporter who had shown the Pennsylvania Railroad Company how to get news of wrecks in and out of the newspapers fast by releasing all the news the first day, advised John D. Rockefeller, Jr., to meet newspapermen personally and to show them that all Rockefellers were not as bad as muckraking journalists had painted them. The program was so successful that the name Rockefeller has since become an asset in politics.

236

Businessmen hastened to adopt the tactics these leaders had developed. U.S. Steel, Bethlehem Steel, General Motors, International Harvester, Pittsburgh Plate Glass, and the New York Central Railroad set up public-relations departments during the 1930s. Pendleton Dudley and Ivy Lee had built modest practices as "public relations consultants" before the Depression. During the 1930s, Carl Byoir, John Hill, and Earl Newsom opened public-relations consulting offices, too. All aimed at creating enduring goodwill rather than tootling isolated sales "messages" by publicity.

A classic incident of the Pecora investigation of Wall Street in 1933 distinguished between publicity, the art of getting attention, and public relations, the art of making oneself understood by the public. In 1933, a Barnum & Bailey Circus press agent popped a midget on the knee of the younger J. P. Morgan when he was testifying before the Senate committee and snapped a memorable picture. That was good publicity for the circus.

Morgan's reaction was a problem in public relations. A natural reflex for this dignified man would have been to brush the intruder off his knee, but this would merely have created a photograph that would have portrayed him in the ungentle and uncharacteristic act of scuffling with a childlike woman. Morgan was startled, and he may simply have been slow to react, but his acceptance of the intruder was good public relations. The picture that resulted went around the world bearing its double message: good publicity for the circus, sympathy for J. P. Morgan. The picture eventually created a tragedy. A few years later, the midget, little Lyra Schwarz, returned to her native Germany, where she was recognized by Hitler's race purifiers and sent to the gas chamber as a Jew, a defective, and thanks to the picture, a "tool of Wall Street."

Capitalists did not enjoy a good press, but many individuals continued to build enterprises in much the same way the founders of the great American fortunes had done. The Hartfords

237

made the A & P grow. Thomas J. Watson expanded IBM. Edgar Queeny more than tripled Monsanto Chemical Company's profits between 1929 and 1937. Lammot du Pont, seventh president and sixth "of the name," added more than $300 million to the assets of E. I. du Pont de Nemours between 1930 and 1940. Walter Chrysler challenged General Motors and Ford during a decade in which automobile companies were going out of business.

These facts were exceptional because manufacturing as a whole did not grow at all between 1930 and 1940. Big business remained virtually unchanged. Seven of the ten biggest manufacturing corporations, according to assets, in 1930 were among the ten biggest in 1940. All but four of the top ten of 1930 on the list below ended the decade with fewer assets than they had started with. The minus sign before the name means that the company lost assets between 1930 and 1940; the plus sign means it gained assets. The numbers in parentheses are, in sequence, rank orders for 1940 and 1963.

— U.S. Steel Corporation (2,4)
+ Standard Oil Company of New Jersey (1,1)
+ General Motors Corporation (3,2)
— Bethlehem Steel Corporation (6,13)
— Anaconda Copper Mining (11,26)
— Ford Motor Company (8,3)
+ Standard Oil Company of New York (Soc-Vac.Oil Co.) (4,5)
+ Standard Oil Company of Indiana (7,9)
— Gulf Oil Corporation (12,6)
+ Shell Union Oil Corporation (15,14)

In 1940, Du Pont, Texaco, and Standard Oil of California replaced Gulf, Shell, and Anaconda Copper on the list of the top ten companies. (Anaconda Copper appeared on the 1930 list only because its capital stock had been bloated by speculative issues.)

238

The most striking aspect of this list is the uncanny lack of movement at the top. But it also dramatizes a significant difference between the companies that gained in assets and rank order and those that dropped behind. The companies that grew and rose were all companies that were no longer run by capitalists. All of them were in the hands of hired professional managers who chose their own successors and ran the show without intervention by the beneficial owners, even in the most unusual crises.

The duel between Ford and General Motors in the key automobile industry is an epic of the change. Henry Ford was the charismatic hero of mass production. He ran the company as a personal possession. He tried to lick the Depression singlehandedly by cutting prices. But he could not cope with the social order he had helped to create, let alone the 75-percent drop in car and truck sales between 1929 and 1932. Like the worst of the decadent Roman emperors, he did not trust anyone who could have coped for him. As Depression deepened, Ford sales fell below those of General Motors and even of Chrysler.

His rival, General Motors, was the model and in large part the creator of the rising management system. This system was born not in the automobile business, but in the chemical industry, where technological advance dealt more ruthlessly with enterprise. In the stock-market drop of 1920, the Du Ponts used their war profits to buy General Motors at a bargain. They managed it the Du Pont way.

Like the Rockefellers, whose oil companies gained on their competitors in the Depression too, the du Ponts did not regard their enterprises as fields for personal expression. Both families disciplined heirs to administer the business as a trust. Du Ponts bred sons and acquired sons-in-law competent enough to run the business. None of the grandsons of John D. Rockefeller went into the oil business. But both families devised ways of separat-

239

ing ownership from control so that members of the family could work in the business, if they chose, without personally exercising the authority of their ownership as distinguished from the moral authority they exerted because they had grown up in the tradition of the business. And in both families, the tradition was to seek out the ablest men, reward them handsomely, and give them authority and status to develop the business as if it were their own.

In 1920, Pierre du Pont and du Pont son-in-law Donaldson Brown took over General Motors. They drafted Alfred P. Sloan, Jr., an industrialist who had followed his Hyatt Ball Bearing Company into General Motors, to bring to the automobile company the management techniques the du Ponts had developed to cope with the complexities of the technologically advanced chemical industry. Because the chemical industry sprouts by-products, the du Ponts learned to decentralize operations by product. Because scientific research threatened existing products, they had to do their own research, and do it well enough to keep new discoveries in the company.

Running an organization of this kind required conscious thought about the authority of each officer. The du Ponts and the Rockefeller companies that faced the same technological problems defined and delegated responsibility, decentralized authority so each decision could be made at the lowest possible level, and developed internal accounting techniques to measure the profitability of each activity so that responsibility could be located and performance rewarded or penalized on an impersonal basis. Both organizations began thinking further ahead than other companies of their time, Du Pont because it was heavily committed to long-range scientific research, of which nylon was a first fruit, and the oil companies because they were using up the oil they owned. Once they had looked ahead, both organizations started to plan beyond the lifetimes of the men at the helm to develop successors on a systematic basis.

240

Under this impetus, General Motors became a federation of business enterprises supporting a top-management policy group that raised money and devoted itself full time to scanning the outside world and the future. When the Depression came, General Motors made a profit and paid dividends every year, and financed a carefully planned expansion entirely out of earnings. Sloan credits the new system of financial and operating controls —"We had simply learned how to react quickly," he says. Instead of cutting prices in hope of expanding the market, as Ford had done to his harm, General Motors was able to figure the market and then cut production to the level that would supply it at the highest profit to General Motors.

Liberal economists blamed this "administered pricing" for prolonging the Depression by keeping prices high, but it was a gyroscopic device for keeping the ship on an even keel by floating with the tide. When Sloan and Brown retired in 1937, they left the company in the hands of a network of managers trained to operate in a self-perpetuating system designed to make the corporation immortal. The system called for two or three backstops for every job attached to the company and compensation so liberal that competitors could not afford to buy GM men away. By 1933, the GM bonus system had made millionaires of 80 employees.

While General Motors was setting an example to the rest of industry, Ford was dropping behind. Henry Ford himself grew more erratic, more suspicious, and more dictatorial. Records were not kept. Good men left. World War II rescued the company and supported it until Henry Ford II, the founder's grandson, inherited it and rebuilt it to health by copying General Motors.

His hardest job was to attract the kind of able managers that General Motors had developed. When he employed Ernest R. Breech, president of Bendix Aviation, Breech was not sure he wanted to work for a company dominated by one family. "I

241

liked my job at Bendix," he recalls. "I named my own board of directors there." By the end of the decade, many salaried presidents were setting their own salaries and deciding on dividends, expansion, and financing.

What really happened to the capitalists was that they simply faded out of power. The uncanny standstill of the economy and the disappearance of speculation as a road to riches put power in the hands of the "executives" and "managers." Management rule—the loaded word is "bureaucracy"—seems inevitable when industry is fully developed. Even Russian industry is increasingly run by professional managers rather than by Communist Party politicians. In the United States, the Depression made manufacturing mature faster than it might have done if growth had continued. The transition was already well advanced in the railroads, the oil companies, and the telephone system.

In the black year 1932, A. A. Berle, Jr., and Gardiner Means shocked even the sophisticated by demonstrating that in 1929, the year of the Crash, two-thirds of the 200 biggest corporations, representing nearly half the nation's wealth, were controlled by their hired managers, in some cases by a legal device that prevented stockholders from influencing operations. Berle and Means were concerned about the threat of this arrangement to capitalist incentives and the concept of private property, but the point was missed. Their book, *The Modern Corporation and Private Property*, became a bestseller because it underlined the helplessness of a small stockholder who had just been wrung out in the stock market. The book confirmed the fear of many liberals that the "interests" were getting firmer control of more of the country's wealth than ever before.

The real situation was both better and in an unexpected way more alarming than the popular forebodings. The speculative stock issues of the Twenties had diluted the holdings of the old founders to "working control"—15 to 25 percent of the stock or less, so they legally controlled far more productive capacity

242

than they owned, but in practice they increasingly left the exercise of this control to self-effacing professional salaried managers. So it became harder and harder to find out who was in charge and hold him responsible for what happened. There were times during the early Depression when U.S. Steel, the nation's biggest manufacturer, floundered like an abandoned battleship.

In America, large-scale enterprises went through three stages. They were founded by a dynamic enterpriser, then administered by his heirs or designees as the "shadow of a man," and finally, if they survived, were handled by a management system in which young managers were reared, which provided for its own succession almost like a living cell. So oil men talk of the "Rockefeller influence" and International Harvester men of the "McCormick influence" quite independently of any particular Rockefellers or McCormicks, or any influence they might be able to exert as stockholders.

The steel industry found the transition hazardous. Stock in U.S. Steel and in Bethlehem Steel was so widely distributed by 1929 that Berle and Means classified them as management-controlled, but they spent a good part of the Depression decade recovering from the one-man rule of their founders. When Judge Gary died in 1927, J. P. Morgan himself became chairman of the board of U.S. Steel and brought in Myron Taylor, a crack reorganizer and refinancer of textile companies, to write off some optimistically valued assets and sort out overlapping subsidiaries. As losses mounted, U.S. Steel spent $3 million on three management consulting firms who produced 204 volumes of analysis. In 1937 the management was streamlined. Ben Fairless, a career steelman, was made president. A new subsidiary company was formed to make policy for all of U.S. Steel, as executive committees were doing for the Rockefellers and du Ponts.

Transition was smoother at Bethlehem, where Eugene Grace gradually took over direction from Charles Schwab, who had

243

lasted until 1939. Both the big steel companies did poorly compared with Republic Steel, which Tom Girdler ran with little direction from stockholder interests, and National Steel, whose board chairman, E. T. Weir, ran the company without interference from the representatives of the 28-percent stock interest held by the M. A. Hanna Company.

The influence of bankers may have a lot to do with the financial, political, and technological conservatism of U.S. Steel, its tin ear for public reaction to price rises, and the subordination of all other business goals, including profit, to making sure it could pay the interest on its bonds. These bankerlike attitudes, in turn, may have had something to do with the poor showing U.S. Steel made in the Depression, compared with nimbler steel companies. The phone company, which has at least as big an appetite for new capital as steel, early freed itself from banker control and made more than a million friends by raising equity money from small shareholders to whom it paid the magic $9 dividend all through the lean years.

A.T.&T., now a model of management, matured into the stage of management control before World War I. Theodore Vail, who became president in 1907, chose his successor, and by the time Walter Gifford became president in 1925 there was no question of his right to do the same. The railroads had bankers on their boards, and those more bankrupt than others were somewhat more influenced by these outsiders, but operations were firmly in the hands of men who had "learned how to run a railroad" from the bottom up. Public utilities had been through speculative fireworks, but the operating companies at the base of the holding companies had settled into bureaucracy before the Public Utilities Holding Company Act of 1935.

Manufacturing companies were not so far along in the evolution to professional management, if only because the big ones were closer to their founders. Of the ten biggest for 1930 listed above, only the four Rockefeller oil companies—Standard Oil of New York, New Jersey, Indiana, and California—went into the Depression under managements clearly able to name their successors. Although the Rockefellers held from 10 to 20 percent of the stock of these companies, the last apparent interventions were the ousting of the president of Standard Oil of Indiana by John D. Rockefeller in 1929 and the sale of Jersey company bonds to Rockefeller foundations in 1936. The tradition of an inside board of directors confined to operating officers of the company who met daily dated from the old Standard Oil Trust, and no Rockefeller would have dreamed of telling "the men who knew oil" what to do.

All four Rockefeller oil companies grew during the decade. Eugene Holman, who presided over the rise of the big Jersey company to the top of the list, was an organization man who came up as a geologist. The only other top oil company to grow was Texaco. Berle and Means classified it as management-controlled in 1929, but in 1935 the directors replaced the president with Torkild Rieber, a Norwegian tanker captain who had helped founding speculator Joseph Cullinan build the 1905 oil strike at Spindletop, Texas, into a major property. In 1940, fiery "Cap" Rieber boasted to reporters that he was responsible only to himself. Shell and Gulf, the two oil companies on the top-ten list for 1930 that lost out during the next decade, were both owner-controlled.

The new managers gained on the old proprietors in numbers as well as in power. Proprietors on and off farms contributed 17 percent of the national income in 1929, but only 11 percent at the census of 1960, while they fell even further in numbers from 22 to 14 percent of the labor force engaged in production. The biggest drop occurred in farm proprietors, down to four percent from 12 percent at the Crash. Meanwhile, professional, technical, and managerial workers steadily multiplied, and by the time of the census of 1960, these brainworkers displaced coupon clippers in the highest income brackets.

The shift involved the same people. Just as the Soviet commissars were apt to be the sons of the bourgeoisie the Revolution supposedly liquidated, so the new managers were apt to be drawn from the families of the old proprietors who had run production as beneficial owners. Many of the sons of the old founders quietly converted themselves into professional managers in the very companies they would formerly have inherited, sometimes working harder to prove their managerial competence than if they had not been burdened with the company name.

Four sons of founder G.F. Swift were active in the management of the meat-packing company all through the decade, although the family had only seven percent of the stock left; by 1940, when assets were far below 1930, three sons were working under a professional chief executive. Fowler McCormick, grandson of John D. Rockefeller and founder Cyrus McCormick, worked in International Harvester under outsiders all through the 1930s, then became president in 1941; the first president of the name since 1922, he was ousted as chief executive in 1951 and replaced by a man who had started with the company as a clerk. Five sons of founder Harvey Firestone spent the decade working at Firestone Tire and Rubber under the presidency of an early associate of their father; Harvey Firestone, Jr., became president in 1941.

Theoretically, at least, the management system opened opportunity a crack wider to talent than it could in the economies of Western Europe, where the family firm prevails in large part to this very day. Careful and even anxious studies of the origins of business leaders agree that the poor, well-educated boy has had a little more chance to become president since the management revolution in the United States than before it, yet the evidence is not conclusive. The men who started working in the Depression and reached the top in the 1950s were better educated than their predecessors in the top jobs, if only because all boys stayed in school longer during the Depression. But the studies show, too, that their fathers were less apt to have been farmers, railroad men, small-business men, or laborers, and more apt to have been executives or company men than the fathers of the men who preceded them in the top jobs. At no time in American history have many really poor and uneducated boys reached the very top.

The management system meant that a founder could find a bright young man and groom him to run the business, if his own sons were not qualified. Sociologists James C. Abegglen and W. Lloyd Warner psychoanalyzed the new management men as mobile in the sense that they were well equipped psychologically to form relationships with father-figures and break them easily when there was an advantage in leaving.

Companies that went through the second stage of management by the founder's crown prince during the 1930s were being run by men who had been chosen for the top job by their authoritarian predecessors. Gerard Swope chose C. E. Wilson of General Electric as his successor; Alfred Sloan chose "Engine" Charley (of the same name but no kin) to head General Motors. President K. T. Keller of Chrysler was a protégé of Walter Chrysler from Buick days. W. Alton Jones of Cities Service became president because he was amiable enough to get along with founder Doherty during his pain-ridden last years. Eugene Grace of Bethlehem Steel was put in by Charley Schwab, who first took a liking to him when the younger man was a yardmaster servicing the chief's private railroad car. The younger men were treated in some ways as if they were sons.

Chance as well as diplomacy played a disproportionate part in a young man's rise to favor under these autocrats. Stanley Allyn, head of National Cash Register, attributes his first big job in the company to an accident that befell its incumbent. John H. Patterson, the dynamic head of National Cash Register, who made selling a way of life, liked to invite his key men to dinner and watch their behavior. On one occasion, he asked each one at the table to tell the story of his life. When one of them paused to finish his soup, Patterson decided he was not eager enough and started looking for a successor. He systematically recruited farm boys because he believed they knew how to work and also knew the value of a dollar. In a short while, Stanley Allyn was moved into the job of the soup-eater.

Those who rose to the top by the arts of political ingratiation were not necessarily equipped to withstand the fearful loneliness when they had arrived at the place where there was no one to ask and no one to please. Neither the divine right of property nor that of kings supported them, and they had been close enough to intuitive genius and luck to mistrust these graces even if they had risen through them, which for the most part they had not.

Old Adam Smith, the ideologue of capitalism, had warned that hired managers would be "disputatious, uninformed and lazy," but the managers, when they took over, proved him wrong. Intelligent, cool, canny, and very eager, they did the very best they could. They prized competence because it was their admission to the élite.

The large-scale enterprises operating under the mature management system, like General Motors and the Rockefeller oil companies, used the loose market for talent to acquire the best. Even during the worst years they sent personnel recruiters to the colleges. Those hired found competition keen and promotions slow, but they worked hard and set standards of diligence that have since become tradition. They did not change jobs lightly. Presidents of the 1960s mostly started with the companies they now head. Fred J. Borch, president of General Electric, says he "camped on the door" of the GE plant at Nela Park, Cleveland, the summer he was out of college, until there was room in the lamp-department budget to hire him at

$115 a month. A Depression pay cut soon had him working for $78 a month. He has never worked for any other company.

It takes a long time to grow an oak tree, and it takes a long time to develop senior management timber. During the long standstill of the Depression, when management as we know it was being created, very few got the chance to learn the art. In the 1960s, men with the experience to be corporation presidents are so rare and so valuable that the industry of executive recruitment has grown up expressly to locate them. Major corporations now pay "headhunters" $3,000 to $15,000 for finding an executive. One obstacle to raiding is that generous fringe benefits tend to keep managers put. The result has been that American corporations have acquired personalities and provided a complete life for managers, from training squad to retirement program. The demand for security and the profit in supplying it to key men have made American corporations feudal in the sense that they exercise political, economic, and social authority without separating these spheres of life. American corporations are a little like the great Japanese zaibatsu or federations of enterprises in different fields that provide employees with lifelong security in exchange for total loyalty.

These chosen men became wary of criticism and eager to depersonalize leadership into system. The old rich had admired Mussolini because he made the trains run on time, but the more bookish of the new managers admitted, among themselves, that there might be a lot to learn from Machiavelli, whose dispassionate analysis of the art of political power had been "misinterpreted" by the liberals. They prized smooth, efficient relationships with Government as well as with employees and customers.

They tried to be scientific. All the factors that the dynamic old man had countered with magic and moralisms were to be analyzed, generalized, and ultimately controlled. Men, money, markets, prices, profits, a better mousetrap, and a good name

249

were to be planned by market research, aptitude testing and training, cost and target price accounting, team scientific research, and professional public relations. One of the unexpected gains was a more decent treatment of labor. The "scientific" labor-relations consultant brought a sheaf of figures on job performance and wage differentials to the bargaining table, instead of injured paternalism. Mill villages, garden plots, and patronizing fringe benefits evaporated unlamented.

The management system aimed to make the corporation live forever. It provided for making business decisions independent of the health or even the wisdom of any one individual, and a system for steering by these decisions that worked automatically. Academic disciplines were ransacked for the job. Behavioral sciences—and even art and literature—supplied techniques for identifying and forecasting what customers wanted, finding customers and selling them, and recruiting talent. Techniques from accounting like the annual budget, and from engineering like statistical quality control, were adapted to spot waste and policy deviation faster than the supervisory eye. Techniques from politics—particularly the Federal ideas of decentralization and the checks and balances of the Constitution —were imported to cope with organization sprawl.

Staff specialists were consulted on more relations than Henry Ford knew he had—industrial, community, supplier, Government, labor, and transcending these, public relations. Invention was no longer to be left to chance, but programmed, priced, and entrusted to teams of salaried scientists hired to keep a watch as well as a jump on technological advance.

In newly professionalized companies, managers did not know enough about these arts to reproduce the success of General Motors, Du Pont, and the oil companies, so they bought outside advice. Management consultants flourished sometimes surreptitiously. "Efficiency experts" were feared because they put men out of work.

250

Efficiency became a bad word. Don't cut costs, Roosevelt begged manufacturers at the Jefferson Day dinner of 1936, for there is no way to do it without hurting people. "One way is by the development of new machinery and new techniques and by increasing employee efficiency. We do not discourage that. But do not dodge the fact that this means fewer men employed and more men unemployed."

Charles Bedaux, a former sandhog who invented a piece-rate system that encouraged pacesetters and penalized the less nimble, was so hated that in 1937 the Duke and Duchess of Windsor hastily canceled plans to visit the United States as his guests. To salaried executives fearful for their jobs—a sizable population in 1932—consultants were Rasputin-like "doctors of business" called in to hatchet for squeamish owners. Professor J. O. McKinsey was widely credited with a "ruthless" reorganization of Marshall Field & Company. As chairman of the board, he put the big store in the black after five years of Depression losses by lopping off its ailing wholesale business, consolidating its sprawling textile mills, and tightening up all down the line. Professor McKinsey died in 1937, leaving his name to McKinsey & Co., Inc., now a leading management consultant so scrupulously professional in its relationships with blue-chip companies that it refuses to recruit executives for them for fear of appearing to raid other clients.

The hated "efficiency experts" had been more active before the Depression. Time and motion studies had been invented before World War I. Productivity per man-hour of factory labor had been more important in the boom when added production could be easily sold, and the only way to get it out of incompletely mechanized processes was, in the quaint phrase of pioneer management scientist Henry Gantt, by "Training Workmen in Habits of Industry and Cooperation."

According to the American Society of Mechanical Engineers, the Twenties saw greatest management progress in worker productivity, cost accounting, budgetary controls, standard costs, waste elimination, job standardization (including "micromotion" methods), materials handling, and dealing with the "human factor" in industries, including understanding the economic value of high wages, short hours, safety, and better working conditions.

In the Depression decade, the consultants attacked reorganization of the front office inhabited by the new professional managers. The ASME review for the 1930s bristles with talk about decentralization, line and staff relationships, freeing top management for policymaking, delegation of authority to the lowest possible level, advisory committee, written definitions for managerial jobs, channels of communication inside the corporation, integrating scientific research with operations, the identification and isolation of "housekeeping" functions.

Opinion was divided on the performance of the professionals. Some felt they were cold-blooded and not as willing as the old millowner to make sacrifices to keep the mill people employed. Austrian-born Harvard economist Joseph Schumpeter thought the managers were dooming capitalism by their timid "employee attitude." Even when the manager is a stockholder, Schumpeter observed, his "will to fight and hold on is not and cannot be what it was with the man who knew ownership and its responsibilities in the full-blooded sense of these words."

Defense came from the other side of the Charles River at Cambridge, where professional managers flocking in to the Harvard Business School for short courses were proving to be the world's most attentive students. There, Professor Sumner Schlichter credited the professional managers with making the economy much safer from depression by scientific management, longer-range planning, systematic scientific research, and better control of inventories, while the new decentralization encouraged experiment and enterprise under the corporate umbrella.

Eloquent and principled defense came monthly from *Fortune*

magazine, a hit with the new managers and a success from the day it started in inauspicious 1930. In 1940, *Fortune* declared that "30,000 managers earning $15,000 to $200,000 plus drive the economic system and coddle 56,000 capitalists." The article reported a rift between stockholders and management in 10 of 14 companies and asserted that the managers could end the Depression if the owners would only give them their heads.

Genuine capitalists, like the Mellons, had no explanation or remedy for the Depression, and when Congressional committees and reporters asked them they genuinely felt that business conditions were beyond analysis or cure by the hand of man. In 1933, even *Fortune* had argued that business had no social responsibility for the suffering caused by the Depression, because noneconomic behavior would interfere with the supposedly benign workings of the free market. Even now there are those who maintain that it would have been better for business to leave social responsibility to the democratically elected Government and confine itself to making a profit within the rules the Government made. We do not know whether it would have been better, because it did not happen.

Like Commodore Vanderbilt, the old millowner may not have cared what the public thought. In his own mind, at least, his right to do as he pleased with his property was written in the laws of God and man. But the hired manager had no such mandate. As this new man surveyed the world from behind his mahogany desk, he was not sure by what right he sat there, or even by what route he had come. Silence on succession to power is as serious a problem to U.S. management as the corresponding ambiguity on the succession of the Soviet presidium. A Soviet board and an American corporate board both follow unwritten customs in choosing successors or deferring to the judgment of one of their number that baffle outsiders, particularly subordinates.

The lack of what the political scientists call "legitimacy"

253

makes both groups more sensitive to criticism than it is quite safe for the wielders of substantial power to be. If American corporate officers sometimes seem to be unduly upset at press comment that is merely informal, the reason is that they are painfully aware that their own power is uncomfortably informal and undefined.

In this predicament, the doctrine of service to distant "publics" was welcome ideological cover. Instead of a hotly contested prize that could be spent in personal grandeur, profit became a bookkeeping device for measuring the competence of the manager in running the enterprise, not for himself, not even for his bosses, but for the employees, the customers, the suppliers, and even the general public. By this time, of course, the beneficial owners were no longer in a position to object. If their hired managers contributed some of the company's money to a college or raised salaries, they could only grumble —their complaint merely made work for the public-relations department charged with treating stockholders as one of the company's publics.

The National Association of Manufacturers adopted the suggestion of General Foods Chairman Colby Chester to promote "The American Way" with an advertising campaign ("What Is America All About?") and a publicity campaign on the high American standard of living and the performance of American business. The public generally yawned at these messages, but the men who paid for them bought them, and that was important.

The very process of getting out of trouble with the public directed the attention of the old-style capitalists to public opinion. Public-relations counselors helped many of them to see the public interest, in some cases for the first time. Broadly speaking, they profited by the conversion. The successful enterprises that have grown big since the Depression have been those that

254

accepted social responsibility and sincerely tried to do more than make a profit.

Most brokers fumed at SEC regulations and New Deal insinuations against the stock exchange. But when a survey showed that people who knew the stock exchange was not a cattle market thought it was crooked, stockbrokers Merrill Lynch, Pierce, Fenner & Beane (now Smith) adopted a policy of no hot tips, no inside dope, and frank disclosure of its interest in recommended stocks. The policy is credited with establishing a new order on Wall Street, but it also helped to earn this firm the nickname "We the People" and make it the biggest broker of all time.

Social responsibility came late to industries like automobiles, which had never known criticism. Neither Ford, an autocrat with his own Gestapo, nor General Motors, brought up in the silent du Pont tradition, realized at first that labor policy could influence customers. The turning point came in the sitdown strike of 1937, when the United Auto Workers aimed fast, fresh releases at newspapers while General Motors could not reply until its statement was approved by a meeting of the board of directors. When newsman Felix Bruner went to work for GM as publicity director, he found President William Knudsen beset by a dozen reporters trying to read a telegram over his shoulder. Bruner suggested copying it for them. "Who the hell are you?" Knudsen asked.

After the two became friends, GM developed a hard-hitting information program under Paul Garret, with a public-relations group sitting in with the high command.

At first the A & P thought that customers cared only about prices. Sometimes they temporarily set prices low enough to drive neighborhood competition out of business. They ran their stores from headquarters and disdained to advertise in local papers. They got the business, but they were cordially hated as murderers of the American dream of a little business of one's own. A middle-aged woman with a good job in New York recalls that as a little girl she was told it was all right to snatch groceries from the A & P, but wrong to steal from little Mom-and-Pop stores. In part to make up for pilferage, for which they were held responsible, some A & P managers systematically short-weighted customers.

In 1940, A & P faced virtual extinction. Representative Wright Patman of Texas pushed a bill that proposed to tax chain stores out of existence. Since the tax increased with every branch of the chain, the bill was more damaging to the A & P than to any other chain. A & P hired public-relations counselor Carl Byoir to help defeat the bill.

There was not time to make the A & P better liked, even if that had been possible. Instead, Byoir hammered away in all media on the money that chain stores saved consumers. J. C. Penney, a well-liked, fatherly merchant who made partners out of his storekeepers, spoke in public for all the chains, while the A & P stayed in the background. In addition to stories in newspapers and magazines, Byoir inspired men and women to pop up in organizations of every kind with resolutions against the chain-store tax bill. The campaign defeated the Patman Act, but it also committed the A & P to better treatment of customers than before its time of troubles. The lesson was valuable.

The new and the old way confronted each other dramatically in the epic struggle between Sears, Roebuck & Co. and Montgomery Ward. Like General Motors, Sears pioneered in all the new management techniques. It countered hostility to chain stores by an elaborate program of community relations that helped local managers win goodwill in their communities. It broke new ground in applying behavioral science to finding and training store managers and locating and designing stores.

Ward was run on the old style by Sewell Avery, the tight-lipped, old-style capitalist who had pulled U.S. Gypsum, a company in which he had a substantial interest, through the worst of the Depression by ruthless cost-cutting. Ward was against the New Deal all the way. He thought recovery could come only when prices dropped. He was a man of principle who was literally carried off the business scene by soldiers when he defied a ruling of the War Labor Board in World War II.

The man who made Sears was just the opposite. General Robert Elington Wood was a West Point engineer who came to retailing from the Quartermaster Corps. Wood was interested in developing employees and in trying new ways, and he thought of business as a service rather than as a moneymaking machine. He originally had gone to work for Montgomery Ward, but he left to take a job with Sears in 1924 when Montgomery Ward would not go along with his ideas. He made a profit for Sears in every Depression year, while Montgomery Ward trailed farther and farther behind in the red.

Wood claimed the formula was simple: "The customer comes first, the employee next, and the stockholder last." Wood studied the consumer. Instead of trying to make existing products as cheaply as possible, he developed new products that fitted into the changing way of life he saw around him. He developed suppliers who could mass-produce "class" products. Refrigerators sold well even in the depths of the Depression, so Wood brought out a low-cost Sears refrigerator to capture this market. He was one of the first marketing men to see the potentials of the automobile. One of his achievements for Sears was to top the tire business he himself had launched at Ward's; another was to offer automobile insurance—at low cost, by mail—before the established insurance companies were willing to promote coverage for the new risk. But most decisively, he saw that the family car meant trips to the store, so he added retail stores to the mail-order business.

The consumer was the key to success in the Depression. The big change the Depression made in business was to reward products, firms, and industries that gave consumers what they wanted. This seems platitudinous in retrospect, but it was not so clear at the time. Money had been made first by investing in railroads, steel mills, construction, mining, and factories. In the boom years, money had been made in financing production and selling stock. The Depression hit these "capitalistic" enterprises much harder than "consumeristic" goods and services people needed in daily living that could often be realized with little investment. Real income per capita—spendable money a family had to lay out—did not grow during the Depression decade, but it did continue to be as high as it had been in the boom. Demand for shoes, drugs, foods, soap, cigarettes, clothes, and gas for the old jalopy grew directly with the population. Buses, trucks, gas, electricity, stores, laundries, beauty parlors, stayed in business.

The list of companies that made more money in 1937 than in 1929 showed no railroads and few of the grand old industrial names. Instead, there were newcomers like Coca-Cola and American Chicle; food-container companies, like Libby-Owens-Ford; truck and bus manufacturers who were supplying the new automotive competition to the railroads. There were mail-order houses, cheap specialty stores like Lerner's and Kress, and consumer credit companies beyond the pale of Wall Street. Macy's had won the heart of New York with its timely slogan, "It's Smart to Be Thrifty."

The financial news of the times abounded in mythical explanations for Depression successes. Stove and refrigerator companies did well, it was said, because well-to-do women had fired their cooks and were appalled at the equipment in their own kitchens. American Tobacco increased its earnings in the darkest days because people smoked more to calm the jitters. Sherwin-Williams Company did well not only because it supplied paint to the dented but surviving automobile industry and was able to cut costs, but because "in good times you paint; in depression, you repaint." The Ball Brothers of Mun-

258

cie did well because they made the jars used by women to put up garden vegetables. The bicycle makers had hoped for a hard-times boom in cheap transportation. When people bought bicycles in 1933 for sport, the makers attributed the fad to "the urge of a weary people to return to the vanished past which, for us, is symbolized by the Gay Nineties." All, of course, were things for people, rather than machines for business.

One of the surprises of the Depression was that people were willing to pay for the convenience of disposable paper cups, paper napkins, paper handkerchiefs, nonreturnable bottles and nonrefillable oil cans for gas stations. Sanitary napkins enlarged their market. In 1938, *Fortune* discovered a growth industry with no advertising or selling expense netting 30 percent on sales: the magazine figured that Americans gave $250 million a year to makers of contraceptives, more than they gave to barbers and almost as much as to jewelers.

Big business had traditionally disdained inexpensive consumer goods. Before the Crash, power companies had given away electric light bulbs in order to increase the use of current, and Muzak was developed later for the same purpose. Before the Depression, General Electric bothered with small appliances only to increase demand for its generators. Broadcasting was started in order to increase demand for radio sets. During the Depression, however, the light bulbs, appliances, and entertainment launched as bait became products worth selling in their own right.

"Consumeristic" companies did better than competitors who were farther away from the retail customer. Both Shell and Gulf lost out to the Standard Oil companies because they were slower to develop gas stations as outlets for their products. Gulf had to build its way back by investing in a national system of leased stations. Little Weirton Steel prospered when U.S. Steel did not, because it was long on tinplate needed for

259

food cans. Du Pont widened its lead over its competitors by beating them to the consumer market with products like nylon. Traditionally, chemical companies had never made anything that a housewife could use directly. Their market had been the manufacturers who made goods for her.

Top management attention focused on selling. The sales department became a better ladder to the president's office than engineering and law. During the boom, the sales department had been charged with selling what the factory produced, if need be by tactics borrowed from the old-time religion. When the Depression increased sales "resistance," the art of selling became the science of "marketing," "distribution," or "merchandising." Salesmen demanded a voice in design, pricing, and volume, as well as in the way products were sold. Henry Dreyfuss, Raymond Loewy, Walter Teague, and other pioneer industrial designers urged manufacturers to build sales arguments at the drawing board. Stationary small appliances and washing machines were "streamlined," because the word sounded good.

Anxiety about sales boomed market research. The essential idea was to find out who wanted what kind of mousetrap, where and how urgently, by asking the potential customers themselves, instead of relying on what the president of the company thought they wanted. Young & Rubicam retained opinion pollster George Gallup to study consumer attitudes. In 1933, A. C. Nielsen, back from Bermuda with a few dollars and a bright idea, launched a service that measured the movement of branded merchandise off store shelves. Daniel Starch resigned from the faculty of Harvard to sell "Advertising Effectiveness" reports to advertisers. Energetic young interviewers flooded the country knocking on doors, to bring back masses of hard facts about the customer for the experts to interpret.

Advertising sold itself hard. It thrived well enough to support radio as well as the old print media. George Washington Hill of American Tobacco Company increased advertising expenditures at the worst of the Depression and made it pay in sales. He once spat on the boardroom table to demonstrate his thesis that advertising could compel customers to buy even as it disgusted them. Advertisers cited the anecdote as proof that consumer objections to advertising would not cut its effectiveness. To counterattacks on the credibility of advertising, copywriters wrote "reason-why" advertisements that mimicked science with unnecessarily accurate statistics ("Listerine reduces germs up to 86.7%"), superfluous laboratory equipment (Old Golds were tested for B.T.U.s in an "Oxygen Bomb Calorimeter"), or technical terms that flattered the erudition of the reader (Victor radios had "impregnated condensers," and "pentode tubes with push-pull amplification"). Agencies competed with each other by offering free marketing and merchandising services to clients.

Publicity proved an effective and often a cheaper way of selling goods than advertising. Airlines limping along on mail contracts attracted favorable attention by inventing a glamorous new job for women, the airline "hostess" or fly-girl. She was supposed to keep the passengers, then mostly male businessmen, from brooding on the distance to the ground. Out-of-work newspapermen thought up imaginative publicity campaigns. Cigarettes were sold by publicizing a midget bellboy named Johnny Roventini, immortalized in the commercial, "Call for Philip Morris."

Effective promotions were the annual "Maid of Cotton," of the National Cotton Council, formed to combat competing synthetics; the Cleanliness Institute, founded by soap companies to promote the sale of soap by engaging professional health educators to teach the evils of dirt; campaigns that acquainted everybody with the vitamin value of oranges and raisins; and the conversion of a lonely mountain peak at a place called Ketcham, Idaho, into glamorous Sun Valley— by Steve Hannegan. Hannegan had worked the same magic on a marshy Florida shore by indefatigable service to shorthanded press-association editors who were accustomed to getting bulletins like "HARRY FLEISCHMANN MILLIONAIRE DROPPED DEAD DON'T FORGET MIAMI BEACH DATELINE."

Advertising was a "growth industry" in the Depression. So was publicity. So were magazines. *Life, Look, Fortune,* and *Esquire* were all launched in the Depression, and all of them did well. Even writers did well by comparison with other professional workers. A list of the new "industries" of the Depression discloses ideas; many of them were ideas like the postage meter and the self-service supermarket, which could be developed on a shoestring with ingenious promotion.

The easy labor market made little service businesses practical, and some of them did well enough to survive prosperity. Chock Full O' Nuts was started by a Columbia University graduate who switched to peddling nuts on a prime corner in midtown Manhattan when the drugstore on the block objected to his selling candy. The day of the Crash, Mike Meehan happened to have put $500,000 into an ice cream company. In order to protect it, he developed the "Good Humor" franchise, which pushed ice cream wherever a customer had a nickel or a dime to spend. Albert Lau, another Wall Streeter, gave up trying to sell stocks and bonds to go into the baby laundry business. He franchised Dy-Dee enterprises all over the country, in some cases to unemployed college graduates who had the time and the enterprise to pursue new mothers in their homes.

Bright boys thought up marvelous ways to make a living and to put themselves through college. A.M. Sullivan, of Dun & Bradstreet, tells about a young man who went from house to house buying up old refrigerators that wouldn't work, repairing them, and reselling them at a profit. Another canvasser built a business ringing doorbells to collect old clothes housewives had been thinking of mending and bringing them to a

262

tailor who did the work at bargain rates. Many a young man took a short course in cookery from his mother before setting out to sell pots and pans by demonstrating them to housewives in their own kitchens.

The very day the money stopped, March 6, 1933, Mary Lasker, the medical philanthropist, then an attractive young working girl, incorporated Hollywood Patterns to bring Paris styles to handy American women like herself who had more taste than money. In 1930, 16-year-old Mary Martin, then a new mother in Weatherford, Texas, had started a dancing school in a storage loft with two pupils who agreed to pay two dollars a month for "class" lessons and one pupil who paid four dollars a month for private lessons. By the end of the first month she had thirty pupils, and in six months she had schools in nearby towns and money enough to go to Hollywood to learn professional dance teaching, and to eventual fame and fortune as a singer.

There was a lush consumer market for goods and services waiting to be exploited, but established firms did not see it. Economists and optimistic public speakers pointed out the opportunities again and again. If industry would only develop new products, they said, prosperity would return. In 1937, sociologist William F. Ogburn of the University of Chicago predicted 13 job-creating innovations. But no one took him seriously.

The only innovation on Ogburn's list that came during the Depression was house trailers. Facsimile transmission, helicopters, and the photoelectric cell remained gadgets of limited use. Tray agriculture, gasoline from coal, synthetic rubber, and, to some extent, synthetic fabrics and plastics were shelved until the commodities they replaced became scarce. Television could have come before the war, if anyone had been willing to put up the money for it. Air-conditioning was not pioneered by the big manufacturers who were equipped to launch it, but by

Willis Carrier, an engineer who had rough going licking the production problems as well as selling it. Theaters and hotels thought they could not afford it and sometimes agreed with their competitors not to install it. Prefabricated housing and the cotton picker were delayed by fear that they would eliminate jobs.

The cotton picker has a significant history. The cotton gin created the economy of poor sharecroppers by making cotton a profitable crop. Almost a century later, Southerners saw any alternative to the unsatisfactory system as economic disaster. When John and Mack Rust demonstrated a cotton picker that would do the work of up to a hundred field hands, Boss Ed Crump of Memphis suggested outlawing the machine. The Rust brothers refused to let a big company develop the invention for fear it would be promoted without consideration for the labor it displaced. They tried to invent a small machine that could be sold cheaply enough to ordinary farmers to recoup the investment and keep control in their own hands. They tried to raise money to build pickers they would lease to farmers who would agree to minimum wages. They offered model machines to farm cooperatives and hoped the Southern Tenant Farmers Union, a socialist organization, would be able to finance mass production. In desperation they tried to set up a nonprofit foundation to develop and sell pickers.

All attempts to raise money with strings attached to the use of the machines failed. In 1942, Mack Rust went into the custom harvesting business in the Southwest, where new cotton lands had no tradition of farm tenancy, slavery, or paternalism. The cotton picker did not become economic until it was developed and sold by International Harvester and Allis Chalmers after the war had shaken up the growing of cotton as a welfare operation.

Rumors that big companies suppressed inventions that would put some product out of the market were exaggerated. But

264

there was a grain of truth in the contention of Charles F. Kettering, General Motors engineering chief, that bankers opposed scientific research as a danger to existing investment. Motels, transistors, neon lights, the self-service supermarket and the oxygenation process in steel were all resisted by the leading concerns already in these fields who by rights should have been the first to adopt improvements. General Foods bought Birdseye's food-freezing process in 1931, but frozen foods did not become popular until after the war.

Locomotives might be chugging along on steam to this day, if PWA had not lent the railroads money to buy diesels. Most lifted not a finger to help themselves fight the competition from cars and buses, which was running them deeper into the red every Depression year. Trucking was little business, but truckers were tough, ingenious competitors in the best free-enterprising tradition. Walter F. Carey, son of a marine engineer on the Great Lakes, built a $5-million business during the Depression devising a better way to carry automobiles on inland waterways. In 1964, he became president of the U.S. Chamber of Commerce.

Many enduring little businesses grew up around the automobile, which surprised everyone by becoming a necessity rather than a luxury. House trailers, auto radios, motels, drive-in theaters—all these small services flourished, none of them developed by people with substantial capital. Established banks did not at first lend customers money to buy cars, and established insurance companies shunned the growing market in automobile liability.

The small business ventures that succeeded in the Thirties often expended as much ingenuity on finding the money as on developing the idea. Soft ice-cream custard sold at roadside stands in summer was pioneered by a young couple, the Carvels, who worked during the winter for five years to help finance it. The United States owes its supply of fluorspar, a

265

mineral needed during World War II to refine aluminum for aircraft, to the ingenuity of Walter E. Seibert, a New York accountant. He borrowed $20,000 from friends to buy a mine in Newfoundland in 1932 and persuaded unemployed miners living on a six-cents-a-day dole to work it on credit, after talking the local merchants into advancing the miners credit for groceries. U.S. Plywood's founder, Lawrence Ottinger, got into manufacturing in 1932 by agreeing to operate a Seattle plywood mill for some bankers who were stuck with it on the basis of half the profits but none of the losses.

The typical success story of the Depression is a consumer product that did not at the time seem worth the notice of a grown man, peddled by a persistent promoter who was not considered eligible for bank credit and had to scrounge for money to expand. A good example is Lawrence Gelb, a bright N.Y.U. graduate in chemistry, from the Bronx, who started manufacturing Clairol hair coloring during the Depression and peddling it himself. Everything about hair dyeing was questionable. Nice women would not talk about it (one of Gelb's contributions was to avoid the word "dye" and use "color" instead). Hairdressers did not know how to apply it, and they feared, with some justification, that their customers might sue them for injuries arising out of accidents in applying the dyes. Banks would have nothing to do with the business.

Gelb was not deterred. For promotion, he wangled a free write-up in *The Chicago American,* which sold out his supply in that city. He wangled credit from bottle manufacturers and extended credit to jobbers so they could put the product into beauty shops on credit. By 1950, Gelb had persuaded young women to change their hair with their moods. In 1959, he sold Clairol to old-line Bristol-Myers for $22.5 million and became one of its vice presidents with a lordly layout in the head office in Rockefeller Center.

While new ventures struggled for financing, established banks were loaded with money they could not persuade businessmen whom they regarded as bankable risks to borrow, even when interest rates fell as low as two percent. Just before the Recession of 1937, commercial bank loans had fallen to half their 1929 volume. There had been too many commercial banks in the boom years. Most of them were reopened one way or another after the Bank Holiday, to face the disappearance of their normal business. For several years, traditional bankers sat in their lonely palaces and bewailed the end of enterprise. No one, they complained, needed money.

The man who really needed credit was obvious. He was, of course, the man with a steady job who wanted to buy a car, a refrigerator, a radio, a suit of clothes, or even a house, before he had saved up money for it. French furniture sellers had discovered early in the nineteenth century that you could sell this man something surprisingly expensive, if you took payment as income accrued to him. The Singer Sewing Machine Company prospered on installment sales of sewing machines in the nineteenth century. After them came pianos, encyclopedias, diamond rings, and vacuum cleaners. In 1910, the Morris Industrial Bank was chartered to lend money to wage-earners without collateral for purposes banks did not consider good risks. In 1915, John Willys began selling automobiles on the installment plan. The same year, Commercial Investment Trust (C.I.T.), a finance company formed out of the May store in St. Louis, moved on from furniture and washing machines to the growing car business.

By 1929, 60 percent of automobiles were sold on the installment plan, and both Ford and General Motors had set up their own finance companies to keep the cars rolling out of the factory. More than $3 billion of installment credit was outstanding, over half of it for cars. But commercial banks held less than five percent of the installment paper. They disapproved of it. They viewed the installment credit outstanding as a weakness of the

267

economy. Spending before earning, they insisted, could only end in disaster. If hard times came, finance companies would reap their just reward in a flood of repossessed cars, radios, refrigerators, and diamond rings that could not be sold at any price. During the week of the Crash, the orthodox blamed installment buying for the collapse; bankers who had prudently stayed with good mortgages and bonds recommended by Kidder Peabody or Goldman Sachs forecast the worst for those who had succumbed to the get-rich-quick temptations of consumer credit.

But the day of reckoning did not come. During the boom, manufacturers never made as high a profit as the Wall Street speculators who financed the production of the goods they made. During the Depression, manufacturers never made as high a profit as the personal credit companies that financed the consumption of the goods they made. C.I.T. and Commercial Credit, the two biggest finance companies, were on the short line of companies that made money in 1932. The installment credit companies had prudently cut their loans to 60 percent of 1929, but they collected all but one percent of the money they lent between 1929 and 1932.

Repayments surprised everyone. Most people, it appeared, wished to pay their debts. Even the unemployed managed to scrounge for the payments rather than lose the car or radio. One reason for the surprise was that bankers had expected the worst of people who were "shiftless" enough to spend "beyond their means." Another was that they had never really looked into the risks. Personal finance companies had actually been very careful in lending to working-class people who had already adopted middle-class values. They were sometimes stricter about repaying than people who did not have to prove they were middle-class, just as lower-middle-class mothers worry more about keeping their children clean than mothers who do not have to establish their status.

The magnificent record of repayment encouraged the more
268

enterprising banks to go after the business of financing consumption. They found it no more risky than commercial loans, and they charged less than the finance companies. Because the money comes back every month, the actual return is about twice the figure usually quoted to borrowers, and much higher than banks had ever been able to make financing production. In 1940, commercial banks held $1.5 billion of the $5.5 billion installment paper outstanding and were set for a major share of the $50 billion outstanding in the 1960s.

It was one of the few changes that expressed itself completely in architecture. When new bank buildings were finally built—and building lags behind the thinking for it—bankers abandoned the old marble mausoleums lined with cages that accused the public of felonious intent, and took to living in glass houses that protested the honesty of the bankers on view inside. Instead of the majestic desks that used to protect First National Bank officers from depositors in the 1930s, when a depositor had to put down $100,000 to be granted a checking account, round desks visible through glass walls now invite the passerby to cocktail-lounge camaraderie.

Banks went after the man in the street. Before the Crash, few householders paid their small bills by check. Banks discouraged small deposits by requiring a minimum balance. They wanted only checking accounts big enough so that the use of the money would outweigh the expense of handling the check. But personal checks were one of the conveniences that found a market even in the Depression. In 1934, Alexander Efron started the Checkmaster Plan, under which anyone could draw a check for a nickel against an account that could be opened with as little as a dollar. By 1938, more than 300 banks were attracting people into the bank by offering small checking accounts and other services.

Others followed the banks in financing consumption. Department stores set up "junior" accounts and revolving credit plans that brought them customers they never had before. Even Macy's gave the Morris Plan floor space to lend to customers who wanted Macy's cash bargains on the installment plan. Between 1934 and 1936, the Federal Housing Administration insured mortgages repayable every month just like rent, pioneering the extensive use of this employee-oriented financing that opened up low-cost housing after the war. Before the Government underwrote the amortizable mortgage, a purchaser had to have most of the cost of the house in cash, and he paid high interest for the mortgage payable in a lump sum at the end of a few years.

Slowly, but at last, the bankers went to work funneling money where it was needed. Increasingly, that place has been consumer credit. The old notion of capital formation and allocation has undergone a big change. No longer is money "saved up" and then invested by individuals in a business of their own or a venture whose risks they are in a position to assess. As a matter of fact, individuals frequently enjoy a high standard of living with very little capital.

The kind of person who before the Crash owned tangible property, securities, or money in the bank is now apt to have only claims to income. Some of the claims arise out of employment—pensions, fringe benefits, expense-account perquisites, medical group insurance—claims that provide the security possible before the Depression only by having money in the bank. And when individuals do have money, they are much less likely than before to decide where it will be put to work. Increasingly, the decisions on where resources will be directed are made by security analysts, mutual fund directors, and other professional specialists who do not have a financial interest in the decisions they make.

The power that investment and commercial bankers held is now scattered. Government puts up the money for enterprises returning too low a rate (river-valley development) or carry-

270

ing too high a risk (basic research) to engage private capital. Big corporations now generate their own funds and allocate them to the development of new products that the managers think will earn high rates, or which they want to pursue for some other reason. Financial intermediaries such as insurance companies, pension funds, mutual funds, and nonprofit foundations of one kind or another now collect the mostly involuntary savings of wage and salary workers.

The Depression could have destroyed corporations and discredited the large-scale corporation as a social invention. Instead, the corporation emerged from the Depression a stronger and better-articulated social organization than it was when the Crash struck. By whom or however the 100 biggest American corporations are owned, all are now self-perpetuating, self-regulating private governments conscious of responsibility to customers, employees, and the public. They all treat profit as an accounting measure of competence rather than as a melon to be sliced. They are all deliberately organized to find new products and improve their methods. And they all provide a "way of life" for salaried employees complete enough to stimulate jokes about the "company cemetery."

During the Depression, business was criticized as antisocial. Professor Robert Brady accused corporations of conspiracy against the consumer in an early book, *Business as a System of Power*. In the 1960s, business is criticized for "bureaucracy." In his 1961 book, *Organization, Automation, and Society—The Scientific Revolution in Industry,* Brady fears "authoritative direction and the erosion of individual initiative."

The new system may not be capitalism as Adam Smith meant it, or even Barry Goldwater. It is "consumer capitalism," or "welfare capitalism." Welfare capitalism seems the more inclusive term because it covers the social responsibility of big corporations, as well as their orientation to the consumer.

Some of the features of the present pluralistic system are not

271

new. Government gave land to veterans and railroads in the nineteenth century. Involuntary saving is not new. On the contrary, the capital for building the American West was extracted from workers who were required to produce more than they consumed as slaves, as underpaid wage workers, or merely as victims of the feverish inflations that were much more common in the nineteenth century than in the twentieth.

But two things about the post-Depression system really are new:

• Ordinary individuals no longer have to save and invest on their own. Social Security (and often private company insurance) is deducted from their salary checks. Pensions are built into their pay. The money saved is invested by salaried professionals working as security analysts for mutual funds, insurance companies, and financial "institutions."

• Ordinary individuals get the money they save in their own lifetimes. The pioneers who settled the West produced more than they could ever consume in hopes that their children would be better off. Now that the country is built, this sacrifice is not necessary.

The first change is a signal advance in efficiency and ensures orderly progress. The second is simply fairer.

11

$ $ $ $ $

THE LIMITED LIFE

THE worst thing I remember about the Depression was watching a friend of the family who had been a captain in the United States Navy take our movie tickets and chop them up in the glass box he then commanded in front of the theater. I don't know how he came to be a ticket-taker. He may have invested in bank stock and found himself owing as much as he had lost. Mother and Father simply told me he had "suffered reverses" after taking early retirement from the service. The embarrassing thing was that he wore his comic-opera usher's uniform as proudly as if it were a real one. He stood bolt upright, gray, smiling, patrician. Mother said he was lucky to get any job at all. I wondered if the theater owner had hired him because of his military bearing.

The story failed to move a friend of mine whose mother and father pressed pants for a living during the Depression. "The people who suffered agonies because they could not buy a new Persian lamb coat give me a pain still," she sniffed. "One nice thing about being really poor was that you could not afford pretenses. When I asked my mother for money to buy a coat so

273

that I could look for a good job, she set me right in a hurry. 'You go out and get a job and *then* you'll buy a coat,' she said. 'If you buy a fancy coat now, they'll think you don't need the job!' "

But middle-class horror stories of the Depression run to the humiliation of "coming down in the world." One woman remembers the first morning her husband ever put overalls on to go to work. Another woman remembers pawning her engagement ring. A man remembers putting his hand five times on the knob of the door of the relief office before getting up courage to open it. Another tells how he used to strike up conversations on trains in order to bum cigarettes.

"I'll never forget watching my mother trying to sell Two-in-One shoe polish from door to door," a successful magazine writer says. "I'll never forget taking turns with my brother to ask for day-old bread in the bakery. The baker would make us say it louder, to get his kicks out of it. Then he would repeat it for the benefit of the other people in the store, 'Stale bread is what you want.' "

Some of the stories can be made to sound funny. Whenever visitors were expected, a successful New York editor remembers, her mother obtained oriental rugs from a dry cleaner who surreptitiously rented them out over weekends when he did not expect their owners to call for them. The possibility of a hurry call and pickup was not funny at the time, however. Stratagems for keeping up appearances hurt too much for words. There was bravado. Columnist Earl Wilson saved the Christmas cards he got and sent them back to their senders the following Christmas, for instance. There were bitter political satires on the New Deal and the WPA, but not on the unemployed. The only Depression song Richard Rodgers recalls is "Brother, Can You Spare a Dime."

The Depression did not mark the initiation of petty economies. Americans had always scrimped and saved, but in the

274

past they had saved "up" for a farm or an education or to go into business. In the Depression, the old saving ways were retained, long after they had ceased to be practical, by people desperately holding on to a house or the "front" necessary to a self-employed business or professional family. "I've taught myself to hold on to money," a thin-lipped, sexless young woman says in an ad of 1933 for an investment trust.

In some circles, the fur coat was the last thing to go. Some men insisted on wearing two freshly laundered white shirts a day even when there was not enough to eat. Keeping clean was one way of proving middle-class status. In other families, jewelry, servants, or having the mah-jong group in, were preserved at all costs. Squeezing out the money for these splurges fell on the women. Like Southern ladies fallen on evil days, some of them tried to make money on the side by selling real estate or taking in roomers. Most people simply cut down. Some middle-aged women still habitually buy day-old bread, save cooking gas by warming up several leftovers in a three-part "Depression pot," and prefer the cheapest canned goods, such as tomato herring.

During the Depression, women saved microscopic and inedible dabs of leftovers and exhorted their husbands and children to "eat up" the last spoonful. They patched clothes, rewove socks, split sheets down the middle and sewed them together to equalize wear, renewed shoulder straps of aging underwear, cut down adult garments for children, relined winter coats with old blankets, saved broken crockery and stored trunks full of rags that might come in handy some day but never did. Smokers rolled their own cigarettes on little machines. People steamed unused stamps off unmailed letters, bought 25-watt bulbs to save electricity, and took uneaten restaurant portions home "for the dog." Men sharpened old safety-razor blades and used them over again. Boys and men repaired the car

275

themselves. Some country people went back to homemade coffins.

Social workers sometimes had trouble getting middle-class families on relief to spend their money for food, instead of for luxuries that seemed necessities to them. "Folks don't see what you eat," one client remonstrated, "but they know where you live." There were status heroes who literally starved themselves to buy new clothes. In Manhattan, a tailer who had been on relief for three years stormed into the relief office just before Easter in 1935 and demanded that the city buy his wife a new dress. "Other women get Easter dresses," he screamed. "My wife, she wants one."

Middle-class conversation bristled with resentment of class distinction. There were stories about how much fun we had although we didn't have money, how we dressed down for parties so that no one need feel ashamed of his clothes, how we closed the big house or put up the yacht because it didn't seem right to spend when so many were unemployed. Or how we winced at eating in a fine restaurant while so many were standing on breadlines, or how people put up a brave front even though they didn't have a dime, or how a businessman kept his office staff on at full pay although he didn't make a sale all year. A bookstore owner recalls with disgust the ostentatious way a well-dressed customer munched an apple to prove he was buying from the unemployed.

Gossip unmasked the pretentious. A socially prominent family gave its daughter a fine wedding, but didn't pay the dressmaker who made her gown for *years*. The wife of a mill-owner fallen on evil days drove up to the A & P after hours and made the manager open up to sell her 15¢ worth of hamburger—in private. As people said, there were a lot of four-flushers around.

During the few prosperous years of the 1920s, more Americans bettered themselves faster than in any previous half-dozen

276

years. Immigrants made good. Negroes came North to freedom. Farmers came to town. Factory workers bought cars on the installment plan. In Detroit, they bought lots and lived in the garages of the houses they hoped some day to be able to build.

Class distinction is scarcely noticed when you are moving up, but when the vehicle that has been carrying you pleasantly forward stops, it feels at first as if you've been flung back. During the Depression there were just enough cases of people who lost their money and their homes, people who disappeared, people who dropped out of sight, to make middle-class families look down—or for many who had recently bettered themselves, behind. Perhaps their children would not be able to go to college after all, or perhaps not away to college. Boys might not be able to go into the professions, but might have to do work of lesser prestige or less to their tastes. Girls might not meet the right men. Boys might be trapped in marriage too soon. The family might lose its home or its business.

Advertising exploited the fear of falling. During the boom years, advertisements were stately exhortations to the fuller life ahead, or recipes for succeeding in business or social life by studying at night or learning to play the piano. Ads opened endless vistas of better jobs, more literate friends, finer homes.

Soon after the Crash, advertisements began to depict disaster. A crestfallen man comes home to a kitchen-aproned girl, unaware that a Gillette shave would have landed him the job. A nice-looking, upper-class girl confides that "like most terrible things, pyorrhea seemed very far away (from me personally)." You could have dreadful new ailments: Armhole Odor, Clogged Pores, Dated Skin, Flour Face, Housework Hands, Monday Blues, Pocket Book Panic, Wash Day Jitters, Yellow Stain. A high-water mark of social uneasiness may well be the Depression ad that pitilessly contrasted men fumbling for trouser buttons with the confident owners of gap-free zippered pants.

All these negative ads exploited a single theme: the fear of

277

being found out for what you really were instead of what you were trying to be. If the negative hard sell was as successful as the advertising men claimed it was, then a great many people must have been worried about relapsing into the "dirty" working classes just below them from which they may have risen. The appeal to fear survives in the Sixties only in small "column" ads directed to the poorest magazine readers.

Increased class consciousness may explain why domestic service continued to decline during the Depression in spite of widespread unemployment. The American case is curious. Except for the Negroes, we have never had a hereditary servant class. Irish and German immigrant girls worked in homes until they learned their way around well enough to find husbands or factory jobs. Vacuum cleaners and washing machines took over some of the housework when the immigrants were barred after the first World War and factory jobs drew girls from domestic work.

The Depression should have halted this shift. Millions of working-class households were left without a wage-earner. Women tried to pinch-hit. Housework was a logical vocation for them, and while salaried families suffered pay cuts, they could have kept more help than they did. In the South, where servant-keeping classes were at least as hard hit as the well-off elsewhere, families cut the wages of their servants, but did not dismiss them. Even in the North, it was sometimes hard to fire servants. My mother had a French-Canadian cook who stayed on although we could not pay her, because there was literally no other place for her to go.

In December 1932, *Fortune* magazine urged housewives to hire servants instead of buying household appliances. Noting with disapproval that there were one million refrigerators sold in the previous year and one million families with servants, the article urged a return to an economy that would surely have put most of the magazine's advertisers out of business. "Only in

278

America could housewives see more merit in the shiny efficiency of a new icebox than in all the minor amenities of extra-clean corners, polished silver, punctiliously served meals . . ."

Women did not listen. They went right on firing their maids and buying new refrigerators. Maid and mistress usually parted company in a snarl of mutual recrimination. In March 1938, *Fortune* found housewives saying they would rather do their own work than stand for bungling servants: ladies who were doing their own work for the first time "liked having the house to themselves."

Something that happened during the Depression made the presence of the poor more embarrassing to the rich than formerly. Those of the rich who were setting up machine guns in the eaves of country houses were relieved to see the servants go because, as they sometimes put it, "You can't be too careful these days." The compassionate rich who were seeing the difficult lot of the women in their kitchens were becoming more uncomfortable with servants and more willing to do without them. Maids were actually dismissed because it no longer seemed safe or right to flaunt upper-class status.

The maids were delighted to go. Girls who worked long hours at piece rates yielding $4 and $5 a week in Lawrence or Fall River textile mills would have been better off in a job that provided room and board, but they did not choose to work in homes. During some of the darkest days of the Thirties, the only want ads in Detroit newspapers were "Live-in maid, $3 wk." Stories circulated about the exploitation of servants by new-rich who were taking advantage of the situation to get servants for room and board. Social agencies refused to let girls do it. "Are Servants People?" Dorothy Dunbar Bromley asked in *Harper's*.

There was truth to the charges of exploitation, but domestic servants had always been exploited. Wages, even in the boom year of 1929, were only $6 a week in Steeltex. Irish and Negro servants had always worked long hours, eaten the leavings, and occupied the least desirable part of the house. Why was all this worse under Depression conditions? The difference was that previously the servant girls had been able to look ahead to the next step: a husband and a farm of one's own, or a job in a factory. No wonder they bitterly resisted going "back" to domestic service when the factories shut down!

Many things are tolerable if they are temporary, or stepping-stones to better things. Cub reporters will work for nothing; so will medical internes. But when the future looks dim, the whole vista foreshortens. The situation behind and below and nearby blanks out the road ahead and above and beyond. The harder the middle classes looked at those below and behind, the less sympathetic they dared to be ("some folks won't work"). The more doubtful the future, the more some yearned for a time when the future had seemed more bright ("back to the land!"; "down with the machines!").

The way the future looks makes a lot of difference in the enthusiasm with which human beings cope with the events of personal life. When you feel good about life and look forward to pleasure, for instance, you enjoy food. Lovemaking, pregnancy, child-rearing and schooling are especially oriented to the future. During the Depression, all four vital activities were pursued more warily than in the boom decade before or in the confident decades after the war.

Food is the universal symbol of life, love, and trust. Extra food is the intuitive way to celebrate happy occasions and show love for children, family, and friends. When these attitudes prevail, as they did in the expansive years before World War I and after World War II, cooking is prized as a fine art. The gourmet sets the style for eating. In the affluent mid-Sixties, women have been encouraged to cook for fun, self-expression, and sociability, or they have been provided with precooked foods that allow them to pay as little attention to the chore as

280

possible. You can eat out or in or together or alone or in **bed** or before the fire.

During the Depression, as in the Middle Ages, the gourmet was a simple glutton. People who lived to eat could not quite shake the specter of the unseen millions who did not have quite enough to eat to live. Housewives thought of food as the inescapable daily expense. The most popular cookbooks taught women how to stretch their food dollars: "New Dishes from Leftovers" and "Better Meals for Less Money." Meanwhile, the science of nutrition was enjoying a golden age. Vitamins had been isolated in the Twenties. During the Thirties, new knowledge about the best kind of food to maintain health was enthusiastically popularized by women's magazines and Government agencies as fast as it came out of the laboratories. Housewives planned meals around the concept of the calorie, the vitamin, balanced diet, "hidden hunger," and the need for a breakfast a man can work on. Welfare workers used the new knowledge to advise relief clients on using food money, to set relief levels, to distribute surplus foods, and to design school lunches that would supplement the diet of children who might not be getting enough of the right things to eat. Families eating on $3 and $4 a week provided accessible examples of the danger of bad food "habits."

Food became a matter of nutrition. Children had to eat their spinach and eat it on time, too. The big old farm kitchens that had been real living rooms were spurned in favor of kitchens as efficient as laboratories and just about as inviting. Gleaming white kitchens engineered to operating-room efficiency were one of the growth industries of the Depression. When Hoover's Secretary Wilbur surmised that children were eating better because the Depression had returned mothers to the kitchen, he was simply reflecting contemporary worry about balancing diets.

Consider, for instance, what the Depression did to the orange. Traditionally, it was a luxury for the toe of a Christmas stocking. During the Thirties, dietitians popularized the daily need for Vitamin C to prevent scurvy and deficiency disease. Orange juice for breakfast, orange juice for baby's first nonmilk food, became dietary duties, the new standard of adequate nutrition. Oranges became the symbol of what everyone should have and would have if things were ordered better in this country. Economists testified that an increase of $2 a day to the income of the lower half of the population would enable them to spend $11 million a year more on oranges. Destruction of surplus oranges seemed especially immoral. Asked how he came to hold left-of-center political views, a college professor produced a vivid memory of childhood guilt at eating an orange while several hungry Mexican boys silently watched. Oranges are good, and that's the way they're promoted in the 1960s. They were put over in the Depression because they were good for you.

The midcentury fad for reducing is a special and an interesting case. Men, women, and even little children starve themselves in the 1960s in order to improve their health and their appearance. Neither motive for reducing received much attention during the Depression. Scientific clues to the danger of eating too much were neither pursued nor popularized in the lean years of the 1930s, although everyone knew that poor people ate too many sweets and got too fat when they were given a chance. Yet perhaps because starvation seemed a real danger, the sick were characterized then as thin much more often than as fat.

In the 1960s, reducing goes much farther than the best nutrition specialists recommend. Something more than science is involved. All sorts of explanations come to mind. New midcentury recruits to the middle classes may be casting off the flabby fatness of their working-class parents. There may even be a spiritual component. The need for periodic self-denial is almost universal, and while it takes many forms (sexual abstinence, rough clothing, humbling gestures, early rising), it usually involves food. Except for the Catholic convention of fish on Friday, twentieth-century American culture has no fast. Since we are too secular to be comfortable in religious penance, we may be using doctor's orders as an excuse for bouts of self-denial that do something for the soul.

Whenever poverty is unrelieved, church calendars provide arbitrary cycles of fasting and feasting. Similarly arbitrary are the cycles of gourmet cooking and dieting popular on the plateau of affluence we now enjoy in the 1960s. Reducing may not have been the style in the Depression because deprivation threatened to strike from the outside. People who needed the experience of self-denial for emotional or spiritual reasons did not have to seek occasions for it during the Depression or during the rationing of the war.

Love can be for many things, and styles change with times and places. Of the wide gamut of interpretations possible—and they have ranged from naked aggression to mystic contemplation—the Depression made love a defense against loneliness.

During the prosperous Twenties there had been a lot of talk about sex. The smart set played the field, self-confidently trying new partners. The Depression reversed this attitude toward relations between the sexes almost overnight. Instead of self-expression, young people sought emotional security against a hostile world. They wanted to marry, but they could not afford to set up housekeeping. When the Lynds returned to Middletown, they found the high-school authorities coping with a rash of secret marriages.

The burning issue was whether to marry on $15 a week. Many waited. The Depression postponed 800,000 marriages that would have come sooner if marriages had continued at the 1929 rate. Brides and grooms were a little older, contrary to the long-term trend toward younger marriages. Girls worried about the waiting. Would their beaux remember them when they were able to marry, or would they marry the younger girls growing up, leaving a "generation of spinsters"?

283

Moralists worried about what the young men were doing about sex while they waited. In 1938, the American Association of School Administrators blamed delayed marriage for an "increase in masturbation, clandestine relations, prostitution, and homosexuality." Others ascribed a rise in illegitimacy to the delay. In 1932, Rabbi Nathan Krass, Patrick Joseph Cardinal Hayes, the Reverend Harry Emerson Fosdick, and Bishop William Thomas Manning agreed that the Depression was forcing many young women "either directly into prostitution or at least into borderline occupations from which the ranks of prostitution are mostly generally recruited."

The simpler moralists assumed that sex was a constant, irrepressible drive that was bound to back up and do harm if deprived of its normal "outlets," to use the mechanistic Kinsey term. A reservoir of unmarried males might break out in rape, riot, and revolution. Sex outside of marriage was discouraged, in part at least, so that young male energy could be channeled into constructive work. If times were hard, more young men had to work longer before they could get enough money to marry and beget children. If productivity improved—as it had when the American West was settled—more men could marry younger and let the babies come. The feedback worked beautifully as long as an ambitious young man could cut down trees and carve out a farm for a wife, but it assumed that if he could find no other work, the devil would find work for him.

The devil was disappointed. Boys and girls had time on their hands, but they had no money for the clothes, the Cokes, the movies, and the carfare that go with even a modest scale of sin. Premarital sex had been rising ever since the automobile provided opportunity, but there was no sudden spurt in the Depression. Army doctors examining CCC boys were surprised to find less venereal disease than among recruits drafted in World War I. The doughboys were older, but they obviously had found it easier to find girls, perhaps prostitutes. Studies of

284

prostitution in Europe, where it is licensed, confirm that the oldest profession is reasonably stable in good times and bad. In spite of newspaper talk, the Depression does not seem to have encouraged vice.

One reason prostitution did not rise, people said, was that the professionals had to compete with amateurs. If so, the motives of the amateurs roaming the streets were not all economic. One of the few stories men tell women about their encounters with prostitutes that sound true is the Depression anecdote about the girl who sidled up to a man and said, "I'll do it if you'll walk with me in the park." For both men and women, "acting friendly," as the Negro folksong put it, may have characterized sex acts that under other circumstances might have been thought of as passion or even rape.

The young people about whom the moralists worried were neither rebellious nor passionate. They were not confident enough to experiment with sex, as their jazz-age elders had boasted of doing. College boys did not flame or rage. According to a study at the University of Rochester, for instance, freshman boys worried about underweight, keeping their minds on their studies, getting jobs, and supporting parents, while freshman girls at the same institution worried about being popular with these rather diffident boys.

To a boy who was not able to get a job, girls were booby traps. Romance took money, even when girls paid their own way. Sex was a threat. "Childish as it sounds," a young man confessed, "I keep away from girls for fear I'll fall in love and make matters worse."

Girls adapted by turning down the heat. The jazz-baby went out with the boom. Flaming Mamie let her hair grow, put on leg-of-mutton sleeves, and discovered that she had breasts and hips. Skirts fell. (As if in response to some mysterious law that links leg appeal with prosperity, skirts dropped with business in 1921; rose in 1927; dropped in 1929; rose during the war, an affluent time, as well as a time of WPB fabric limitations; and hit a new high over the knees with the record Gross National Product of 1965.)

The down-playing of sex is reflected in the attitude mothers were advised to take toward sexual gratification in babies. Martha Wolfenstein of the University of Chicago studied the change in advice given mothers in the authoritative United States Department of Agriculture *Infant Care* manuals. In 1929 these manuals reported masturbation, thumb-sucking, and cuddling as dangers. Mothers were advised to tie a baby's hands so he could not suck his thumb. In 1942, mothers were allowed to cuddle their babies, provided they did it only at certain times of day. Masturbation was downgraded from the fierce impulse of 1929 to idle exploration from which the child could be diverted by a toy.

Love affairs of the Depression tended to be rather high-minded, sexually subdued partnerships for mutual support and companionship. "Perhaps one should not get married when one hasn't a job, but we did," a typical contribution to *The Atlantic Monthly*'s column of letters from readers "Under Thirty" begins. Young couples sounded as if they were spending more time together and exploring each other's company more eagerly than marriage partners before or since. There were fewer places to go and things to do than on traditional farms or in the mid-Sixties suburbs. And there were fewer children because the wife had to work.

Although the young people worried about it, many marriages were possible only because the wife had a job, sometimes the only job in the family. This childless, companionate type of marriage was heartily approved as a steadying influence. The Rockefeller General Education Board's Commission on Human Relations urged sex education in the schools and early marriage, financed if necessary by the wife's earnings. When the University of Missouri had to raise tuition fees, it relaxed the rule

286

against married students so that a man could get through school by marrying a girl with a job. In the 1960s, Margaret Mead has been urging girls not to marry until they are through college. In the 1930s, she was willing to let the girls support the boys so that they could get married younger.

The new marriage had endless possibilities. Love and sex and marriage could at last be private. With children postponed, with economic support shared or even passed from husband to wife in turn, all sorts of life styles could be created. Private life could be organized to accommodate adventure, scientific research, exploration, or periods of intensive devotion to art or literature.

Those who waited for marriage had years of uncommitted single life to invest. A nose-counting survey of a small reunion of the Vassar class of 1935 disclosed that the average alumna attending had remained single for more than three years after graduation, a fate that would alarm mid-Sixties graduates, a large proportion of whom are married the very month they get their diplomas.

Nonmarriage was more acceptable. Even girls considered it a possibility. A book telling them how to *Live Alone and Like It* became a bestseller, and the subject lives on as a magazine-article chestnut. "I am lonely less often than many married women, for I have long ago learned to depend on myself for amusement," a self-styled "fortunate spinster" wrote. "Deprived of one great sense experience, I have learned to value the small things of life." Like others of the same view, the lady sounds as if she were exhorting a generation of spinsters to make the best of it. Many of them made superb use of the years alone, and even better use of the new freedom to build a marriage around a life of public service.

They had as models for a life of public service many well-known women, married and single: Ruth Benedict, Margaret Mead, social worker Helen Hall, Eleanor Roosevelt herself.

287

Some of Roosevelt's so-called "dedicated old maids" were quietly married, like Secretary Perkins, or determined Lucy Stoners like Caroline Ware. Journalist Dorothy Thompson inspired her husband Sinclair Lewis to write a novel explaining career girls: *Ann Vickers* became a bestseller of 1933. According to Sinclair Lewis, it was timely because women had recently become "almost complete, full-sized human beings, with ideas, reasons, ambitions, force—with virtues and faults." Later on, when he parted from Dorothy Thompson, he ridiculed her as the "talking woman."

The characterization was apt. Like the pioneer career women now emerging in African and Asian nations, the women of the Depression who became public figures did not pull their punches. They were more self-confident, original, and "masculine" than any of the more numerous women holding important jobs in the 1960s. In part, at least, they may have profited in peace of mind by renouncing the attempt to be feminine according to conventional definitions.

Once embarked on her own course, the old-style feminist did not mind clipping her hair when other women were wearing theirs long. She did not waste emotion over the babies she might have had, and she may even have referred to menstrual periods as "the curse," at least before counterfeminists like Marynia Farnham (*Woman: The Lost Sex*) read rejection of femininity into the slang term. If the implications were called to her attention, she might have queried the politics of the ladies so belligerently declaring their femaleness. By no accident, she would have said, all the Fascists flourished on repairing damaged male pride: Hitler, Mussolini, and our self-confessed home-grown Fascist, Lawrence Dennis, were all for sending women back into the home.

Pregnancy became a disaster. Marriage was "okay," people said, even if the wife had to work, but "kids were out." Young people seriously debated whether they had a "right to bring

288

children into a world like this, perhaps to starve," the way a few self-doubters now question bringing children into a world facing atomic explosion. "Is it our bounden duty to bring non-being into being?" a 25-year-old wife wrote in 1938. "Would our child be wanted in 1958?"

I am keenly aware of the distance we have come, because I had my first baby in 1935 and my second in 1961. The first time, the women pregnant along with me took the news of pregnancy as if it were a misfortune and concealed it as a disgrace; maternity clothes were designed to "keep your secret." In 1961, the news was joyously imparted to all and sundry the day the rabbit confirmed it, and pyramid styles were helping women to look pregnant when they were not.

In the 1930s, the first thing intimates asked a pregnant woman was whether she had considered "doing something about it." Solicitous friends sometimes undertook to recommend an abortionist, or to relive their own gory experiences with one. The same sort of female talk in the 1960s is likely to revolve around "what we went through to become pregnant." Abortions were reported on the rise in the 1930s, in part at least because doctors were hard up themselves. Treatment of infertility is an increasing part of gynecological practice in the 1960s.

Having a baby was only slightly more hazardous in the 1930s than in the 1960s, but more was made then of the discomfort. Civilized women were supposed to have a much harder time giving birth than peasant women who worked in the fields until the last minute. After learning that you intended to "go through with it," friends in 1930 assured you with hollow brightness that pregnancy was "really" a natural business, or they extended forthright sympathy: "You must feel awful." Obstetricians say that women who don't want babies have a harder time in childbirth than those who do. If so, some of the commiseration of Depression childbearing may have been warranted. In 1937, for instance, two doctors blamed hard times with "their immediate

289

and remote effects upon personal and domestic harmony" for a steady increase since 1931 in "madness after childbirth."

In the 1930s, the moment of birth was dreaded as an ordeal. Breast feeding was supposed to ruin your figure, and bottle feeding was on the rise. In the 1960s, some women like to be pregnant because it "feels good," the birth itself is exhilarating, and breast feeding is pleasurable. Women have actually become so snobbish about nursing their babies that the authorities feel constrained to reassure those who "can't" that their babies will be all right. Hospital practice reflects the change in attitude: in 1935 I was knocked out with chloroform for the birth of my daughter and recuperated for ten days in the hospital; in 1961, I saw my son born, was on my feet as fast as the peasant women, and went home in five days.

In the 1930s, the expense of raising children was on everyone's mind. News of pregnancy inspired comment about how much it was going to cost to straighten the baby's teeth, how much it was going to cost to put him through college. "Will he smile when he needs work?" an insurance ad of the time made a baby ask. The baby in the picture was smiling, the caption explained, because "the money for his start in life will be ready when he is, and his mother and I will not have to back him with heavy payments from current funds." Economic reasons were given by about half the respondents to polls asking why couples did not have more babies.

But there was something remote about the budgeting problems. Teeth-straightening and college do not become expenses for many years, and the immediate medical costs could be modest. In 1935, medical and hospital expenses for the birth of my daughter at Presbyterian's Sloane Clinic in New York City were $65, paid $10 a month with $5 saved from each biweekly paycheck. In 1961, private hospital care for the birth of my son in New York City cost upwards of $600, of which half was covered by medical insurance. Sylvia Porter figures, however,

290

that shorter hospital stays, cheaper maternity clothes, and hospital insurance have cut the constant-dollar cost of having a baby with a private doctor since Depression days.

Child Rearing became a burden. At a time when having a baby seemed dangerous, confining, expensive, and even disgusting, theories of child training provided no emotional rewards for the financial burdens of raising a family. Vulgarizations of Freud spread the false notion that "Mom" was responsible for every fault a child would develop at any point in his life. Progressive education had elaborated the "child-centered school" and directed parents to be "permissive" on pain of crushing a child's initiative. The evils of early toilet training were publicized before the automatic washing machine made it possible for mothers to take the relaxed attitude recommended.

Parents told each other about the man who had never eaten a breast of chicken at his own table: when he was a child, it was reserved for the grownups, and when he was a parent it was reserved for the children. In 1938 George Boas, professor of philosophy at Johns Hopkins, deplored the "maleficent paidocracy" of progressive education in an article entitled "The Century of the Child." As psychoanalyses of the 1960s are disclosing, parents of the 1930s struck back at the avalanche of advice by nagging at their children or magnifying deviations from the standards of health and development with oversolicitous concern that was correctly interpreted by the children as hostile.

Mothers worried about handling children the way they worried about balancing their meals. "Parenthood became predominantly a matter of know-how," Wolfenstein concludes on the basis of the *Infant Care* manuals 1929–1938. "The parents had to use the right techniques to impose routines and to keep the child from dominating them." In the 1920s and earlier, children's impulses were feared as potentially evil. Between 1929 and 1938, the *Infant Care* manuals warned that children might demand too much attention from their mothers.

291

In the postwar baby boom, child specialists urged parents to stand up for their rights, and more formal family life is returning as the big families grow out of babyhood. In the 1960s, model houses have "parents' suites" forbidden to the children, who have their own wings. Togetherness can now be intermittent. And parents are no longer to blame for everything. Child psychologists now talk of "rejecting children" as well as of "rejecting mothers." Some of the big families are going back to chores for all. Discipline is staging a comeback. A questionnaire sent to Vassar alumnae disclosed that more graduates of 1956 than of the classes 1929 to 1935 valued "obedience and respect for authority" as "the most important virtues that children should learn." The idea seems to be to make the children behave at least well enough so that you can genuinely enjoy having them around the house.

Some of the big families now give and take beneath an umbrella of discipline in the same unselfconscious way that built the character of farm boys growing up before World War I. By contrast, the solicitude and worry about children that were expressed during the Depression sound as though parents, and particularly women, genuinely disliked children, or at least doubted the fundamental proposition that human life was worth perpetuating. There was a lot more talk then about children "interfering with one's freedom" than before or since.

College women openly bewailed the drudgery of diapers and housekeeping. Complaints about the burden of children were a magazine staple of the times. College women sometimes wondered whether they would not have been happier if they had never been exposed to the temptations of higher education. "There is no job that *looks* so easy and is so difficult for a conscientious woman as bringing up a family," one of them commented, while another went so far as to confess, in print, that she hated her own children and would "resign from motherhood" if she could.

292

Part of the trouble was that families were cooped up together in close quarters without enough diversion. Women suffered most from the rub of nerve upon nerve of sisters, cousins, aunts, and grandparents who came home to roost when there was no longer work or place for them elsewhere. Sometimes an aged foreign-born parent returned to "interfere" in the lives of adult Americanized children. When money was scarce, mothers did not get away from the overflowing nest as easily as did other members of the family.

The very decline in divorce rates cited by optimists as a sign that the Depression was good for family life meant that couples were staying together for no better reason than a lack of funds for escape. In affluence, when everyone gets out, home is the place you come back to. In the Depression, it could easily become the place you had to stay in because you couldn't get out. In other words, a jail.

Education. The Depression disillusioned young and old with education. Even college did not guarantee a living. In 1936, one out of three members of the Harvard class of 1911 confessed they were frankly hard up, and one out of eight was on relief or dependent on relatives. Cartoonist Gluyas Williams won first place among his classmates for achievement, but second place went to stockbroker Richard Whitney, not yet fallen from grace. John Tunis dished up the sad figures in a report that bore the questioning title "Was College Worth While?" So many people were asking the same question that the Fidelity Investment Association hastily calculated that the more schooling a man had, the more money he would earn in his life. According to their figures, every day in college added $100 to the total lifetime earnings a student could expect.

It did not look that way to men who got out of college in the early 1930s. They had so much trouble getting jobs that it sometimes seemed that their college degrees were a hindrance. The liberally educated are most needed when an economy is expanding, because they are better fitted than the routinely experienced to start new projects. But at the routine level, where most college graduates had to start, higher education could be a positive disadvantage.

Croswell Bowen, later a successful writer for *The New Yorker*, confessed in 1935 that he soft-pedaled his college degree to land a $17-a-week job handling furniture in a store. At that time he counted among his acquaintances a Harvard man and a Yale man in the uniformed police and fire departments of New York, a matron whose butler had a master's degree in engineering from M.I.T., a Harvard Business School graduate selling furniture on the installment plan, and a doctor of music selling radios in Macy's. "How we would have shuddered in the old days if the thought had struck us that any Harvard or Yale man would ever come to sell neckties or stewpots or be a carnation-lapelled floorwalker," he wrote at the time.

The college boys shuddered, but they took the jobs, and in spite of occasional misgivings, employers preferred them to the high-school graduates who normally filled minor posts. Some office managers actually boasted that they could get college graduates living at home to work for $8 or $10 a week and "experience." The practice did not endear college graduates to workers of less education who were displaced, but it made the boys and girls who had to give up going to college feel a little better.

The Depression made college even more of an upper-class luxury than it had been all along. During the early Thirties, enrollment in colleges actually fell, and it was easier for a poorly qualified applicant to get into the college of his choice, if he had the money to go. Good colleges lost some of the students they had accepted in the freshman class because at the last minute their families could not raise the money, and every upper class lost students who could not afford to continue.

The most ambitious struggled to make it. A majority of stu-

294

dents on some Midwest campuses were "working their way through" at jobs ranging from undertaker's assistant to photographic tinter to tutor to dog-sitter to soda jerker. Colleges tried to help by giving as many jobs as possible to students, opening unused buildings for cheap living quarters, organizing cooperative houses where students could get room and board for as little as $15 a month, and serving balanced meals for as little as 12¢. NYA made many of these plans possible.

College enrollments did not resume their normal rise until we lost a generation of college graduates in the classes of the early Thirties. Almost everyone knew someone who couldn't go to college because of the Depression. Buford Ellington, Governor of Tennessee in 1958 and President Johnson's disaster chief in 1965, says that he would have become a Methodist minister if the Depression had not cut short his plans to go to college. College has always been the royal road to success. When poor boys could not go as easily, liberals questioned whether it was right for the rich to monopolize the educational resources of the country. In 1938, President James B. Conant of Harvard, later to make the famous Conant report on higher education, was complaining that college was out of the reach of the 80 percent of American families with incomes of less than $2,000 a year.

The loss hurts today whenever we have trouble finding people to train for a new white-collar skill, whenever we lack scientists and executives. It helps to explain why more than half of the people in this country with above-average intelligence have not been to college. Lack of money barred the bright boys during the Depression, but poor motivation—in part ascribable to the disillusion with opportunity dating from the 1930s, is the legacy which perpetuates this loss of human resources in the 1960s.

Alert poor boys sized up the situation. The frustrating job experiences of college graduates during the Depression and the limitation of colleges for so long to the upper middle classes

295

made it hard to convince bright boys from the working classes that college was really for them. The Depression increased the snobbery of college in another way. Ivy League schools supported by endowments, mostly in gilt-edged bonds, got richer, while tax-supported colleges often had trouble getting appropriations out of hard-pressed states and cities.

While bright boys and girls were giving up plans to go to college, high schools were overloaded with youngsters who were there only because they could not get a job. This meant that high schools had more students at a time when their budgets were being cut. The first year of Depression, high-school dropouts fell one third. In 1930, half the youngsters of high-school age were in high school; in 1940, three-quarters. When the textile mills shut down in Fall River, Massachusetts, the town had the biggest high-school graduating class in its history. At the same time, and by the same token, the city had a harder time collecting property taxes than ever before. From the point of view of the school budget, the logical thing to cut was the remedial reading, the guidance counseling, the school paper, the library, art and music, extracurricular activities. Yet these were just the enrichment that the children of mill hands needed to make use of the schooling to which they were so unwillingly exposed.

Standards seemed to drop. High-school students couldn't spell, the critics complained. Schools were not teaching children history or mathematics. The handwriting of students was clearly getting worse. Parents, taxpayers, and some teachers blamed the failure to learn on lax discipline encouraged by progressive education. Actually, of course, high school was flooded with students for whom it had never been designed. Boys and girls who were in school only because the mill was not hiring were the first to see that the curriculum was not intended for them. They understood quite clearly that they were merely marking time.

296

The schoolhouse was warm, less interesting than a movie, but free. With a little ingenuity it was possible, especially when the school was overcrowded, to avoid the effort that seemed required. In some cities, you could get a hot lunch at school, and even clothes. The poor trooped in, and teachers were amazed to see how many there were. Because the poor had big families (or, as we would now say, because big families were more apt to be poor), there were more poor children than poor adults. Forty percent of the 20 million Americans on relief in 1935 were children under 16. Schools were inundated with children who were not well enough off to profit from schooling.

Enriched programs, "fads and frills," and kindergarten might have rescued some of the poor who took refuge in the school building, but there was no money for them. Education was regarded as a sort of boondoggle that could make work for adults. Teachers were frankly hired in part on the basis of need. Schools were built to make construction jobs for the local unemployed. Curriculum enrichment benefited no vendor. Yet there was a good side to this.

Teaching jobs were so highly prized, in spite of pay cuts, that teaching attracted people who in better times sought other careers. Many of them were better motivated than teachers in the prosperous postwar years when schools have had a hard time finding staff. They were willing to correct English themes. They organized extracurricular activities after school without a thought to the extra time. Teachers in the mid-Sixties seem less "dedicated." Instead of a determined teacher making a sullen mill boy stay after school for extra drill, we now have a college-bound youngster demanding extra attention that a clock-watching teacher may resent as an encroachment on "his" time—if not a grievance to take up through the teachers' union.

Most of the changes are for the better, but we still think of the schools as a cushion for the job market. During the Depression, some schools added a "postgraduate" year to the high

297

school. Roosevelt suggested raising the legal age for leaving school to keep young people from being labeled unemployed. In 1964, President Johnson suggested the same device to cut or at least conceal high unemployment among teenagers. Thirty years ago, when President Johnson was heading the National Youth Administration in Texas, NYA scholarships for college students were defended as the most economical way of keeping young people out of the labor market. Learning for fun or for its own sake is still an alien concept.

Adaptation to the limited life takes many forms, none of them pleasant. The apathy of American Negroes before the 1963 uprisings is one form; the earlier ritual lynching of Negroes by whites is another. During the Depression, almost everyone felt limited. To a remarkable degree, successful adaptation meant finding acceptable ways not to enjoy, marry, have children, move, try, protest, or participate. To the generation of strivers before them, the "Lost Generation" of Depression young people seemed amiable, pliant, and uncritical.

12

$ $ $ $ $

WAR OF LIBERATION

THE Sunday President Roosevelt proclaimed the Bank Holiday, the German people went to the polls and voted in to power
the National Socialist Party of Adolf Hitler. The following
Thursday, when the United States Congress convened to vote
President Roosevelt emergency war powers to deal with the
banks, President von Hindenburg of Germany proclaimed that
the hooked cross of Hitler's Nazi Party would henceforth fly
over all German public buildings.

Time put Hitler on the cover the week that Roosevelt was
inaugurated, but it was offbeat casting. People were more interested in where their next dollar was coming from than in the
end of civil liberties in Germany, even when the storm troopers of *Time's* "pudgy little vegetarian with the Charlie Chaplin
mustache" roughed up American Jews there.

Americans were not in a mood to see the relationship between
the two crises. Hitler had risen to power because he promised
to stop paying the reparations the liberal German Republic
had agreed to give the victorious World War I Allies. During
the American boom, the German government had paid repara-

tions installments by selling bonds to American investors. When the Crash cut this financing, the Depression spread to Germany. Europeans accused the United States of "exporting" its collapse, but Americans were too busy with their own troubles to care what Europeans were saying or doing.

The Depression had preoccupied Hoover so completely that he ignored the reports of diplomats on the rise of a militarist Japanese government and its adventures in Manchuria. He compromised with tariff lobbyists who argued that languishing American companies needed protection against foreign competition. Military strategy seemed so irrelevant that many Americans favored giving the Philippines their independence so that a tariff could be charged against Philippine imports. Twenty professors of economics urged President-elect Roosevelt to make jobs by lowering the tariff so that foreigners would be able to earn dollars to buy our goods, but no one paid any attention to them.

Roosevelt sacrificed foreign to domestic policy from the very start. He withdrew from the London Economic Conference that Hoover had called, so as to be free to devalue the dollar. His attempts to raise farm prices by cutting the dollar price of gold did not work, but they were politically popular. Townsend, Coughlin, and Long were for inflation and against foreigners. "Radio talks of people like Coughlin turned the tide against us," Roosevelt told Senator Elihu Root in 1935, when the Senate voted down Root's lifelong dream of United States participation in the World Court.

Meanwhile, Depression abroad strengthened the dictators. They adopted warmongering as work relief. They put their unemployed boys into uniform and their idle factories to work making arms. Few Americans saw this as a threat to world peace. The Depression had forced the expatriates to come home, and they were busy discovering America. Americans who might

300

have brought home firsthand reports of what Hitler and Mussolini were really doing were not vacationing in Europe.

Dorothy Thompson was one of the first to see the parallel between Fascism at home and Fascism abroad. Like Hitler, Father Coughlin and Gerald F. K. Smith blamed the Jews and the international bankers for the Depression, but when Miss Thompson talked about the loss of civil liberties in Europe, people shrugged, "It can't happen here." This apathy disturbed her so much that she persuaded her then husband, Sinclair Lewis, to write a novel of that title, which appeared in 1935.

Americans thought that war enriched cynical "merchants of death," but they failed to see that war mobilization could stimulate the whole economy. If anything, they thought war boomed prices for an inevitable crash to follow. Hoover had blamed the Depression on the first World War, and many agreed with him. Roosevelt told Hoover's Secretary of State that he did not think the Japanese could afford to mount a war in China. He himself cut back the armed forces, to balance the budget, until in 1935 we did not have enough modern rifles to arm a single regiment. The stock market went down on the news of gathering war in Europe, instead of up, as it would have done if its crystal ball had been unclouded.

The first trickle of war stimulation picked up the slump of 1938. Toward the end of 1938, when British Prime Minister Neville Chamberlain sought to make "peace in our time" with Hitler in Munich, foreign military missions began hunting through the United States for idle factories that could take on war orders.

The year 1939 opened with the fall of Madrid and the surrender of the Loyalists in Spain to the Fascist-sympathizing Insurgents. On March 13, Hitler took Austria; on March 15, Czechoslovakia. In April, the British authorized conscription, and in June their King and Queen visited the Roosevelts and

301

ate hot dogs at Hyde Park to display Anglo-American solidarity. Capital poured in to the United States, some of it in diamonds Jewish businessmen were able to smuggle out of Germany. On September 1, Hitler invaded Poland, forcing France and England to come to her rescue under their treaty. The next month, Roosevelt called Congress back and forced through repeal of the embargo on shipping arms to Europe so that France and England could get war supplies.

In 1940, Hitler rolled over Europe with terrifying speed. Norway and Denmark fell on April 9, Holland on May 15, Belgium on May 28. Next week the British forces in Flanders retreated to the Channel at Dunkirk and eventually escaped to England in small boats. On June 14, the Germans took Paris. During that year, the British spent $4.5 billion on arms in the United States, and unemployment dropped to 15 percent.

Roosevelt asked "millions for defense." Congress appropriated the money, but neither the empty factories nor the idle men were equipped to make the war goods the armed forces wanted. Our biggest forges could handle only bathtubs and automobile frames, and the first howitzers were made on machines designed to turn out streetcar axles.

Ten years of standstill had rusted America's productive capacity. Since 1929 we had worn out houses, factories, and machines faster than we had replaced them. The fundamental machine-tool industry had all but disappeared. Enterprises had survived Depression by gearing down to make a profit on low volume. Manufacturers had learned to demand proof that output could be sold, before investing in new plant and equipment. Policy was built around avoiding "excess capacity."

War orders did not look attractive to managers trained in this school. Everyone thought the war would be short. When it was over, who would buy tanks and guns and millions of gallons of fuel? The country could not rely on capital to invest voluntarily in the means of production that were needed to win the war. When the Japanese attacked Pearl Harbor, the Government took over direction of the nation's resources and managed them for high production.

Industry cooperated, but controls voted by Congress gave the Government unquestioned authority to enforce its suggestions, if necessary by Army operation of plants. The Government "interfered" with private enterprise in all the ways that had been rejected as politically "impossible" when suggested as remedies for the Depression. After Pearl Harbor, the bureaucrats really took over. A partial list includes:

• DPC (Defense Plant Corporation) built war plants and leased them to the manufacturers to make war goods on contract at set prices. Competition disappeared.

• WPB (War Production Board) directed raw materials, labor, and even plant facilities to production that the Government approved. The controls planned civilian output. WPB determined the kind and number of refrigerators and dresses available for civilians.

• WMC (War Manpower Commission) counted, trained, recruited, and deployed skilled labor.

• WLRB (War Labor Relations Board) settled labor disputes that would have led to strikes in peacetime.

• OPA (Office of Price Administration) rationed butter, meat, sugar, coffee, and rubber tires, and set price ceilings on essential consumer goods so that war workers would not be outbid by the rich.

• PAW (Petroleum Administration for War) coordinated the tankers, pipelines, refineries, and oil reserves of competing companies.

• RRC (Rubber Reserve Corporation) made competing chemical companies pool their patents and resources to develop synthetic rubber.

• OSRD (Office of Scientific Research and Development)

303

put American scientists to work on war problems and organized manufacture of the atomic bomb.

Even when Government supplied the capital, manufacturers hesitated at first to go into war work. They feared the new factories would overload the civilian market after the war. When Roosevelt asked for 50,000 planes a year, some privately groaned that the new aircraft industry had not been able to produce 1000 combat planes the year before. Roosevelt admitted he had picked the figure out of the air because it sounded good and round. "Oh, the production people can do it if they really try," he told Hopkins.

Incredibly, he was right. Under the spur of war, production rose almost vertically. By 1944 we were making a plane every five minutes, and everyone was having fun doing it. As chief of industrial production for the National Defense Advisory Council, "Big Bill" Knudsen of General Motors wandered around Washington with long lists of military needs stuffed in his pocket. "George, in that plant of yours—Plant Four, I mean—I'll make sure you get the tools, see? Now the Army people need . . ." And with no more than a confirming "letter of intent" George went ahead and did it. This was Paul Bunyan style, and red-blooded Americans could not resist it.

For ten years there had not been enough jobs to employ all the skilled mechanics in the country, much less train new ones. Now there were not enough shipyard workers to build the ships to carry the war gear to the fronts. In some trades that took years to learn there were 50 jobs for every qualified man. Processes were redesigned around the skills available and broken down to small repetitive tasks that could be taught in a few days to an illiterate man or a housewife who could work a swing shift.

New ways of training workers were devised. Visual aids were used to help uneducated people see the point. The exploded blueprint bypassed the conventions of traditional blueprints to

304

show a machine part the way it would look if you could see into it. Old hands at production shook their heads, but the exploded blueprint worked for people without the education to learn mechanical drawing even if there had been time to teach them. Instead of arguing, one Air Force colonel demonstrated.

"Do you know anything about planes?" he asked a red-necked roustabout admiring a new four-engined bomber on the runway.

"Not much. Fact, I've never been in one. I know tractors pretty good."

"Read this," said the colonel, handing him a new instruction manual. "Do exactly what it says. I want you to get those engines going." The farmhand climbed into the cockpit, stared at the bewildering array of instruments on the dashboard of the biggest bomber the world had up to then produced, and in 18 minutes got all four engines going.

Manpower could no longer be wasted. Negroes were needed in factories and stores and offices. Women were needed so desperately that the Federal government supported nursery schools for their children so that they could work in aircraft factories. To draw the idle into the labor force, war contractors raised wages for unskilled work. Negro income rose from 41 percent of the income of white workers in 1939 to 54 percent in 1947. A substantial part of the lower one-third that Roosevelt had defined as poor earned enough to support middle-class living.

War created a mass market. Salary and profit ceilings and progressive taxation limited the consumption of the highest-paid. Price control and rationing of meat, sugar, coffee, gas, and tires made sure that the essentials were available to the lowest-paid. The Crash had reduced the share of the very, very rich by burning up inflated stock values, but the war was the great social leveler. The share of the richest one percent fell from an all-time high of 17 percent of all personal income in 1929 to 13 percent in 1939, and 9 percent in 1945.

War necessity put innovations to work: diesel power, prefabricated housing, catalytic cracking of crude oil, quick-freezing of foods, the "electric eye" for automatic controls, radar, powder metals. Construction of the atom bomb showed what technology could do when the engineers and scientists "really tried."

War necessity worked reforms New Dealers had never been able to put over. Welfare provisions were routinely written into war contracts. When war plants were relocated to avoid air attack, they were quietly established in areas that were pockets of poverty. War industry permanently rescued depressed communities in Oklahoma and Georgia.

Americans hated war, but this one felt like a war of liberation. For millions of men, idle at home, the war meant a job, and a job meant an end to the degrading trade of time for pennies to which so many of them felt reduced. There is psychological if not quite literal truth to a story newspapermen are still telling each other about the reaction of a Boston newspaper editor when he was unexpectedly offered a job at many times his frugal pay in another city. According to this legend, the man was accustomed, on coming home in the afternoon, to taking two empty milk bottles to the store and trading them in for the refund of five cents apiece. The afternoon the good news came he simply picked up one bottle and smashed it on a rock. Then well pleased with the sound, he smashed the second bottle.

Getting a job was release from pettiness and boredom as well as from privation. It was like getting out of jail. For millions imprisoned by Depression and poverty, the war meant getting out of the house, out of town, out where the action was. They were needed, and the work was not made up to keep them occupied. Writers moved from WPA, where the object was to write 300 words a day, to the Office of War Information, where the object was to inspire the home front and explain the war to Allies overseas. Women lonely at home tied bandanas around their heads and went out to learn how to rivet bombers. Mrs.

Staples, of Akron, Ohio, had the satisfaction of inspecting, packing, and stamping the very safety belt that saved the life of her son when his cruiser went down off Guadalcanal in the Pacific. Some of the women salted away their unexpected pay for the house they had always wanted. Some of them went ahead and had the baby they had denied themselves when there were no jobs in the family at all.

War killed fewer than 300,000 American soldiers. Each one paid the total price. But the number who paid was relatively small. During the five years 1959–1963, we sacrificed to the joys of riding around in automobiles two-thirds of the number of American lives lost in combat during the five years following Pearl Harbor. Except for those who were killed or disabled, or who lost someone they loved, it is hard to find an American who did not come out of the war better off in some way then he went into it. Stimulation to the economy gave everyone what he had been denied.

Manufacturers made profits, limited as to rate, but high in dollars. Farmers got good prices. Girls met and married boys. Boys who had lounged sullenly around street corners marched off to become war heroes. Men whose pride had been damaged by unemployment were restored to full manhood. The armed forces put Southern white boys under the command of Negro noncommissioned officers and proved to both of them that the heavens did not fall when the races were "mixed." Depression had delayed the integration of the Italian immigrants, the last to come before immigration was cut off. All through the Depression they had huddled together, keeping to their language and their food, supplying manpower for illegal activities such as gambling. The Army Americanized them by the thousand.

The armed forces were a vast educational service for the disadvantaged one-third. The military services uncovered talent. They fixed teeth. They diagnosed and treated physical and mental illnesses. They taught boys to live together. They gave ambitious poor boys the hope, and under the GI Bill of Rights, the funds to go to college and make something of themselves.

War proved we could manufacture plenty. It proved that we could plan production without creating an unbearable police state. It proved that the poor were willing to work if given a chance. It proved that the uneducated could learn if they were taught. It showed what we could do if we "really tried." But it also proved that it took a lot more spending than the New Deal had ever suggested to get the economy moving.

Roosevelt himself had taken fright when the Government spent $3.5 billion more than it collected in 1936, even though unemployment fell the next year to 14 percent. His efforts to balance the budget cut the deficit for 1937, but unemployment shot up to 19 percent the year after. Yet even as businessmen were absorbing this lesson, war spending began to work the other way. In 1941 the Government's cash deficit rose to $4.8 billion, and unemployment fell to 10 percent for the year. In 1942 the Government spent an unheard-of $20 billion more than it collected, and unemployment fell below five percent. In 1943 we had everyone who could hold a job out earning. Unemployment was less than two percent, but the deficit was more than $50 billion.

At war's end we were making both guns and butter. The Government alone was buying more goods and services than the entire economy had ever produced in any Depression year, and on top of that, civilians were consuming 10 percent more than they had ever been able to get during the Depression. Consumer goods seemed scarce to people who had always enjoyed them, but the reason was that they were going to millions of the poor who had never been able to buy them before. The bonanza seemed too good to last.

As soon as victory was assured, everyone started worrying about peace. Sensible people were sure that there would be a dreadful Depression. When the Government stopped buying, the economy would collapse like a pricked balloon. Forecaster Leo Cherne saw a "cold breeze sweep through America..." Returning servicemen would be restless, he thought. "Occasionally you will see them in strikes and riots... The newly set up employment offices, particularly at first, will grind slowly... An occasional soldier will be found on a street corner selling a Welcome Home sign. Others will start house-to-house convassing in their uniforms."

Some expected revolution. Estimates of postwar unemployment ran as high as 17 million. All sorts of remedies were suggested, including keeping the soldiers in the Army until jobs could be found for them. But politicians knew what opinion polls confirmed: the lesson of war boom following Depression had not been lost on the American voter. He expected the Government to do something about hard times.

The Full Employment Act of 1946 proposed to set up a permanent Council of Economic Advisers to report on the state of the economy and suggest Government action if unemployment should rise above a level they regarded as high. The measure was bitterly debated. Government "interference" was again denounced. Conservatives saw the rise of Washington "jobocrats," but liberals urged holding the war-won gains. "Are we concerned about the health and care of mothers and children only when the husband and father is being killed or mutilated?" Philip Murray, president of the Congress of Industrial Organizations, asked. "Are we willing to provide housing on the basis of people's needs for it only when soldiers in foxholes have no home or place to lay their head?"

Congress provided for returning veterans by voting funds to help them find jobs, go back to college or take job training, go into business for themselves, or buy a house on easy terms. They also voted the Full Employment Act of 1946, with machinery to implement the lessons the Government had learned

309

in Depression and war. But it was politically impossible for them to slow down demobilization until jobs opened up, as many economists urged.

When Japan fell, we stampeded into peace. Between victory in Japan (V-J Day), in August 1945, and the end of the year, more than five million servicemen were released to the civilian job market. In 1946, the Government spent $52 billion less than in 1945, throwing millions more out of war work.

But the Depression never came. People cashed their war bonds and bought themselves new clothes, new houses, new anything that could be bought. Businessmen put their war profits into reconversion. Veterans flocked back to school; by 1947, a fifth of the younger veterans were studying. Women stopped working and had babies.

The peak of the "goodbye babies" had come in 1943, the year after the men went to war. Births dropped in 1944 and 1945. Then, a year after the men came home, more than half a million *more* babies were born than the year before. The rise continued. Millions more babies were born right after the war than the most optimistic forecasters expected. By 1965 there were 20 to 30 million more Americans than the postwar planners had estimated. Since all their forecasts started with an assumption about the population, all were too low.

Babies and consumption kept the economy moving after war had started it going. In 1946, the Gross National Product dropped less than $3 billion, and less than four percent of the labor force was unemployed. Ironically, John Maynard Keynes died during the year that proved his contention that we could, after all, spend our way to prosperity.

13

$ $ $ $ $

THE INVISIBLE SCAR

IN 1964, Lady Bird Johnson campaigned to help elect her husband. "Tell them about 1929!" advised a sympathizer in the audience at Richmond, Virginia. "Do you remember 1929?" The First Lady did not smile. "We remember," she said.

But most did not remember. The war babies overloaded the population with so many young people that by 1964 fewer than a quarter of the voters had been grownups during the Depression. Most of Lady Bird's audience were too young to remember that Eleanor Roosevelt had supported her husband in much the same way. This public-minded independent helpmate who had made a success in business during the Depression while her husband was rising in politics was not a model for most of the women in the audience. They identified more readily with Jacqueline Kennedy, the young wife and mother who sounded as if she were not interested in politics. Jacqueline Kennedy did not remember 1929 because she was an infant in her bassinet.

Americans forgot the Depression after the war as abruptly as Germans forgot Hitler. Most people my own age were surprised to hear that I was writing a book about it. "What do you want to write about *that* for?" some of them said in distaste. But younger friends were simply ignorant. The Depression was clearly dead history, something that could have happened any time between Fort Sumter and Pearl Harbor. In the fall of 1963 I asked a class of 20-year-old Vassar girls taking an advanced course in "The Roosevelt Era" what the Depression had meant to their families. Not a single girl was aware of any relationship at all.

Whenever they could, middle-class parents concealed their financial troubles from their children. "I never told her about the Depression," a dinner-jacketed man tells another in a cartoon of the 1930s. "She would have worried." I knew my own family was cutting down, but I discovered only by accident that they were not heating a part of our house while I was away at college.

There was another reason for the blackout. The poor people that Roosevelt set out to rescue in his Inaugural Address of 1937 were the one-in-three that he saw "ill-housed, ill-clad, ill-fed." The poor that Johnson set out to rescue from the trap of self-perpetuating poverty in 1964 numbered only one in five. By these rough definitions, more than 25 million in Johnson's America had escaped from their own or their parents' poverty. They could not be expected to remember the conditions under which their parents lived, even if they had wanted to remember. And many simply did not know because their parents did not tell them. The poor are short on family history.

Those who escaped from poverty were pushed up out of it during the few short years of the war. After the war, the door of the iron trap clanged shut on those who had not been lucky enough to get out and doomed them to poverty more isolated than the world of the poor during the Depression, when poverty was a national issue to be shared among those suffering it.

War restrictions and labor shortages had narrowed the differential between the highest- and lowest-paid. During the 1950s the differentials widened once again: managerial and professional workers made the biggest income gains, skilled workers less, while the service workers who had leaped ahead during the war made the least gains of all. It was a little harder to get ahead, suggesting why the sociological term "status" has become one of the most popular and most charged slang words of the prosperous postwar plateau.

But if the escapees from poverty did not tell their children about it, they did accumulate things with a ferocity that looked pathological. The children of Depression seemed to be acting out the resolve of a girl who wrote *The New York Times* the day of the Bank Holiday that she intended to spend every cent she would ever lay her hands on and enjoy it, rather than "wait for it to be swallowed up by others in some mysterious fashion." Margaret Mead's service with the rationing authorities during the war convinced her that the Depression made people teach their children to grab instead of to plan.

The veterans and their wives grabbed for the good things as if there were no tomorrow. They wanted everything at once—house, car, washing machine, children. Like the culturally poor from whom many of them were descended, they did not look very far ahead. They had babies without worrying about how much it would cost to straighten their teeth or send them to college. Some of the escapees from poverty revenged themselves for the snubbing they took in middle-class high schools when as postwar taxpayers they got a chance to vote down school bond issues. Marketers were startled at how blithely they took to life on the installment plan. Older people who had coped with Depression were appalled.

In the 1950s, the young were fair game for criticism. Political activists deplored their apathy to causes and called them "the uncommitted generation." Cartoons depicted them

313

as empty Brooks Brothers suits, critics called them unambitious "organization men" and faulted them for "togetherness" at home and oversociability in the new suburbs. College teachers were shocked at the apathy of their students. "What we need," said one, "is a moral equivalent of Depression."

Much of the criticism was snobbish. Many of the young people were apathetic because they had grown up in underprivileged homes. Some had never heard their parents talk politics at home. Others were politically stunted by the failure of their fathers to make a living and to relate them constructively to the outside world. Boys who grew up in Depression were apt to be strongly influenced by their mothers, if only because mothers were less damaged by Depression than fathers. Above all, Mother wanted Father to have a steady job, so that is exactly what boys brought up in the Depression set out to get. When they set up homes of their own, these boys took a livelier interest in domestic life than an earlier generation did. They washed the dishes and diapered the babies. Home became a center for recreation and companionship, rather than a haven from a hostile world or the place where you had to stay because you could not get a job. Grown children and grandmothers trooped off to work and to live alone if they chose.

Once the escape hatches opened by the war were closed, those who had scrambled out of poverty did not want to look back. Just as the lower middle classes were sometimes hysterically vicious in dissociating themselves from the poor, so the gregarious householders of the new suburbs were hysterically blind to the underpaid hospital workers, prison guards, laundry workers, kitchen help, and other laggards in income who were struggling along much as their own parents had done. In a surprising number of cases their parents were still living this way in another city while their children were "living modern." If the newly affluent were rootless, the reason was

314

that they had no background that could help them cope with the world they had entered. Even if they did not disown their parents, they could draw no strength from their example.

At the top, in business and politics, we have men whose views were distorted by the Depression. Policy is now made, as it generally has been, by men between 55 and 70. Our leaders in this age group formed their opinions and achieved their initial successes during the Depression. Age and class always separate leaders from their constituencies, but this "leadership gap" is specific in two ways: many of today's leaders come from more priviliged families than (we hope) will be the case in the future, because back in the Thirties there was little chance for poor boys to get ahead; and because they distinguished themselves in attacking the problems of economic standstill, these leaders are more cautious and less imaginative than (we hope) tomorrow's leaders will be.

(This situation is in the process of change. While Negroes and Italians are still rare at the top, most organizations have promising ones in their middle ranks, and there is some evidence that the most recently promoted top managers are a little more likely to have come from disadvantaged homes than their immediate predecessors.)

Leaders of the 1960s have often had to cope with the exact opposite of the problems on which their competence was built. A manager who was promoted because he knew how to keep costs down and hold a company together through stagnation becomes president at a time when the company is planning expansion. A politician who rose to power because he fought the domestic battles of the New Deal must cope with the nuances of foreign policy dominated by atomic strategy.

This "leadership gap" causes the most trouble in organizations whose leaders choose their successors, yet depend on support from the rank and file, such as unions. Labor leaders bemoan the lack of militancy of their members; men who are punching time clocks in factories today are almost all of them too young to remember the struggle to unionize. The rank and file of doctors may not be as bitter against "socialized medicine" as the officials of the American Medical Association, who restricted entry to medical schools and insisted on high "standards" in order to limit competition among doctors. The gap shows up in trade associations and in the disenchantment of business with the National Association of Manufacturers and the U.S. Chamber of Commerce, both of which still fight Government much as their leaders learned to do in the New Deal days.

A great deal of the Government-business dialogue of the 1960s is an echo of earlier battles that do not rouse strong feelings. Young wives simply do not understand why Esther Peterson, President Johnson's consumer counsel, is so excited about deceptive packaging, because they do not remember the old consumer movement or the resentment of big business on which it was based. The late Senator Estes Kefauver had trouble whipping up popular indignation against the pricing practices of the drug industry. During the Eisenhower years, public-relations counselors complained that the climate for business was "too good for us." When almost everyone has a job, almost no one in the United States seems to care what business does.

As successful politicians, the old New Dealers in control of the Democratic Party are professionally alert to the leadership gap. Barry Goldwater threw them into a last-minute panic in 1964 because they knew that a very large proportion of the voters did not remember the Depression and had not even heard much about it. To anyone who remembered Hoover's Presidency, Goldwater's endorsement of Hoover's economic policies on the occasion of Hoover's death during the 1964 campaign was a political blunder. No one imagined Goldwater to be politically bright, but it was just conceivable that

316

he would get away with this boo-boo. It was possible that young voters simply did not know what would happen if Social Security were repealed, TVA sold off, or welfare policy laid down by Federal grants-in-aid turned back to the states.

Those who talk about the Depression belong to the very small group that made good during it. Some of them recall fondly the rent parties, the ferry rides, the quarter movies, the stadium concerts, and the spirit of sharing that made Greenwich Village life on a shoestring gay. Some romanticize the exhilaration experienced in fighting. "The Twenties were a time of things," a veteran labor reporter recalls. "The Thirties were a time when fathers and sons got acquainted and people were kind to each other."

Many others romanticize obstacles overcome, now that they are securely past them. Company histories sometimes boast about how close a company came to bankruptcy during the bank crisis. Occasionally, you hear about a man who repays a bill he could not meet during the Depression. Hazel Bishop, who is rich now, told a reporter that she went to work as a biochemical technician in 1929 after graduating from Barnard, because the Depression discouraged her dream of being a doctor.

Class reunions of the 1930s stimulate memories of early jobs and hardships endured, and everyone agrees that life in the thin old days was more fun and more challenging. A New York City physician, swapping stories with colleagues about what they had gone through to stay in medical school, tells how a pretty college girl who was listening burst in to exclaim, "You don't realize how lucky you are. *You* had the Depression. We kids have nothing."

Some of the attractions of the Depression for those who survived it without emotional damage are subtler and more sinister. The social pyramid was much steeper in those days. A college graduate was more exceptional a person, even if he could not get a job and was reduced to clerking in a store. Although sincere liberals who spent the Depression working for the New Deal would be shocked at the thought, many of them found it more comfortable because their relative status was higher and an easy labor market supplied people to smooth the way for them. People who are usually compassionate sometimes fail to see how the full employment of the 1960s is responsible for what they experience as a general decline in morals, competence, courtesy, energy, and discipline.

To those who lived reasonably well during the Depression, people were better then in many concrete ways:

There were fewer people on the street in those days, and they weren't in such a hurry that they pushed each other off the sidewalk. There was less litter. Snow did not pile up downtown, but was shoveled into wagons and hauled away the night of the day it fell. Cars could be parked anywhere. Tables were always available in a good restaurant, and it was never necessary to share one with strangers. Waitresses said "Thank you" for 10-cent tips.

Shopping was a pleasure. Women spent days "just looking." The salespeople knew the stock and enjoyed showing it. Alterations were free. Stores didn't charge for credit. Banks didn't charge for checks. Repairmen didn't charge for estimates. Barbers came to the house if desired. Hairdressing salons didn't think they were performing a favor by giving a manicure. Shoeshine boys were everywhere.

Mail and milk were delivered along with the newspapers in time for breakfast. Western Union delivered messages by boy instead of by telephone. Elevators were run by operators who said "Good morning," reported the weather, and took in messages and parcels. There was a cop on the beat, and he said "Good morning." Groceries were generally ordered over the telephone and delivered to the door.

Butchers cut meat to order, and did it cheerfully. Instead of

318

automatic washers and Laundromats to help do the washing in a jiffy, there were laundries and washwomen who did the whole thing. Music teachers came to the house. So did dressmakers. And so, more importantly, did doctors.

It was possible to be sick in dignity. The doctor came when called. He did not ask the ailing to jump into a taxi and come to him. If they did, he did not keep them waiting. Dentists and specialists did not overschedule so that any loss of time would be at the expense of the patient rather than the doctor. Hospitals were so nice and quiet that they attracted people who simply wanted a good rest. No one tried to send private patients home before they felt like going. It was always possible to get a private nurse. Women stayed in the hospital ten days after having a baby instead of tottering home with a baby three days old.

There were no jet planes, but there was dignity in travel. Dining cars had real linen tablecloths and full-course menus. The roadbeds were maintained so that the soup didn't spill. The waiters did not snap at diners. The train windows were clean. There were porters to carry bags. Hotels always had room for people who walked in without a reservation.

Offices were serious places of business. Stenographers could spell, and they knew how to look up words in the dictionary. They didn't make as much noise or take up as much space as they do in the Sixties. They arrived on time even in snowstorms. They had eaten breakfast and removed their hair curlers. They were fully clothed. They stayed at their desks. Girls did not smoke at work. If they made personal phone calls they did it so surreptitiously that no one was disturbed. They did not take time off to go to the dentist or the psychoanalyst. Most of them brought lunch in an inconspicuous brown paper bag and ate it in the ladies' room. Everyone stayed late without extra pay, if there was extra work, and took vacations at the convenience of the boss, if at all. The boss was a big man in those days and the girls looked up to him. . . .

The list is worth elaborating because it explains why poverty is so hard to fight. The poor will be with us as long as poverty is useful to those who are not poor. One "benefit" of poverty is that it keeps people from crowding streets, stores, restaurants, theaters. The poor take up less space. They do not occupy the attention of doctors, teachers, and waiters so that these skilled servants do not have time to lavish attention on those who can afford to pay them. Another "benefit" of poverty is that, at least in the past, it has been the only way to provide doormen, busboys, delivery boys, porters, and domestic workers whose services are not economic if they are paid as well as production workers. But the "benefits" of keeping some people poor are not all economic. Some of them are social, too. There is no point in getting ahead unless there is someone to get ahead of. The Depression threatened the middle class so much that they needed the poor more desperately than ever.

Almost all Americans put themselves in the middle class, whatever their income or education, but the word "middle" implies a class below and a class above. In practice, the middle class is a moving class. It comprises everyone who is moving up from the lower class toward the upper class. If upper and lower classes did not exist, they would have to be invented in order to define the middle class. The upper class may not be generous, the lower class may not be lazy, but the traits are ascribed because they are directional signals for the mobile. In the nineteenth century, Americans invented an upper class of Southern plantation owners to provide a goal for the mobile; in the affluent Sixties some warriors on poverty sound as though they are relieved to find some poor still around to define the lower boundary of the middle class.

During the Depression, the sadistic treatment of the unemployed bolstered the status of the middle classes who were

320

closest to disaster. Just as the poor whites are hardest on the Negroes, so the people who barely managed to keep off relief had most to gain by convincing themselves that the poor were poor through their own fault. Those who were newly risen from marginal poverty during the prosperous years had the strongest need to dissociate themselves from their former condition. They needed to believe that the poor were a different and a lower order of human being, to which they could not possibly belong.

Those fearful of falling would have been more comfortable if the unemployed on relief had been forced to wear the equivalent of the Star of David enforced on the Jews in the Warsaw ghetto. Those who had recently risen or hoped to rise had a total stake in the notion that a man gets what he deserves. They could not blame poverty on the system without barring their own chance to rise. For if the poor are not poor through their own inadequacies, then I cannot rise through my own merit.

Roosevelt hoped to build a country that would leave nobody out, but the New Deal explicitly confined itself to "helping people to help themselves." Its deliberations excluded the helpless poor. When the war widened opportunity, those who grasped it first were those who were ready to move: organizable labor, farmers, people who once had had small homes, jobs, or bank accounts, or the will to go to school. Those left in poverty after the war rescued the mobile were the poor who could not help themselves: the migrants, the sharecroppers, the industrial rejects, children of big families, the unskilled, the uneducated, the Negroes, people damaged by physical or mental handicaps or isolated in depressed areas.

One consequence of this sifting was that the poor left behind were cruelly forgotten. The escapees did not help those who but for the grace of God they might have been. They ran away from them. If there are few pockets of poverty left in

321

Germany and none in Scandinavia or New Zealand, it is not because each member of their lower classes made the heroic individual effort to pull himself up by his own bootstraps. It is rather because the underprivileged made common cause politically. If Americans had given up the dream of social mobility, they might have identified their real interests and demanded "socialized" medicine, civil rights for Negroes, clean rivers, decent cities, responsible labor unions, and such amenities that other parts of the civilized world have long enjoyed.

It is interesting to speculate, for instance, whether the same people would now be poor if the Federal Government had spent as much money helping politically unorganized children get an education as it spent on politically articulate farmers. A Federal system of education and Federal guarantee of voting rights would surely have rescued many Southern Negroes from the impoverishing handicaps of illiteracy and discrimination before the law. A Federal commission with powers over the charters of national corporations, similar to that exercised over broadcasters by the Federal Communications Commission, would surely have found ways to protect consumers against high prices for installment credit and overpromoted drug and cosmetic products. Such a commission might even have scrutinized pricing, employment, promotion, and investment policies that exploit the disadvantaged. It could have kept plants from migrating in search of cheap labor and found ways to take the profit out of seasonal and cyclical employment patterns that still keep migrant workers in peonage.

The Depression did not encourage high dreams. It encouraged defensive rather than progressive policies. By their own life experience, policymakers of the 1960s aim at avoiding Depression, rather than building a greater society. Their caution contrasts sharply with the optimism of economic thinking before 1929. Most authorities now concede that the Government has the tools and the will to avoid a downward spiral like the

Great Depression, but they are content to point out why it can't happen again.

Yet after saying this, the graying policymakers talk about inflation, unemployment, budget deficits, and the danger of "big spending programs." Fear of Depression still defines all economic problems. The very terms are timid:

Is prosperity dangerous? How fast do we dare grow without inviting a ruinous Depression?

Opinions differ on whether unemployment is worse than inflation and where to strike the balance between them, but Depression-bred observers assume that we have to put up with one or the other. The trick is to "heat the economy up" enough to make jobs for everyone, or almost everyone, without boiling off in steam the dollars of people living on fixed incomes.

By 1965, performance had been exemplary. According to the index of the Bureau of Labor Statistics, the cost of living has been rising little more than one percent a year since the late 1950s. People think that prices are going up, but it is their own standard of living that is rising. It costs more to live because people add to the list of necessities. Yet overoptimism is stigmatized as "growthmanship." *The Wall Street Journal* continues to editorialize warnings against "boom psychology" and praise business organizations for "recession planning" to contract in a hurry if there is a downturn. In May, 1965, William McChesney Martin, chairman of the Federal Reserve Board since Truman's day, warned of disturbing parallels with the boom that ended in the bust of 1929 and there were enough traders who remembered the crash to cause the stock market to drop.

Can we afford to take care of everybody? How much poverty can we relieve, and where should we put the floor beneath which no American family should be allowed to fall?

The heritage of Depression persists in the notion that a bal-

323

ance must be struck between social equity and prosperity. Roosevelt had to mediate between New Dealers who wanted to reform first and those who wanted to make the economy grow first. Now, as then, liberals contend that a better distribution of wealth is a cause, not a consequence, of prosperity. The debate continues in the diagnosis of mid-Sixties unemployment. If unemployment is "structural" to industrial progress, as the reformers claim, then the Government has to protect the victims so that we can afford the human cost of increasing productivity; if it is merely a symptom of "inadequate demand," then all we need is a little pump priming, and the less specific the better. A stimulant popular with political conservatives has been defense spending.

The brief Presidency of John F. Kennedy and his unexpected succession by an older man contrast post-Depression and Depression styles of liberalism. Kennedy was elected President of the United States at the freakishly youthful age of 43. In 1929, Kennedy was 12 years old. His acquaintance with the Depression was as a Harvard student with a million dollars waiting for him. He became the first President to propose deliberately stimulating the economy by cutting taxes, but almost immediately he had to reckon with the fears of older men who controlled the economic machinery. The policymakers at normal ages for their jobs were alarmed.

In dealing with the Federal Reserve Board, Kennedy had to contend with William McChesney Martin, who had started working as a member of the New York Stock Exchange in the wake of the Crash. At 29, Martin succeeded Richard Whitney as Governor of the Exchange and had to pick up the pieces of that institution after the speculators almost wrecked it. He has cautioned against inflation ever since. In heavy industry, Kennedy confronted men like Roger M. Blough, president of U.S. Steel, who was advising big corporations through the lean years as a bright young lawyer with White & Case. Even the

324

news reporters were older. Policy at the influential *Wall Street Journal* was made by publisher Bernard Kilgore, who had reported the Crash and its aftermath as a cub reporter for that paper. To men who had been through the Crash, the tax cut looked like dangerous inflation, inviting boom-and-bust.

Kennedy fought back. "Some conversations I have heard in our country sound like old records, long-playing, left over from the middle Thirties," he complained. "It is our responsibility today to live in our own world, and to identify the needs and discharge the tasks of the Nineteen Sixties." The needs did not sound particularly new: "generate the buying power which can consume what we produce on our farms and in our factories"; take advantage of automation without putting people out of work; eradicate barriers to equal opportunity; and "make our free economy work at full capacity." The distinction, Kennedy implied, was one of method. "I am suggesting that the problems of fiscal and monetary policy in the Sixties as opposed to the kinds of problems we faced in the Thirties demand subtle challenges for which technical answers—not political answers—must be provided."

Before he could develop new "technical answers," Kennedy was succeeded by a man nine years his senior who had cut his eyeteeth on the "political answers" Kennedy appeared to deprecate. When he unexpectedly succeeded his junior, Lyndon B. Johnson duplicated the moves of the President whom he had watched take control of the crisis of 1933.

Most adults were too young to see how closely Johnson followed in FDR's footsteps. Like Roosevelt, Johnson started by promising to cut waste in the Federal establishment, and he set a personal example by turning off lights in the White House, as Roosevelt had done by eating 19-cent lunches there. He next took the sketches for a war on poverty that Kennedy had bequeathed him and implemented them by renewing the New Deal. Johnson's "job corps" to put unemployable boys to work

325

in the woods was the old CCC. Work-study plans and help for college students was Johnson's own NYA. Federally supported local nonprofit work was the old WPA. The Appalachia program was based on the parts of TVA that could be separated from a river. The food-stamp plan, extension of the minimum wage, Federal loans to businessmen to make jobs, and even rural resettlement, were proposed. Planners talked about raising the school-leaving age and cutting the work week to spread the work, as they had done in the Thirties.

All this is fine, if a bit warmed-over, but it is too bad that we cannot define our goals in mid-Sixties rather than in Depression terms and apply machinery that economists have developed since then. If we are no longer content to leave out those who cannot respond to offers of help, then it might be possible to accomplish the end more simply by guaranteeing everyone a minimum income. Yet even now, the notion is unacceptable. People are still supposed to earn their share of the national pie. More sinister is the obsolete fear that since a war cured the Depression, peace might bring it back again.

Do we dare disarm? How big a defense or space effort do we need to keep everyone employed?

Opinion divides on how much defense we need, but the Depression-bred see no way out of an agonizing choice between unemployment and the risk of atomic war. The choice is confused because no one likes to put it that bluntly, and only the specialists have learned to accept the enormity of atomic war. To men of policymaking age, the word "war" means the war that ended the Depression, a wonderful bonanza for everyone.

Talk with Russians, and you detect a different intonation to the very word "war." They lost 7.5 million in battle in World War II. School grades that bulge with war babies here at home are empty there; many women my age are living alone because their men were killed. A million lost their lives in Lenin-

326

grad alone. Russians I met in Moscow in 1958 smiled patronizingly at me, "No, you are an honest woman and you do not want war, but your Government needs war to make jobs."

The accusation was nettling because, in a less gross sense than they meant, there was some truth to it. Our own General Eisenhower warned against a war-based industry when he left the Presidency. Cancellation of war contracts causes a hue and cry in Washington. And while the defense contractors are less blatant than the munitions manufacturers Senator Gerald Nye investigated long ago, defense contractors have at times mounted elaborate public-relations programs to "awaken" the public to the need for national defense.

When the cold war became too tense, and we came to realize the risk of mutual deterrence, we tried to substitute a harmless "race for space." It soon became clear, however, that we could not mobilize the enthusiasm for space that would make a race to the moon the economic or moral equivalent of war. The new technology may be to blame. Missiles and rockets employ fewer men and women than the bombers that Rosie riveted, and they do not create work anywhere near as efficiently as the old WPA, but disarmament efforts stimulate business press headlines that I hope my friends in Moscow do not see, such as "If Peace Does Come—What Happens to Business?"

Economists put various spending and taxing conditions through model formulas that calculate by computer the outcomes of a change in one of many related factors and produce unemployment figures to go with each level of cutback. Dr. Emile Benoit, of Columbia University, figured that "all-out peace" would add four to eight million to the 3.4 million unemployed in the early 1960s unless plans were laid to ease the transition. Like most economists, he recommended a large-scale and long-term rebuilding of the public investment in roads, schools, and hospitals, and more welfare and urban renewal to

327

create a new, higher plateau of demand for privately produced goods.

In addition to these economic issues, we have inherited from the Depression a brace of phony social "problems" which simply conceal values that need reexamining in the light of new technology. Because the Depression was experienced as unemployment, we worry about leisure, automation, and population growth instead of welcoming them as good things.

Leisure-as-problem is a problem in itself. Billions of words of print now guide retirees to the attitude they should take to staying home. Predictably, and pathetically, the solution for most of them is to find some other employment, ideally employment that does not compete with younger people. An economy of plenty would do better to make moral or even spiritual achievements the price of inclusion, yet we cannot break the notion that each of us must rise every morning and "earn his keep" by productive work. We can see the way to provide material decency for our senior citizens, but we cannot think of anything for them to do. It takes someone with one foot in an Oriental culture, like Santha Rama Rau, to ask the key question: Why do they have to *do* anything?

Fear of unemployment makes offices slow to mechanize. Real work is becoming a scarce commodity. While waste has been identified and attacked in factories, business managers appear to have avoided seeing it in offices. I once asked a management consultant what would happen if all business enterprises were as efficiently managed as the best. "Fourteen million unemployed," he said, after scribbling some figures. "Don't worry, no one really wants a revolution."

An extensive literature on the social conscience of business centers on the dangers of automation and the helplessness of businessmen to do anything about the people displaced. "I shall be told that the very machines that threw men out of work create new lines of endeavor that absorb the jobless," a Senator

328

wrote. "Once that statement might have been true in part; but we know now that machines have thrown men out of work faster than new industries could absorb them." This sounds midcentury, but it is not. The Senator was Bronson Cutting. The year was 1934. Automation simply activates the old fears.

Population growth is fearsome not only because it uses up limited natural resources, such as water, but because we have difficulty in imagining any other reason for living than working. Future projections of a crowded earth suggest to us a vast poorhouse of unemployed, apathetic, limited, useless subhumans. These "superfluous people" would be poor not only materially, but culturally, of "no use."

Ideological lumber in the form of phony problems is one of the burdens of Depression we still bear, but we have inherited real problems, too. Three worth mentioning are the city, the role of women, and the culture of poverty.

Cities are corrupt, confused, shabby, dirty, expensive, inefficient, and so unworkable that they can hardly perform the essential function of bringing diverse people together to keep the society in touch with itself. American cities are worse off than many European cities or, for that matter, than Toronto and some cities in Latin America. While the causes are complex, they have been attacked in other countries. Why not in America? Part of the answer may be that Roosevelt and the New Deal defined the Depression as primarily a farm problem.

Or consider that awkward piece of unfinished social business, the role of women. Women don't know "their place" because they have been shunted between home and job as a buffer for the business cycle. As long as "women's work" is whatever needs to get done at the moment in a society that values people in terms of what they "do," preferably for money, women can never afford the luxury of a settled character. Until we solve the economic problem with less human waste, the American woman will remain a distraught figure

329

jockeying a carpool of children to school before she delivers herself to office or supermarket, depending on the economy's need for production or consumption. We still value people so exclusively in terms of their economic roles that all talk about the contributions of women in responding to the emotional needs of their families sounds patronizing.

There are signs, now in the Sixties, that we may free ourselves from the blinkers of Depression. The children of the war-boom babies, the first big group to escape from poverty, are now in their twenties. To them, the Depression is merely quaint, something that was going on at the time of the old advertisements they frame as "Pop Art."

The apathetic Fifties have already given way to the moralistic Sixties. These youngsters who have never known want are more concerned with public issues than their parents. They are better supplied but less greedy for consumer goods. They take material comfort for granted. They buy the economical compact cars now being made in America so that they can afford to buy art, and they are painting pictures of people, not merely abstractions. They are turning away from objective method in the social sciences and asking the old questions about what is right and what is wrong in the relations between people. They worry personally about alienation and isolation because their world is more heavily populated.

College students of the Sixties have marched for Negro rights, much as their Depression grandparents championed the rights of labor. As for the Negroes, they were not able to demand their rights under the Supreme Court decision on school integration until they could be led by a generation of Negroes who had never known the discrimination of the Depression. The "new Negro leadership" was confident enough to move ahead because it grew up in the full employment of the war.

The time is ripe now for a war on poverty that will rescue the poor the New Deal forgot. In spite of the accident that puts old New Dealer Johnson in charge, in spite of the creaky old New Deal machinery he is reviving, the idea of a war on poverty was started by Kennedy, our first post-Depression President. The children of the war babies do not need the poor to define their middle-class status as urgently as the poor were needed in the Depression. They want poverty eliminated not so much to stimulate the economy, for they have never known stagnation, but as a matter of simple justice and compassion. They favor using the resources now tied up in defense spending more daringly than the Depression-bred watchdogs. And because they were never rescued from anything bad by a war, they are able to listen calmly to the reports the specialists give of what atomic war would really mean. From what they hear, the risk of a Depression is nothing, compared with the risk of triggering a single bomb.

The coming of age of a post-Depression generation makes it possible to see what the Depression has really done to us. It helped us to discover, if not cure, poverty. It taught us how to avoid slumps. It may have helped us to adjust to advancing technology by slowing it down just long enough to give people a chance to think about the changes that had to be made. If the economy had remained as hot as it was in 1928, for instance, people would have poured into Detroit faster than they could have learned to live there. Cars could have multiplied faster than we could have built roads or traffic conventions to handle them, resulting in a heavier death toll.

A great many foolish predictions were made of what the post-Depression generation would be like. Most were gloomy. At one point, anthropologist Franz Boas surmised that the children of Depression would be stunted. One prophet scored a bull's-eye. In 1930, John Maynard Keynes decided that the conventionally wise needed cheering up, so he dashed off a chatty little essay entitled "Economic Possibilities for Our

Grandchildren." Of all the analyses of the stock-market Crash made since, it remains the most accurate:

"We are suffering not from the rheumatics of old age, but from the growing-pains of over-rapid changes, from the painfulness of readjustment between one economic period and another. The increase of technical efficiency has been taking place faster than we can deal with the problem of labour absorption; the improvement in the standard of life has been a little too quick; the banking and monetary system of the world has been preventing the rate of interest from falling as fast as equilibrium requires ... I draw the conclusion that, assuming no important wars and no important increase in population, the economic problem may be solved, or be at least within sight of solution, within a hundred years. This means that the economic problem is not—if we look into the future —*the permanent problem of the human race.*"

Since then we have had another war. Our real economic problems center on growing population. But we are just beginning to realize that the economic problem is not the permanent problem of the human race.

NOTES

Complete documentation has been deposited in the library of Vassar College at Poughkeepsie, N.Y.

CHAPTER 1

An important book for its interpretation and many of the facts about the period is J. K. Galbraith's *The Great Crash, 1929* (Houghton Mifflin, 1954). Also valuable are H. A. Smith's unpublished autobiography, *Fifty Years on Wall Street,* Frederick Lewis Allen's *Only Yesterday* (Harper, 1931), and David Alexander's *Panic!* (Regency Books [Evanston, Ill.], 1960). I am indebted to many eyewitnesses, in addition to accounts in *The New York Times, Time* magazine, *The Literary Digest, The Commercial & Financial Chronicle, The Bronx Home News,* and the old New York *World,* a mine of colorful detail. Statistics came from the anthology put out by the U.S. Bureau of the Census, *Historical Statistics of the United States, Colonial Times to 1957,* facts about events largely from the year-end chronologies published by *The New York Times.*

The somewhat scandalous suppression of J. J. Riordan's death was reported at the time and is covered extensively in Galbraith's *Great Crash*.

One of the National City Bank employees forced to continue paying for bank stock contracted for at pre-Crash prices was a cousin of mine, who was living with us at the time. My father was so outraged at the bank's double standard of morality—strict for employees, loose for Charley Mitchell—that he tried to figure out a legal way out for her. The bank continued to pursue her for the amount owing when she left the bank and refused to pay the balance.

The failure of the Bank of the United States, which had 440,000 depositors, was set forth in *The New York Times* of the period, and the frauds for which two officers were convicted were described from the court testimony and in a book by M. R. Werner, *Little Napoleons and Dummy Directors*, published by Harper, appropriately, on March 6, 1933, the day the money stopped.

CHAPTER 2

Social workers who could write and were not afraid of getting into politics lobbied brilliantly for the poor during the early Thirties; among them were Frances Perkins, Helen Hall, Edith Abbott, Beulah Amidon, Lorena Hickock, Clinch Calkins, Ewan Clague (recently retired as Commissioner of the Bureau of Labor Statistics), and Paul Douglas (now Senator from Illinois). A storehouse of information about the poor can be found in reports of the La Follette-Costigan Senate investigation of unemployment, and in *Survey*, the now defunct social work magazine that bristled with lively, indignant, and informative facts about poverty.

Fortune magazine is to be commended for digging out the facts of deprivation and presenting them forcefully; "No One Has Starved" (September 1932) is a magazine classic.

Harry L. Hopkins, in *Spending to Save* (Norton, 1936), is authoritative on the relief situation he and Roosevelt inherited; his book is the source (p. 26) of my quote about the Nichlos leftover system. The surprising objection of John Barton Payne of the American Red Cross to accepting money from the Federal Government because "the people have plenty of money" to donate to the Red Cross is also set forth in Hopkins's book (p. 34).

Irving Bernstein's book, *The Lean Years* (Houghton Mifflin, 1960), is a scholarly but spirited review of the source material on the condition of the working class in the Depression.

CHAPTER 3

The best journalistic, sociological, literary, and political talent of the 1930s described how it felt to be jobless. Edmund Wilson reported the unemployed, Malcolm Cowley the Bonus Marchers. Dorothy Dunbar Bromley's "Birth Control and the Depression" in *Harper's* (CLXIX [1934], 563–574) and Thomas Minehan's participant-observer *Boy and Girl Tramps of America* (Farrar & Rinehart, 1934) are prime contemporary sources on their respective phenomena that demonstrate the sociological quality of Depression journalism. Mirra Komarovsky's study, *The Unemployed Man and His Family: The Effect of Unemployment upon the Status of the Man in 59 Families* (Dryden Press, 1940), illustrates the academic bent of the time and builds emotional impact with quotes in a manner that midcentury sociologists would deprecate as sensational.

Two recent cool-headed studies underline what the indignant journalist-sociologist-novelist-reformers of the period were saying: Brian MacMahon, Samuel Johnson, and Thomas Pugh, in "Suicide and Unemployment" (U.S. Public Health Reports, 78:285 [1963]), and Norman M. Bradburn in National Opinion Research Center Report No. 92, "In Pursuit of Happiness" (University of Chicago, May 1963), measure statistically the relation between unemployment and misery.

For my first clue to the damage sheer boredom can do I am indebted to Dr. Alvan L. Barach, chest specialist, who urges handicapped patients to live it up instead of "conserving their strength."

Fortune, Time, and *Survey* articles supplied most of the news material. The story of the suicide of Albert R. Erskine, including collection of his $900,000 life insurance policy, comes from *Fortune,* February 1935. The divorce mill for schoolteachers was reported in *Time,* July 29, 1935.

The coal miners' statement is quoted from a La Follette Committee report on "Violations of Free Speech and Rights of Labor" (Government Printing Office, 1937, Part 2, p. 414).

Jack Conroy's description of hole-in-shoe problems is from his book, *The Disinherited* (reprinted by Hill and Wang, 1963, p. 234).

The Stuart Chase passage on the gloomy future with fewer babies is from his *Idle Money, Idle Men* (Harcourt, Brace, 1938, p. 65).

Opinion polls compiled under the editorial supervision of Hadley Cantril in *Public Opinion, 1935–1946* (Princeton University Press, 1951) helped clinch prevailing views on jobs, women working, family size, and birth control. Birthrate figures come from Freedman, Whelpton, and Campbell, *Family Planning, Sterility and Population Growth* (McGraw-Hill, 1959).

Discrimination was not a Depression issue, but the reason is easy to reconstruct from Gunnar Myrdal's *The Negro in America* (Beacon Press, 1944) and *Black Metropolis* by St. Clair Drake and Horace R. Cayton (Harcourt, Brace, 1945). For the frank prejudice against Jews, as for much else in this chapter, I have relied on what I and a dozen friends remember.

CHAPTER 4

Arthur Schlesinger, Jr.'s *The Crisis of the Old Order* (Houghton Mifflin, 1957) presents Hoover as a well-intentioned bungler. Eugene Lyons's *Our Unknown Ex-President* (Doubleday, 1948) and the authorized account of the Hoover administration by William S. Myers defend him.

Fortune, Time, The Literary Digest, The New York Times, and public opinion polls edited by Hadley Cantril reported the economic schemes and thinking of the period in great depth, including the rich and extensive lunatic fringe of remedies. The thinking of economists is discussed in Robert Heilbroner's readable *The Worldly Philosophers* (Simon and Schuster, rev. ed., 1961); Joseph A. Schumpeter's analytical *Ten Great Economists from Marx to Keynes* (Oxford University Press, 1951); and the encyclopedic *Main Currents in Modern Economics: Economic Thought Since 1870,* by Ben B. Seligman (Free Press [Macmillan], 1962). A handy catalog of diagnoses and prescriptions is David Lynch's summary of the protracted inquest on the Depression conducted by the Temporary National Economic Committee, *The Concentration of Economic Power* (Columbia University Press, 1946). The benchmark, for economists, is *The General Theory of Employment, Interest and Money*, by Maynard Keynes (Harcourt, Brace, 1936), addressed "chiefly to my fellow economists," but Lord Keynes put his remedy more bluntly in an article entitled "Can America Spend Its Way Into Recovery?" (*Redbook*, December 1934).

CHAPTER 5

Much of the material on the bank crisis was used in my article, "The Day the Money Stopped" (*Look*, March 12, 1963). Randolph Burgess, former chairman of the New York Federal Reserve Bank, and the late Jules I. Bogen of *The New York Journal of Commerce* gave me the benefit of their firsthand expert experience with the crisis, and many excellent anecdotes of the moneyless days were told to me by Raymond Rubicam, Henry Wallace, Mort Weisinger, J. K. Galbraith, A. A. Berle, Jr., and many others. Anyone who doubts human ingenuity under stress will be heartened by the listing of strange hiding places under "Gold" in *The New York Times Index* for 1932 and 1933.

My interpretation of the Hoover-Roosevelt exchanges during the interregnum between Roosevelt's election and his inauguration is, of course, pro-Roosevelt, following William E. Leuchtenburg (*Franklin D. Roosevelt and the New Deal, 1932–1940*, Harper, 1963) and Arthur Schlesinger, Jr., but useful detail came from Lawrence Sullivan, in his *Prelude to Panic* (Statesman Press [Washington, D.C.], 1936), Raymond Moley, and others of the Hoover camp. Similarly, interpretation of the Ford-Couzens struggle in Detroit follows Jesse Jones, who was RFC administrator and pro-Roosevelt, but some facts were taken from the biographies of Ford and of Couzens that were somewhat more charitable to these titans.

My husband, Tom Mahoney, has a letter from William McGaw, editor and publisher of *The Southwesterner,* documenting the bank failure mentioned on page 97.

337

CHAPTER 6

Raymond Moley, A. A. Berle, Jr., and Randolph Burgess told me what they recalled of the confused events over the inaugural weekend, and Mr. Berle was kind enough to give me a typewritten copy of the notes he took for his own use during the meeting. Most of the conversation quoted at these meetings comes from this source. Raymond Moley's recollections have been printed in several of his books, principally *After Seven Years* (Harper, 1939) and *27 Masters of Politics* (Funk & Wagnalls, 1949). Letters to the President, in the Franklin Delano Roosevelt Memorial Library at Hyde Park, and the Hickock-to-Hopkins file there provided source material for the early New Deal measures. Frances Perkins, Harry Hopkins, Hugh Johnson, and Rexford Tugwell have all written accounts of their part in the Hundred Days on which Schlesinger, Leuchtenburg, and James MacGregor Burns (*Roosevelt: The Lion and the Fox*, Harcourt, Brace, 1956) have relied. Ernest K. Lindley's *The Roosevelt Revolution* (Viking, 1933) is a valuable contemporary report.

Inventory, An Appraisal of Results of the Works Progress Administration (Government Printing Office, 1938) by Harry Hopkins is a handy compendium of the far-flung accomplishments of WPA. The Chronology of *Banking Magazine*'s Reference Supplement lists briefly the major events in the nation's money and banking system from 1932 to 1935.

The New York Times and *Time* magazine covered the inaugural and holiday period in detail and perspective. *The Daily Worker* is authoritative on the Communist line in the Bank Holiday.

CHAPTER 7

My purpose in naming the intellectuals who strayed left and returned is to show that everybody who was alert was a little bit Red for a short period in the early 1930s, and Red baiters must take this wholesale flirtation into account. Red involvements of the period have been overstudied. Books I consider most useful are Murray Kempton's *Part of Our Time* (Simon and Schuster, 1955); *The American Communist Party* by Irving Howe and Lewis Coser

338

(Praeger Paperbacks, 1962); Daniel Aaron's *Writers on the Left* (Harcourt, Brace, 1961); and the well-researched but admittedly witch-hunting exposé by Eugene Lyons, *The Red Decade* (Bobbs-Merrill, 1941).

"Marxist" or Communist leaning has been based on signature of the letters supporting Foster and Norman Thomas, standard-bearers of the two leading Marxist parties in America at the time, and on statements of political faith such as those in the symposium "How I Came to Communism" in *The New Masses* (September 1932). *Time* magazine alertly reported the Reds during the 1930s.

I am indebted to The Macmillan Company and to the author for permission to quote from Stuart Chase's 1932 book, *A New Deal* (p. 156), and to Edmund Wilson for permission to quote from his essay of that year, reprinted in *The American Earthquake: A Documentary of the Twenties and Thirties* (Doubleday [Anchor], 1958). Lawrence A. Cremin's book, *The Transformation of the School* (Knopf, 1961), is authoritative on the social leanings of the Progressive educators. Leslie A. Gould's *American Youth Today* (Random House, 1940) is helpful on the left-wing youth movements.

Malcolm Cowley's articles in *The New York Times Book Review*, especially a long one of December 13, 1964, put the Depression social conscience in perspective. Cowley counts *U.S.A.* as a novel of the Thirties in tone although it was completed earlier.

The cartoon referred to at the beginning of the chapter is in the book *Everything Correlates* by Anne Cleveland and Jean Anderson (Vassar Cooperative Bookstore, 1946).

CHAPTER 8

The Ford Hunger March of 1932 has been curiously neglected in the folklore of the Depression. *The Detroit Free Press, The Detroit News,* and *The New York Times* covered in detail, but were at a loss for interpretation. *The Nation, The New Republic, The New Masses,* and of course *The Daily Worker* sympathized with the strikers, and after a day or so even the conservative press followed, although there seems to have been some reluctance to feature the rather dramatic Red funeral the Communist martyrs were given. Details on Harry Bennett were checked against lives of Ford and Harry Bennett's own account in *We Never Called Him Harry* (Fawcett [Gold Medal Books], 1951). John L. Lewis's threat to Governor Frank Murphy is reported by Murray Kempton in *Part of Our Time* (Simon and Schuster, 1955, p. 60); it is quoted here with the author's permission. Dick Frankensteen's report on his beating up at the overpass is from *Time* (June 7, 1937, p. 14), quoting a *Daily Worker* interview.

The role of the Communists in the labor union movement follows the scholarly study by Irving Howe and Lewis Coser, *The American Communist Party* (Praeger Paperbacks, 1962), which deals only with on-the-record material; the list of unions dominated by Communists is from their footnote on page 385. Nathan Glazer, in *The Social Basis of American Communism* (Harcourt, Brace, 1961), analyzes why Communist Party membership appealed to urban intellectuals.

Bergoff's activities were thoroughly covered by a *Fortune* article, "Strikebreaking" (January 1935). Anyone who doubts that a reign of terror held down unions should dip into the hair-raising testimony taken by Senator Robert M. La Follette's Civil Liberties Committee. Clinch Calkins told the story about the Detroit man on the employment line who got the job by offering to work for $10.

The story of the rise of the CIO follows Schlesinger and Frances Perkins; *Time* carried a running account.

CHAPTER 9

Major Dyer's proposal for euthanasia was reported by *The Newark Star-Ledger*. A man sent it to Roosevelt with the suggestion that Major Dyer be the first to go (Roosevelt Library). The early fight against unemployment statistics is described in Irving Bernstein's book, *The Lean Years* (Houghton Mifflin, 1960), and the recent attempts to obfuscate are set out in "Employment and Unemployment," Hearings before the Subcommittee on Economic Statistics of the Joint Economic Committee, December 18–20, 1961.

The quote from Roosevelt on cradle-to-the-grave security is from

Frances Perkins's account in *The Roosevelt I Knew* (Viking, 1946, p. 282). The inserts in pay envelopes exploiting the deductions are set forth in the Social Security Box in the Roosevelt Library at Hyde Park. The files at the Roosevelt Library also contain crank letters illustrating the Hate-Roosevelt mystique.

Hostile libels circulated against President Roosevelt are summarized in David Cushman Coyle's *The Ordeal of the Presidency* (Public Affairs Press [Washington, D.C.], 1960), and Marquis Childs' *They Hate Roosevelt!* (Harper, 1936). The McClure Syndicate item about the businessman hoping for a couple of well-placed bullets was submitted by Roosevelt himself to Press Conference #367 (May 18, 1937) off the record and has since been made public.

James Agee's *Let Us Now Praise Famous Men* (Houghton Mifflin, 1941) supplied vivid detail on the mountaineers, and the Tennessee Valley Authority's report, *Valley of Light, 1933–1963,* is authoritative on TVA's accomplishments. TVA's Paul L. Evans compared the Tennessee Valley with Appalachia for me.

The relief programs are described by Harry Hopkins in his *Spending to Save* (Norton, 1936); Harry Hopkins himself, in Searle F. Charles's *Minister of Relief: Harry Hopkins and the Depression* (Syracuse University Press, 1963).

Frederick Rudolph, in "The American Liberty League, 1934–1940" (*American Historical Review*, LVI [1950], 19–33), covers everything essential about the Liberty League.

David Lynch, in *The Concentration of Economic Power* (Columbia University Press, 1946), digests the voluminous testimony of the Temporary National Economic Committee (TNEC) and provides a handy guide to the economic thinking of the time.

Richard Whitney's downfall is chronicled in the reports of his trial and in SEC hearings.

Martha Gellhorn's description of rural rehabilitation is from *The Trouble I've Seen* (Morrow, 1936).

The Keynes comments on the nature of businessmen, from his letter of Feb. 1, 1938, are quoted in a paperback edited by Basil Rauch, *Franklin D. Roosevelt: Selected Speeches, Messages, Press Conferences, and Letters* (Rinehart, 1957, p. 193).

CHAPTER 10

Shifts in the actual control of major companies are documented by Robert A. Gordon's scholarly *Business Leadership in the Large Corporation* (Brookings Institution, 1945), which analyzes the situation in the 1930s. Monograph No. 29, "The Distribution of Ownership in the 200 Largest Nonfinancial Corporations" (Government Printing Office, 1940), made under the direction of Raymond W. Goldsmith for the Temporary National Economic Committee, is an exhaustive account of stock interests of the richest families. The concept of separation of ownership and control, of course, was formulated by A. A. Berle, Jr. and Gardiner Means in their classic study, *The Modern Corporation and Private Property* (Macmillan, 1932).

The list of ten biggest companies was taken from a compilation appearing in the *National City Bank Bulletin,* June 1949. Peter F. Drucker was first to expound the management system; my description is indebted to his account in *The Practice of Management* (Harper, 1954). Details of the systems at General Motors and at Sears come from Drucker, too. Views of Ford have been published by Harry Bennett in *We Never Called Him Harry* (Fawcett, 1951) and by Allan Nevins and Frank Ernest Hill in *Ford: Decline and Rebirth, 1933–1962* (Scribner, 1962). The influence of Du Pont management thinking on the system at General Motors is disputed by inside observers and may have been minimized to avoid antitrust litigation, but it is attested by Gordon and Monograph No. 29, at least for the early days of General Motors.

The Image Merchants (Doubleday, 1959), by Irwin Ross, gives data on the rise of public relations; Pendleton Dudley gave me firsthand data on the early days.

The decline of proprietors numerically has been dealt with by Herman P. Miller in *Rich Man, Poor Man: The Distribution of Income in America* (Crowell, 1964). Mabel Newcomer's book, *The Big Business Executive: The Factors That Made Him, 1900–1950* (Columbia University Pres, 1955), documents the shift in the origins of top managers, and a recent, unpublished extension of her study to 1960 discloses an even bigger increase in opportunity for the less advantaged to rise to the top. James C. Abegglen and William Lloyd Warner reported the same trend in their *Occupational Mobility in American Business and Industry, 1928–1952* (University of Minnesota Press, 1955). Revealing details of the "adopted sons" of management were inadvertently disclosed in the laudatory profiles of *America's Fifty Foremost Business Leaders* (B. C. Forbes & Sons Publishing Co. [New York], 1948). For a paean to the new managers, see Herrymon Maurer on "The Age of the Managers" (*Fortune*, January 1955). I am indebted to John F. Maloney, Princeton '35, for an analysis of biographical data supplied by his classmates which disclosed that the highest incomes were reported by those who had had the fewest jobs in their careers, the lowest incomes by those who had changed jobs most often. The information on J. O. McKinsey comes from *Time* (December 27, 1937).

The changing focus of management consulting was pointed out in a 1956 study published by the General Electric Company, *Some Classic Contributions to Professional Management*. The chain store tax campaign is discussed in Tom Mahoney's *The Great Merchants* (Harper, 1955), as is the contrast between Sears and Ward.

The relative health of consumer goods industries is indicated in a list of companies with net profits larger in 1937 than in 1929 compiled for the 1945 Congressional hearings on the Full Employment Act, as well as in accounts of corporations in *Fortune* and the business press. General Electric's campaign to sell appliances is described in Kent Sagendorph's anniversary biography of Charles Edward Wilson published in 1949 by the General Electric Company. Information about the early history of marketing research came from an unpublished speech by Russ Colley. Material on advertising is available in a book by Otis A. Pease, *The Responsibilities of American Advertising: Private Control and Public Influence, 1920–1940* (Yale University Press, 1958). I am indebted to Tom Mahoney's judgment for the selection of significant publicity campaigns of the 1930s.

Berton Braley, the late Charles Bonner, and other writers active during the Depression recalled getting along better than acquaintances in other fields. The new little service businesses were reported

343

in short form by *Fortune* over the years. The cotton picker story is told in James H. Street's monograph, *The New Revolution in the Cotton Economy: Mechanization and Its Consequences* (University of North Carolina Press, 1957). For delay in applying invention, see *Technological Trends and Their Social Implications*, a June 1937 report of the Subcommittee on Technology of the National Resources Committee. Growth of the small businesses is attested by reports on them in *Time*. Lawrence Gelb told me the story of his start personally.

I am indebted to J. A. Bancroft, president of The Morris Plan Corporation, for lending me a company history, *Banking on Character for a Quarter Century,* that shows the lack of consumer credit for wage earners before World War II. For an early orthodox view of installment credit, see "The Anticipated Dollar" in *Fortune* (January 1933). For the new outlook, see David Rockefeller on *Banking's New Look* (Chase National Bank).

The role of the midcentury corporation is analyzed in an anthology, *The Corporate Takeover* (Harper, 1964), edited by Andrew Hacker.

CHAPTER 11

Almost everyone who knew I was writing about the Depression contributed at least one horror story of suffering and humiliation. Most of my friends, including some professional sociologists, agreed that the Depression perpetuated class consciousness, but there was sharp divergence on my theory that the Depression stimulated a companionate rather than a passionate style of life. Frederick Lewis Allen noted a toning down of sexiness right after the Crash in his *Only Yesterday* (Harper, 1931), but many middle-aged people, particularly men, insist that they suffered no sex repression in their youth.

Reuel Denney first pointed out to me that in times of stress, women's breasts are featured, while leg appeal seems to go with periods of affluence and self-confidence, and he put me on to Martha Wolfenstein's study of the U.S. Department of Agriculture's *Infant Care* manuals for changes in fashion in child rearing. It is set forth

344

now in a book by Margaret Mead and Martha M. Wolfenstein, *Childhood in Contemporary Cultures* (University of Chicago Press, 1955). Dorothy Swaine Thomas, in *Social Aspects of the Business Cycle* (Knopf, 1925), reports the constancy of prostitution during good times and bad in Europe.

Alice Leslie Koempel, Professor of Sociology at Vassar, recalls greater freedom for women to remain unmarried during the Depression. Her doctoral dissertation, *Measurement of Changes in the Standard of Living During a Depression* (Bryn Mawr, 1937), was a mine of data for testing theories.

CHAPTER 12

Robert E. Ferrell, in *American Diplomacy in the Great Depression* (Yale University Press, 1957), summarizes what most diplomats say about the appalling disregard of world affairs before World War II. Francis Walton's *Miracle of World War II: How American Industry Made Victory Possible* (Macmillan, 1956) provided statistics and facts that back up my own observation of the war effort as secretary to the job manager of the contractor building the Army Air Force base at Trinidad and later on *Newsweek* and *The New York Journal of Commerce*.

The domestic revolution brought about by World War II has not yet been analyzed as seriously as it deserves to be. It may be a little unfair to quote prophesies of postwar depression from Leo M. Cherne's book, *The Rest of Your Life* (Doubleday, 1944), when everyone else was as far off the mark as he, but Mr. Cherne was more vivid than the others. A lot of wise men predicted the Crash of 1929, but I have not run across any serious thinker of 1945 who foresaw the smooth postwar reconversion.

CHAPTER 13

Michael Harrington's book, *The Other America: Poverty in the United States* (Macmillan, 1962), defines the midcentury poor who were left out by the New Deal. Emile Benoit and Kenneth E.

345

Boulding, editors of *Disarmament and the Economy* (Harper, 1963), calculated the dependence of the midcentury economy on war. The reasons why another 1929-style debacle is unlikely today have been summarized in *Fortune* magazine (February 1955) and *U.S. News & World Report* (June 11, 1962).

Russell Lynes, in "Take Back Your Sable! Or What's So Good about Good Times?" (*Harper's*, June 1956), takes the nostalgic view of the Depression as stimulating that a surprising number of people expressed. The same people beat the apathetic suburbanite organization men of the 1950s over the head, following David Riesman and Holley Whyte. The deprecation seems snide now, including my own article, "Born 1930: The Unlost Generation" (*Harper's Bazaar*, February 1957).

I am indebted to Edna Macmahon for the phrase "moral equivalent of Depression" and to Alice Leslie Koempel for insights into the nature of midcentury poverty.

The concluding quote from John Maynard Keynes is on p. 361 of an anthology of Keynesiana published under the title *Essays in Persuasion* (Norton, 1963).

INDEX

A & P, 238
  anti-unionism, 184
  public relations, 255–56
Abegglen, James C., 247
accounting practices, 240 ff, 250 ff
Adams, Norval W., 217
advertising
  agencies, 260–61
  attacks on, 149–51
  booster, 72, 73
  consumer-oriented, 260–61
  fear philosophy, 277–78
  public relations and, 254
  regulation, 226
aged
  leisure as problem, 328
  pension plans, 202, 203
  Social Security, 205 ff
Agricultural Adjustment Act (AAA),
  125, 137
  food costs, 136
  Negro sharecroppers hurt, 228
  surplus crop payments, 127, 130, 216
  crop and acreage limitation, 127
  unconstitutionality, 127, 220
Aid to Dependent Children, 32
air conditioning, 263–64
aircraft industry, 304
Akron, Ohio, 186, 192
Alabama, 157–58
Alaska, 215
Allen, Gov. Oscar, 103, 119
Allis Chalmers, 264
Allyn, Stanley, 247–48
American Association of School Ad-
  ministrators, 284
American Bank Note Co., 106
American Bankers Assoc., 217
American Civil Liberties Union, 173
American Economic Assoc., 71
American Express, 99, 122

American Federation of Labor (AFL),
  166, 178, 181 ff
American Federation of Teachers, 177
American Friends Service Committee,
  27, 235
American Institute of Public Opinion,
  86–87
American Management Assoc., 217
American Medical Association, 162–63,
  205, 206, 316
American Piano Co., 14
American Society of Mechanical Engi-
  neers, 251–52
American Student Union, 157, 177
American Telephone & Telegraph, 244
American Tobacco, 258
  advertising and consumer, 260–61
American Youth Congress, 141
amusements, 8, 10, 20–21, 61 ff, 71, 97,
  121
Anaconda Copper Mining, 238
Anderson, Sherwood, 156
Anthracite Miners Assoc., 47–48
anti-Semitism, 54, 55–56
antitrust action, 223
apple sellers, 2, 26
Architectural Record, 82
Arkansas, 215–16
Armour, Ogden, 234
Arthurdale, W. Va., 215
artists
  topicality and realism, 152 ff
  social consciousness, 140 ff, 146 ff,
  151 ff
  radicalism, 140 ff, 146 ff
  work relief projects, 133–34
Association Against the Prohibition
  Amendment, 72–73
Atlanta, Ga., 186
atom bomb, 165–66, 167, 315
Auto Workers Union, 169

347

351

Dy-Dee, 262
Dyer, Maj. Edward, 197

Eccles, Marriner, 88, 222
economic goals, today's, 325–26
economizing
  government, 80–81, 98, 125
  industries, 19, 72
  institutions, 20
  personal, 12, 20–21, 46, 273 ff
  services, 21
Economy Act, 125
Edgerton, John E., 78
Edison, Charles, 135–36
education
  adult, 132, 133, 139, 140, 304–305,
    307–308
  Army as, 307–308
  careers and, 204, 246–47, 293 ff
  colleges, 293 ff
    See also colleges.
  of the poor, 29, 32, 83, 87, 296–97
  high schools, 296 ff
  progressive, 159–60
  training methods, 304–305
  training programs, value of, 207–208
  social consciousness, 159–60
  veterans, 309, 310
  work relief projects, 132, 133, 134
"efficiency experts," 250 ff
Efron, Alexander, 269
Eisenhower, Dwight D., 316, 327
El Paso, Tex., 72
Elks, 24
Ellington, Buford, 295
Ellison, J. Roy, 87
embezzlement, 8, 9, 97
Emergency Banking Act, 123 ff
Emergency Relief Appropriation Act,
  132
employment
  age, 23, 86, 87
  "boondoggles," 131
  codes, 126–27
  discrimination, 53 ff, 198, 228
  downgrading of skills, 23, 43–44
  Federal projects, 130, 131 ff
  forced, relief and, 31, 32, 86
  full, 201, 304 ff
  government, 231
  guaranteed income, 202, 204
  inflation vs, 323–24
  Negroes, 53 ff, 228, 279–80, 305
  part-time, 24, 61, 79, 202
  post-World War II, 309–10
  private, creation of, 213

psychological effects of re-employ-
  ment, 306
ratio of, 42–43, 198 ff
recruitment at management level,
  249–50
"Reemployment Agreement," 128
search for, 43–44, 48–49, 181
self, 45 ff
shared, 61, 79, 87
war and, 54 ff, 201, 300, 301, 303,
  304 ff, 326 ff
endurance contests, 64–65
entertainment and entertainers, 8, 10,
  61 ff, 71, 97, 121; see also theaters,
  movies
Ernst, Morris, 143
Erskine, Albert, 50
Esquire, 167, 262
Europe, World War II, 299 ff
extremism, right-wing, 202 ff, 222

Fadiman, Clifton, 143
Fair Labor Standards Act, 226
Fairless, Benjamin, 189, 243
families
  broken, 50, 66–67
  corporate management, role in, 239 ff
  isolation of poor, 39, 60 ff
  loyalty within, 29, 34
  psychological impact of Depression,
    57–58, 313–14
  size, 51–53
  women as breadwinners, 56 ff, 286–
    87
Farley, Jim, 120, 220
Farm Holiday Assoc., 193
Farm Security Agency, 153, 222
Farmers Union, 140–41
farms and farmers
  acreage limitation, 79, 125, 127, 230
  Communists, 140–41, 192–93
  conservativism, 192–93
  drought, 16, 27, 80, 82
  electrification projects, 134, 208 ff
  income, 16, 127, 207, 229–30, 245
  laborers, 136
  marginal, 44–45, 125, 136
  mortgages, 82, 125
  power cooperatives, 211–12
  prices, 81, 84
  production, 127
  relief, federal, 130
  relocation, 125, 214–15
  road work, 35, 136
  self-sustaining, 44–45, 87
  submarginal, 130

352

Johnson, Lyndon B. *(cont.)*
  work-sharing, 87
Johnstown, N.Y., 185
Johnstown, Pa., 68
Jones, Jesse, 124
Jones, John Price, 185
Jones, W. Alton, 247
Josephson, Matthew, 146, 156
journalism
  photographic, 152–53
  trade unions, 177

Kallet, Arthur, 149–50, 151
Kansas City, 68, 187
Kaufman, George, 143
Kefauver, Sen. Estes, 316
Kelly, George "Machine Gun," 195
Kempton, Murray, 167
Kennedy, Jacqueline, 311
Kennedy, John F., 86, 112, 194, 226, 324–25
Kennedy, Joseph, 10, 233
Kenosha, Wis., 108
Kent, Atwater, 234
Kentucky, 26–27, 35, 158, 204
Kern, Jerome, 11
Kettering, Charles F. "Boss," 72, 265
Key West, Fla., 132
Keynes, John Maynard, 74, 89, 135, 222, 223, 231, 331–32
Kilgore, Bernard, 325
Kimball, Dr. Justin Ford, 162
Knudsen, William S., 145, 188, 221, 255, 304
Kokomo, Ind., 43

labor
  conservativism, inherent, 191 ff
  "exploited," 148–49
  practices, management, 44, 170, 178 ff
  quit rate, 180
  ratio of employment, 42–43, 198 ff
  relations—*see also* specific industry, 181 ff
  skills, downgraded, 23, 43–44
  superfluous, 42–43, 49–50, 198
  unemployables, 197–98
labor-saving
  appliances, 258, 278
  machines, 44, 87, 182, 229
La Follette Civil Liberties Committee, 165, 178–79, 184, 188, 189–90
La Follette, Sen. Robert M., 36–37
LaGuardia, Fiorello, 126–27
Lamont, Corliss, 235
Lamont, Thomas W., 4, 17

landlords, 33, 34–35
Lasker, Mary, 263
Lau, Albert, 262
Lauchran, Martha, 109
lawyers
  Communist, 157–58
  New Dealers, in government, 135
  organization, 177–78
Lawyers Guild, 177–78
leadership, today's, Depression-trained, 42, 207, 210, 315 ff
League for Industrial Democracy, 186
League of Women Shoppers, 186
Lee, Ivy, 236, 237
Lehman, Herbert, 110
leisure
  aged, 328
  Depression problem, 60 ff
Leon, René, 74
Lerner, Max, 144, 167
Lewis, John L., 74, 182 ff, 187–88, 190, 192, 194
Lewis, Oscar, 39
Lewis, Sinclair, 204, 288, 301
Liberty League, 217–18, 233
libraries, 134, 140
Life, 152–53, 262
Life Extension Institute, 163
Lindbergh kidnaping, 194
Lions Clubs, International Assoc., 72
Literary Digest, 220
literature
  radicalism, 141 ff, 146 ff
  topicality and realism, 152 ff
Livermore, Jesse, 5
living standards
  middle-class, 22, 273 ff
  Tennessee Valley, 208 ff
  poverty-stricken, 22 ff
loans
  to banks, 80, 104
  corporation, 267, 270
  housing, 80
  tightness, 98
Loewy, Raymond, 260
London Economic Conference, 300
Long, Sen. Huey S., 203, 204, 300
Look, 153, 262
Lorentz, Pare, 153
Louisiana, 103, 203
love, 283 ff
Lowell, Josephine, 31
Lundberg, Ferdinand, 145–46
lynchings, 194, 195
Lynd, Robert and Helen, 61, 151, 167, 184

357

money (*cont.*)
"real" and paper losses, 11–12, 83–84
scrip, 100, 105, 106, 107, 114, 116, 120–21
silver, 74, 88, 125
substitutes for cash, 99 ff, 117–18, 122
monopolies, 86
Monsanto Chemical Co., 238
Montgomery Ward, 256–57
morality, 283 ff
crime, 8, 9, 63, 97, 108–109, 120, 123
Moran, Joe, 64
Moran, William, 105
Morgan, J. P., 20, 73, 95, 219, 237, 243
Morgan (J. P.) & Co., 4
Morgenthau, Jr., 222
Morris Industrial Bank (Plan), 267, 270
mortgages, 18, 82
moratorium, 126–27
Morton, Charles, 9
Mt. Kisco, N.Y., 24
movies
refuge of poor, 38, 62, 64, 297
Communism, 155, 165, 177
work relief projects, 133, 134
muckrackers, 236
Mumford, Lewis, 144, 167
Muncie, Ind., 72, 102, 184
Munich, 301
Murphy, Gov. Frank, 30, 171, 188
Murray, Philip, 189, 309
Muscle Shoals, 209
Mussolini, 68, 113, 249, 288, 301

Nassau County (N.Y.) Medical Society, 164
National Association of Manufacturers (NAM), 78, 181, 185, 254
National Association of Women Lawyers, 57
National Cash Register, 247–48
National Chain Store Assoc., 19
National City Bank, 4, 12, 95, 120
National Defense Advisory Council, 304
National Industrial Conference Board, 199
National Conference of Social Workers, 34
National Industrial Recovery Act (NRA), 126, 127–28, 136, 137, 182–83, 184, 215–16
National Labor Board, 183
National Labor Relations Act, 184

National Labor Relations Board (NLRB), 190
National Recreation Assoc., 61–62
National Steel, 244
National Youth Administration (NYA), 133, 207–208, 213, 298, 326
natural resources, conservation, 125
Nazis, 157, 299 ff
Negroes
civil rights, 157–58, 194
Communists, 54, 149, 175, 176, 177
diet, 38
discrimination, 54–55, 170, 228–29, 307, 321
domestics, 279–80
employment, 53 ff, 228, 279–80, 305
New Deal and, 228–29
riots, 157, 195
Nielsen, A. C., 260
Nevada, 103
New Deal—*see also* specific agency
"brain trust," 134–35
evaluation of, 227 ff
philosophy and aims, 204–205, 226 ff, 321, 324
New England, 180, 212
New Masses, 143, 151
New Mexico, 23
New Orleans, 103
New York City, 106, 108, 109, 158
apple sellers, 26
arson, 63
bank holiday, 117, 118
building, 16–17
charities, 29
medical care, 161–62, 163
private work relief, 26
real estate, 16–17, 18, 82
relief, 26, 33
starvation deaths, 35
teachers, 30
work relief, 131
New York Central Railroad, 237
New York Post, 167
New York State, 24, 31, 33, 161, **163,** 185
New York Stock Exchange, 224 ff
year-end festivities, 15
stock market crash, 4 ff, 224–25
New York Telephone Co., 236
New York Times, 6, 11, 12, 15, 16, 17, 23, 55–56, 75, 77, 81, 99, 313
New Yorker, 139, 146, 158, 167, 294
Newburgh, N.Y., 31
Newsom, Earl, 237

358

359

362